Couple Counselling

PRAISE FOR THE BOOK

'Martin Payne, the writer of perhaps the best British introduction to narrative therapy, presents, in his own words, "a clear, succinct and above all practical guide" to how
narrative therapy can be used in the complex area of couple counselling. The book is
aimed primarily at individual counsellors and I particularly like the way Martin
emphasises the counsellors' transferable skills. The book can also be used as a training
tool, as it includes suggested experiential exercises, role plays and discussion topics,
together with plentiful and highly relevant examples from Martin's own work. Much
of what Martin writes reverberates closely with my own experiences as a systemic
psychotherapist using mainly narrative therapy, but borrowing from other therapies
where appropriate. I strongly recommend this book to any individual counsellor who
wants to work effectively with couples, and also to any couple counsellor who wants
to enrich their practice.'
Barry Bowen, Systemic Psychotherapist, editor of David Epston's recent book Down Under
and Up Over – Travels with Narrative Therapy

'This book is well overdue and fills a gap in the market for accessible, pragmatic and
sophisticated writing about therapy with couples. Martin Payne manages to make
links with other approaches where others see divisions. He describes a clear breakdown of session structures – process and content – together with the detailed
exposition of a variety of strategies for more effective practice. This book is inclusive,
user-friendly and always loyal to narrative principles.'
Mark Hayward, Institute of Narrative Therapy

Couple Counselling
A Practical Guide

Martin Payne

Los Angeles | London | New Delhi
Singapore | Washington DC

SAGE Publications Ltd
1 Oliver's Yard
55 City Road
London EC1Y 1SP

SAGE Publications Inc.
2455 Teller Road
Thousand Oaks, California 91320

SAGE Publications India Pvt Ltd
B 1/I 1 Mohan Cooperative Industrial Area
Mathura Road
New Delhi 110 044

SAGE Publications Asia-Pacific Pte Ltd
33 Pekin Street #02-01
Far East Square
Singapore 048763

Library of Congress Control Number: 2009934035

British Library Cataloguing in Publication data

A catalogue record for this book is available from
the British Library

ISBN 978-1-84860-048-5
ISBN 978-1-84860-049-2 (pbk)

Typeset by C&M Digitals Pvt Ltd, Chennai, India
Printed in Great Britain by CPI Antony Rowe, Chippenham, Wiltshire
Printed on paper from sustainable resources

Mixed Sources
Product group from well-managed
forests and other controlled sources
www.fsc.org Cert no. SGS-COC-002953
© 1996 Forest Stewardship Council

In memory of my parents, Ted and Em
A great couple

CONTENTS

ACKNOWLEDGEMENTS

I am grateful to:

The persons who generously gave me permission to use disguised versions of their counselling as examples of practice;

My partner and colleague, Mary Wilkinson, who by her reading and detailed commenting on many drafts of the manuscript saved me from the embarrassment of spelling, punctuation and grammatical errors, repetitive, obscure and wordy phrasing, and my wilder ideas;

Dulwich Centre Publications for their excellent online library of narrative therapy texts, and permission to quote from their publications;

Sharon Cawood, Alice Oven, Susannah Trefgarne and other staff at Sage Publications, for their patience and helpfulness.

INTRODUCTION

A PERSONAL NOTE

When I began counselling in GP surgeries, I met a far wider range of people seeking counselling than in my private practice. The extent of presenting problems was enormous. I like to think that my initial person–centred training, together with good supervision, generally enabled me to assist these people reasonably competently, though I was by no means free of misjudgements. There was, however, one group which produced reactions in me ranging from unease to severe anxiety: around 20% of referrals were for couples unhappy in their relationship. My training had been entirely about counselling individuals; the only advice we had been offered about working with couples was to use person–centred techniques in joint sessions in much the same way as with individuals.

My attempts to do this were, if not actually disastrous, certainly highly unsatisfactory, both to myself and to the couples I attempted to counsel. I vividly remember a husband and wife having a huge and escalating row, after my naive suggestion that they 'attempt honestly to communicate their feelings', while I sat helplessly listening. Some couples, in contrast, were not openly angry with each other; rather, they brought a contagious sense of hopelessness into the counselling room. I tried evermore desperately to work effectively with couples, but very little I had learned seemed to help.

I needed guidance on what I should *actually do*, but the books I read were too theoretical and too generalized. None gave really practical help by suggesting how ideas about couple counselling might be translated specifically into practice moment by moment.

Fortunately, I found supervisors who were family therapists, who introduced me to a variety of unfamiliar yet relevant approaches. One of these was solution–focused therapy, a down-to-earth way of working which, when applied to couple counselling, encourages people to identify their relationship's strengths and then to define and monitor realistic goals. Using solution–focused practices seemed to improve my work with couples, though at times I missed the more open-ended nature of person–centred therapy.

I then discovered narrative therapy, developed by Michael White and David Epston, pioneering family therapists from Australia and New Zealand. Their values and practices seemed to have much in common with both solution–focused therapy and person-centred therapy (Payne 1993). As I saw it then, narrative therapy appeared to combine the person-respecting and exploratory nature of Rogerian therapy with the practical, brief, resource-identifying nature of the solution-focused approach. Studying with Michael White at The Dulwich Centre in Adelaide, together with seminars in the UK with my supervisors, enhanced my understanding and practice of narrative therapy and increased my confidence when counselling both individuals and couples.

I wanted to share my discovery of narrative therapy. In 2000, Sage published my book *Narrative Therapy: An Introduction for Counsellors*, which contained some examples of counselling couples, and at this time I also began to present workshops for counsellors who wished to expand into couple therapy. The second edition of my book (2006) contained a longer section specifically on couple counselling.

I wish I could time-travel back to when I first recognized my limitations in counselling couples, and hand a copy of this present volume to my former self! As that seems unlikely in the present state of theoretical physics, I offer it to present-day readers, trained in individual counselling, who wish to extend their practice to working with couples. I hope that it will enable them to take the first steps towards undertaking this work, which can be more difficult, demanding and open to error than individual counselling, but which, when it succeeds, is intensely rewarding and heartening.

A NARRATIVE APPROACH

In the workshops on which this book is based, I presented narrative therapy to groups of counsellors trained in a wide range of other approaches. Since most participants had not previously heard of narrative therapy, they were rather wary, but (as I had anticipated) they found it sympathetic. Although perfectly suitable for use with individuals, narrative therapy originated in family therapy, where multiple viewpoints are taken into account, and course members immediately recognised this as relevant to working with couples. It was different and intriguing, but had enough in common with their usual ways of counselling to form a semi-familiar yet fresh base on which to build new skills in this unfamiliar context. For readers unfamiliar with narrative therapy, Chapter 2 comprises an outline of its theory and main practices; the chapter may be omitted by those already familiar with it.

Although narrative therapy forms the basis of this book, I sometimes suggest the use of practices from other therapies where they mesh with narrative practices and values.

AIMS AND STRUCTURE

I aim to provide a clear, succinct and above all practical guide to couple counselling. Clearly, the book cannot attempt to cover all aspects, and cannot alone teach the reader to develop full competence – attending workshops and courses, together with good supervision, are essential. However, I hope it will provide a reasonably comprehensive starting point.

Parts I and II describe ideas, issues and practices around this area of work, including an exploration of social and cultural influences on counsellors and couples, and an exposition of narrative therapy that identifies its common ground with other approaches. Part III is the core of the book, the step-by-step, what-to-do 'nitty-gritty', where I offer a framework of practice for first and subsequent sessions, transferable to most situations likely to be brought to couple counselling. Part IV extends this overview to consider how these practices may be adapted to several specific situations frequently presented by couples.

Most chapters include experiential reinforcing exercises and/or suggestions of topics for discussion. The role-play exercises which end the chapters on practice aim to reinforce and consolidate participants' learning around part or all of the chapter's content through experiential enactment, and to encourage the consolidation of this learning by the interchange of ideas and discoveries arising from the exercises. The topics for discussion which conclude chapters exploring concepts and principles also have the aim of encouraging further thinking and discussion, and of encouraging the participants to relate ideas to the practicalities of working with couples. The exercises and discussion points are intended to be useful for training purposes, but I hope they will also stimulate creative thinking in readers who are using the book as an introductory guide to practice without the assistance of other people.

By the term 'couples', I follow common usage, meaning two people who have chosen to form a close relationship. Narrative therapy is also suitable for working with other dyads such as siblings, parents and children, or friends, but I do not include these situations here. I use 'partners' as a generic term for committed couples whether or not they are married. Throughout the book, I follow Michael White's practice of referring to people who come to counselling as 'persons' rather than 'clients'. 'Counselling' and 'therapy' (also 'counsellors' and 'therapists') are used interchangeably, and male and female pronouns are introduced at random. All examples of therapy are based on my work with couples unless otherwise stated, with names changed and circumstances disguised to protect confidentiality.

MICHAEL WHITE

Shortly after being contracted to write this book, I was shocked to hear of Michael White's death from a heart attack, in April 2008, at the age of 59. He was a man of great compassion, and enormous energy and commitment, who loved life and lived it to the full. Michael's writing, teaching and practice embodied an outstanding breadth of reading and originality of thought, indisputably making him one of the most important and influential therapists of our time.

PART 1
IDEAS AND PRACTICES

1
INDIVIDUAL COUNSELLING AND COUPLE COUNSELLING

In this chapter, I discuss some of the differences between working with individuals and working with couples which need to be taken into account by counsellors trained in individual-based models who branch out into couple counselling. I also make the case that experienced counsellors new to couple counselling will bring many appropriate assumptions and much skill and experience to this work, and that these will stand them in good stead as a foundation for practice.

THE NEED FOR COUPLE COUNSELLORS

The market for individual counselling has now become pretty well saturated in the UK, and I know of many counsellors who find it hard to get paid work because of the competition. At the same time, there is an unsatisfied demand for couple counselling, with Relate (formerly the British Marriage Guidance council), for example, having long waiting lists of many months in some areas of the country. Very few qualifying courses seem to offer training for working with couples, with obvious exceptions, such as those run by Relate. Courses in family therapy largely exist for employed practitioners. For the individual-trained counsellor hoping to work with couples, there is an additional problem – the most common theoretical approaches used in work with individuals are person-centred, psychodynamic and, more recently, cognitive–behavioural, all originally developed for one-to-one counselling and not adaptable to a wider context without further training.

A DILEMMA

A counsellor trained only in individual therapy faces a dilemma when approached by couples asking for help with their problems. The obvious solution is to suggest that they see a colleague experienced in couple work, but the shortage of such counsellors may make this difficult or impossible. The individual-trained counsellor may be the only resource to whom unhappy and conflicted partners may be able to turn, if they are unwilling to join a long waiting list for couple therapy and risk their problems worsening or becoming intractable while they wait for an appointment. The counsellor may decide with some trepidation to take the couple on and try to adapt individual-counselling methods with them, whilst seeking help from supervision, books, articles, workshops and more extended training.

My own past experience shows that there are many traps lying in wait for the novice couple counsellor, even if he or she already has considerable experience in individual counselling. If these traps are not anticipated and prepared for, they will soon impact on the work and threaten its effectiveness, or at worst even exacerbate the couple's difficulties. However, my experience also indicates that an individual-trained counsellor can learn to counsel couples successfully if he or she is willing to consider new approaches, go to workshops, read widely and discuss the work with a good supervisor.

So what are these traps? Below, I outline some differences between counselling individuals and counselling couples which, I suspect, may sometimes prevent individual-trained counsellors from taking up couple counselling, and/or create problems once counselling has begun for those who do take it on. These and other differences, and the problems and misjudgements they may result in, should not be underestimated.

Time constraints

Counsellors new to couple work are likely to find that their usual sessions of about 50 minutes to an hour are uncomfortably tight for ensuring that two people, rather than one, are adequately heard and for ideas to emerge and be explored. A willingness to depart from the conventional amount of time allocated to a session is usually necessary. My own practice is to allow an hour and a quarter for the first session and at least an hour for further sessions, occasionally extending time if the progress of the session makes this necessary. On the other hand, there is no need to assume that sessions must always be held at weekly intervals; especially at later stages, gradually widening the length of time between sessions can be helpful, as it allows the couple to gain confidence in their ability to put their discoveries and decisions into practice and to monitor their progress.

Three-way interaction

Many individual counselling approaches are rather loosely structured, with pauses for thoughts and feelings to emerge, and further exploration dependent on what the person has just said. With just two people conversing (the counsellor and the person seeking help), this is appropriate and manageable. The dynamic of counselling couples is much more complex than this. If the counsellor begins by waiting for one of the partners to speak, then reflects back and summarizes when he or she does, the other partner may feel unheard, and interrupt or build resentment and impatience. If the couple are encouraged to discuss their problems with each other, without the counsellor firmly controlling the dialogue, they will probably repeat familiar and abrasive complaints, dispute or argue, with the atmosphere heating up and the session becoming unproductive.

Once the session is under way, but not necessarily in this order, the counsellor talks to A and A talks to the counsellor; the counsellor talks to B and B talks to the counsellor; A talks to B and B talks to A; sometimes, when they are under emotional pressure, B may try to talk to A at the same time as A is talking to B, and vice versa; and at times the counsellor may address A and B simultaneously … this can be a minefield for counsellors used only to one-to-one dialogue in the counselling room!

Counsellors new to work with couples need to learn and practise more structured ways of running sessions than when counselling individuals, to prevent interaction between three people becoming unwieldy or losing coherence. The counsellor needs to be tactfully but firmly in charge of the proceedings, and she may find this rather different from her usual way of working, or may even object to it as too directive compared with individual counselling. But structuring the session is not directive in the sense of telling persons what they should feel, do or think. Couple counselling does not need rigid or invariable procedures, but should nevertheless be based on clear frameworks. The counsellor new to couple counselling can bear these frameworks in mind, perhaps referring during the session to memory-joggers such as those given in the Appendices at the back of this book. In narrative therapy, the base model of this book, the session frameworks are designed (among other things) to allow each person to be heard, acknowledged and validated, and to eliminate interruptions, aggression or other counterproductive elements. Once the frameworks become familiar and habitual to the counsellor, they will allow her to be wholly spontaneous and natural with the couple, and create conditions for the couple to explore their problems and concerns fully and without rancour.

Immediacy of conflict

Michael White admits (2004a: 5) that he sometimes experiences impasses when working with conflicted couples. That even such an exceptionally experienced and skilled therapist could sometimes find a couple session almost going out of control is either heartening or worrying for the rest of us, depending on how you look at it! Emotions in the counselling room are frequently intense, as with some individual counselling, but resentment, exasperation, disillusion and despair may be immediately expressed, directed at a partner physically present in the room who is likely to respond in kind. When this happens, emotional interactions both expressing and creating conflict are powerfully present to the therapist *there and then,* with conflict taking place in front of her in all its raw, messy and distressing reality, not, as in individual therapy, being limited to emotions arising from the memory and description of events distant in time and place from the consulting room. Immediacy of couple interaction will also be present if the conflicted couple's feelings are bleak and held in rather than expressed in open anger, with the session just as potentially at risk if the therapist tries, in these circumstances, harder and ever harder to evoke a response. The couple will feel under pressure, and may withdraw even further into their defensive shells and fixed positions.

Echoes from the counsellor's private life

Conflict between two persons can be daunting for the counsellor contemplating taking up couple counselling if it resembles past or present difficulties in his own relationship with a partner or other close individual, or triggers painful memories of parental conflict in his childhood. The difference between this situation in couple counselling and coping with personal echoes triggered in individual counselling lies primarily in the difficulty of resisting identification with the person who appears to be in a position similar to the counsellor's in the past or the present, an identification that might distort objectivity and be noticed and resented by the other partner. Conversely, the counsellor may recognize this impulse, and overcompensate. In either case, failure to achieve appropriate objectivity can skew the therapy. Keeping to a clear method and structure is the answer. If this is achieved, sessions will usually be productive despite personal echoes, which will be kept at bay. If the counsellor's personal reactions do continue to affect his objectivity despite this, the problem should of course be addressed in supervision.

Neutrality

Many people who come to individual counselling are unsure of their aims, other than wishing in a general way to overcome their uncertainties and unhappiness. Specific aims emerge during and arise from their counselling. Counsellors who work with individuals are well used to giving undivided attention to the person's problem-story and, through reflecting, checking out and empathic responses, conveying that they understand it, take it seriously, and accept it as an accurate representation of the person's felt experience. Counsellors who work with individuals will already know that a person's being heard and believed can be powerful factors in producing emotional relief, and a reassuring and calming prelude to the exploration of emotionally charged difficulties and confusions.

When counselling couples, whether in joint sessions or separate individual sessions, the situation becomes more complicated. The counsellor needs to maintain a 'dual-viewpoint' stance at all times, and continuously to communicate this to both persons. This is *neutrality* – not meaning a distant and disengaged manner, far from it – but consistently ensuring that both persons feel heard and believed even if they have very different perspectives on the same events and experiences. Very often there is blaming, with resentment and anger from the original source of the conflict exacerbated by the frustration of each partner believing the other to be blind to their obvious faults and responsibility for the problem, and stubborn to boot. Inexperienced couple counsellors can swiftly become lost in these situations, which present challenges very different from the individual-focused, one-to-one empathic attention they have been used to giving to one person. Neutrality is a core skill of family therapy which also needs to be learnt and practised by couple counsellors, and narrative therapy embodies this principle – one of the reasons why it is particularly suited to couple counselling.

Split agendas

Individuals are often rather uncertain about exactly what they want to get from counselling, but they are usually clear about their *reasons* for coming. They know what the problem is, though they may be confused about how to deal with it, or conflicted about different or apparently irreconcilable possibilities, and good counselling can usually aim to help them to unravel these confusions and make choices.

Conflicted couples may also be unsure about quite what they want from counselling, and in addition each partner may be mired in different interpretations and contrasting understandings of the same events. Even more confusingly for the novice couple counsellor, each partner may bring a quite different agenda, a situation by definition not found in work with individuals. One partner may want the couple to move to a different area but the other may want them to stay where they are; one partner's aim may be to minimize contact with the other's relatives, whereas the other partner may wish to see more of them; the partners may be wholly opposed on how to deal with their children's misbehaviour; one partner may want the other to give up drinking alcohol or smoking pot whereas the other may want, and be determined, to continue. At worst, one partner may wish to rescue the relationship whereas the other may wish to end it (I describe an example of this in Chapter 12). Each partner will probably hope that the counsellor will validate and support their own aims and attitudes, and will convey to the other partner that their viewpoint and wishes are mistaken. An inexperienced couple counsellor runs the risk of swiftly being pushed towards an unproductive 'referee' position, and possibly of frustrating both partners by refusing to take sides. Following the session frameworks offered in this book will go a long way towards assisting the couple to see each other's point of view, but negotiating compromise is not always possible, and where the issues are such that the partners cannot agree to differ, the counsellor may be left with the unenviable task of assisting them to explore and face up to the disturbing implications and consequences of their fixed positions.

Unrealistic expectations

Persons sometimes have unrealistically high expectations of counselling. Often couples, even more than individuals, come at a late stage of their problems, with a corresponding sense of unhappiness, pessimism and urgency. One partner may have resisted coming to counselling and the other, in increasingly desperate attempts at persuasion, may have exaggerated its potential benefits. When the couple find that there is no offer of immediate and brilliant advice that magically sorts things out, and no immediate reassurance that everything will undoubtedly be resolved through counselling, they may feel let down and disappointed. The counsellor may then experience anxiety and a self-generated pressure to produce a breakthrough in double-quick time. Such pressure always makes it difficult to slow down and follow a more realistic and work-able agenda, and to assist the couple to find their own solutions, with the counsellor in a facilitating role.

Ethical dilemmas

When two people are being counselled rather than just one, it may sometimes be difficult for the counsellor to determine exactly where her ethical allegiance lies. For example, if a woman claims that her partner is sometimes so verbally violent that she lives in continual fear that he will attack her physically, yet the man sorrowfully denies this and claims that she is exaggerating the occasional spat, whom should the counsellor believe and what should she do about it?

Sometimes the mere fact of having ethical responsibility to two people rather than primarily to one person can produce ethical problems. Consider this example:

> At their first, joint session, Ken and Mary's relationship appeared to be basically sound, though there were many differences and disagreements about money, and other conflicts which they were finding very hard to resolve. The atmosphere of the session was cooperative and quite relaxed, and sometimes humorous glances passed between the couple. I certainly did not detect any undertones of possible violence or abuse. We discussed whether to continue with individual or joint sessions, and agreed to continue with the latter. Two days later, Mary rang me to request an individual session for herself, saying she had not told Ken of this request and was not going to.

The reader might like to think about what he or she might have done in this situation, where agreeing to Mary's request would have meant colluding with secrecy, yet refusing it might have meant an important issue being excluded from the couple's counselling. At the end of this chapter, I say what I did.

Most ethical *positions* apply equally to individual and couple counselling, but the generalized ethical guidelines of the counsellor's professional organization, such as (in the UK) the British Psychological Society, the British Association for Counselling and Psychotherapy, the Association for Family Therapy and Systemic Practice and other bodies affiliated to the United Kingdom Council for Psychotherapy, will not always provide clear guidance on how to resolve a specific *issue*. Where ethical dilemmas in couple counselling differ from those in working with individuals, they usually, as in the examples I have given, arise from the counsellor's having equal responsibility to two persons, and also a duty of protection if one or both appears to be at serious risk in any way.

What should a counsellor do when one partner continually arrives late for joint sessions, or misses appointments altogether, with the other partner making what sounds like lame excuses for this? More urgently, what action should be taken if one partner inadvertently reveals that the other is involved in serious criminality such as drug dealing? What ethical responsibility does a counsellor have towards a person who is violent or abusive to his or her partner, as distinct from responsibility to the victim? Good supervision is essential; here such dilemmas can be unravelled, action decided upon in relation to BACP or other ethical guidelines, and consequences monitored.

TRANSFERABLE SKILLS

I am rather worried that after reading about these difficulties and dilemmas, individual-trained counsellors might be frightened away from couple counselling! I hope they will read on.

As I say earlier in this chapter, I believe that experienced individual counsellors will already have many transferable skills, and a grasp of many appropriate concepts, which perhaps they have come to take for granted or do not fully recognize because of familiarity. I also believe that these skills and concepts can be brought to bear in the unfamiliar context of couple counselling and form a solid foundation for successful work.

Previous counselling experience concerning couple conflict

Many counsellors new to working with couples will have counselled individuals who are unhappy or conflicted with a partner or spouse. It is also likely that these counsellors will have played a significant part in the person's resolution of these issues. Since assisting a person to cope with the breakdown of an intimate relationship is one of the most difficult and complex issues individual counsellors can be faced with, the skills and knowledge developed in such counselling will be wholly relevant when counselling two people rather than just one, even though the way these are deployed will need to be modified by the new context. The advantages of seeing both partners rather than just one will soon become evident, with more detailed and full information being revealed, including a more balanced view of the issues affecting the couple.

Empathy combined with neutrality

The capacity to enter imaginatively into the world of the person, yet not to identify so wholly with her that a wider perspective is lost, is an ability developed by individual counsellors both during their training and as a consequence of their later experience with persons whom they counsel. Person-centred training, for example, puts great emphasis on developing skill in empathic listening combined with alertness to significance, allowing the counsellor to gain and communicate an understanding of the person's experience and at the same time objectively to select cues that might fruitfully be expanded into more detailed exploration. Therapists trained in approaches where empathic listening is not specifically taught develop the same skills through the application of inherently respectful practices specific to their own model. These skills are certainly central to good narrative therapy, and are essential to all couple counselling, with the additional dimension, as Wilkinson suggests when describing therapy with families, of assisting conflicted persons to develop a degree of empathy *towards each other* (Wilkinson 1992). It is easy for counsellors to lose sight of how rare the ability to empathize is in wider social life. Persons sometimes say that even close friends listening to their account of a distressing or worrying episode, and genuinely trying to be of assistance, are likely to interrupt, lengthily turn the conversation round to their own experiences, or offer unhelpful, top-down and unsolicited advice.

A non-expert stance

A truism of all counselling is that the person herself is the expert in her life, not the counsellor, and that the counsellor's role and professional expertise lie in assisting the person to move from distress and despair, and to recognize, activate and consolidate previously overlooked skills, abilities, personal resources and feelings. Obviously, these core aims are achieved differently according to the counsellor's therapeutic approach. At different stages of my own professional life, I have worked in three different approaches (person-centred, solution-focused and narrative) and I hesitate to say whether there was any significant difference in success according to which I used, judging by persons' feedback about how far my counselling was helpful to them. I am now a narrative therapist because this approach matches my present assumptions and beliefs about people and about counselling, but I believe that the factor of respecting and enhancing the person's own capacities was also present in my previous ways of working. Counsellors beginning couple work will bring these assumptions to it as a matter of course, and this will be a major factor in their undertaking it effectively.

Reflexivity and professional development

Counsellors new to working with couples will take certain professional practices for granted, such as a commitment to regular supervision and to continuing professional development through self-reflection, reading, and attending courses and workshops. These practices embody continually reviewing one's work, both in specific learning contexts and through regular conversations with an experienced colleague, in a spirit of (in the most positive sense) critical self-examination. Acceptance of the importance of supervision and professional development, no matter how experienced the counsellor may be, is something the profession can be proud of, as it demonstrates an ever-present acknowledgement that there is always something to learn and to improve, and a permanent commitment to this process. Particularly through supervision, the novice couple counsellor will identify and discuss issues and difficulties in working with couples before the problems become urgent or disabling, and also explore possibilities of how to assist couples more effectively.

Choice and role of supervisor

Good supervision is, of course, crucial to good counselling – but what if the counsellor's usual supervisor has little or no experience of working with couples, and/or no knowledge of narrative therapy, the model used in this book? Should a different supervisor be sought for this area of work, and the current supervisor consulted only in relation to the counsellor's work with individuals? Perhaps the ideal couple-work supervisor for readers of this book would be a narrative therapist experienced in couple counselling, but such people are thin on the ground at present!

I think this apparent problem can be overstated. A supervisor doesn't necessarily need to work to the same model as the supervisee, though some degree of common ground is helpful. Good supervisors respect their supervisee's way of working rather than try to impose their own, possibly different approach. They also recognize that a *two-way* process occurs in their consultative sessions; that these are not top-down situations where a superior practitioner puts a less skilled colleague right, but collaborative conversations where (as in counselling itself) the supervisee is primarily encouraged to identify, articulate and develop his or her own ideas, competencies, skills and solutions. Where dilemmas and difficulties occur in a novice couple counsellor's work, a good supervisor will encourage him to recognize and draw on his reading, thinking and experience, and through this to find a way forward. A good supervisor's suggestions for consideration will be tentative, related to the counsellor's model and fully open to discussion. When I began using narrative therapy, firstly with individuals and later with couples too, my supervisor was a colleague trained in person-centred therapy, who worked mostly with individuals. My sessions with her were always immensely beneficial.

Ethical practice

The counselling profession's emphasis on ethical practice, embodied for example in the various counselling organizations' guidelines, should inform couple counselling in exactly the same way as when working with individuals. The counsellor new to couple counselling will bring an adherence to ethical concepts, policies and practices as a matter of course – for example, counselling being for the benefit of persons rather than the counsellor, the need for clear contractual agreements, the maintenance of appropriate boundaries, lack of exploitation, maintaining confidentiality, and accepting persons for counselling no matter what their sexuality, ethnicity or personal beliefs. Although (as I say earlier) BACP's and other organizations' ethical guidelines cannot, and do not claim to, provide solutions to all ethical dilemmas, consulting these guidelines will often clarify matters, especially when the supervisor is also recruited into the discussion. Having the ethical dimensions of professionalism already firmly in place will be an important and reassuringly familiar element when working in this new context.

Personal experience

I believe that the dangers posed by persons' problems triggering echoes from the counsellor's personal life, with those echoes becoming a threat to the counselling process and also forming a threat to the counsellor's own wellbeing, have been rather exaggerated in the traditional counselling culture. I am dubious concerning the still widespread notion that all counsellors should, as a matter of course, have personal therapy in order to identify unrecognized psychological traumas and emotional danger areas and address these. Rather, I am inclined to think that counsellors will usually recognize this potential situation should it threaten, and deal with it, perhaps in supervision.

Nevertheless, I suggest that there is truth in the idea that the counsellor's own experience is relevant to her counselling. In couple counselling, for example, as I suggest above, painful relationship issues in the counsellor's life may inadvertently incline her towards over-identifying with the partner whose situation most resembles her own, and this needs to be guarded against. On a contrasting positive note, when properly recognized and taken into account, the counsellor's experience of life can be brought to bear on the couple's problems and assist her to work creatively. Very few people escape painful relationship issues at some time in their lives, and when a counsellor has been through such experiences, they may well enhance her ability to understand the reactions, thoughts and feelings of couples going through similar crises. I think this positive factor has been undervalued in the traditional counselling culture, with its perhaps rather nervous emphasis on how echoes from the counsellor's life may distort her objectivity by reactivating painful memories. Common ground of human distress can be a powerful resource when brought to bear in couples work, and narrative therapy in particular has developed practices where the counsellor's own experience can be drawn on openly and appropriately in the service of the couple.

Mary and Ken (see above, page 12)

I asked Mary whether she wanted this secret individual session so as to tell me in confidence about abuse, violence or criminal acts which she felt unable to raise with Ken present. If she had said this was so, I would have agreed to the individual session on the terms she was requesting.

However, Mary had simply changed her mind about all sessions being joint, and had decided she would like an opportunity to explain her point of view to me in more detail. She was embarrassed at the idea of Ken's knowing her change of mind, and anxious in case he might be angry about it, but she assured me there was no way he would be violent. I said that I would be happy to have some individual sessions with her after the next, agreed, joint session, but that Ken must know about these, and must also be told about her phone call and request. I would have to mention the call to Ken at the joint session unless she had told him about it already, and if she had, I would need her to tell me this in front of Ken at the start of the session. Mary said she understood the position, apologized for the mistake she had made, and undertook to tell Ken what she had done. At the joint session, Ken himself began by saying that Mary had told him about her phone call and why she had made it, and that although at first he was hurt that she had gone behind his back he did realize why, as he knew he could be quick-tempered at times. We then agreed that each partner would have an individual session after this joint one.

DISCUSSION POINTS

Consider these questions, if possible in discussion with a colleague:

1. What has led you to consider working with couples?
2. What previous personal and professional experiences will contribute positively to your couple counselling?
3. What existing personal and professional qualities and skills will you bring to this work?
4. What qualities and experience will you need in the supervisor whom you consult about your couple counselling? How will you help your supervisor to help you?

2
NARRATIVE THERAPY

This chapter describes the philosophical assumptions and some of the practices of narrative therapy, with adaptations, simplifications and practices from other therapies, since this is the model used in this book. As already suggested, readers fully familiar with narrative therapy might like to skip this chapter.

AN APPROPRIATE THERAPY

Counsellors trained to work with individuals may possibly be unfamiliar with narrative therapy, as it developed in the context of family therapy rather than traditional one-to-one counselling. In my workshops on couple counselling, participants trained in various different individual-based models have told me that it has been easier to learn this unfamiliar approach than to try to adapt their existing way of working. As the workshops progressed, participants who normally used psychodynamic, person-centred or cognitive methods, for example, agreed that narrative therapy offered a detailed, clear, consistent and unified approach which they found sympathetic, and clearly geared to the unfamiliar area of working with couples. However, most of them also found, slightly to their surprise, that narrative therapy had enough in common with their usual way of working to give them a sense of continuity and consistency. I hope that readers of this book who are new to narrative therapy will also find it stimulating, appropriate and above all practical, and that this chapter's overview will help them to orientate through the rest of the book.

NARRATIVES OF LIFE AND PROBLEMS

Narrative therapy originated in Australia and New Zealand in the early 1980s, in the thinking and practice of Michael White, Co-Director of the Dulwich Centre for Family Therapy and Community Work in Adelaide, and David Epston, Co-Director of the

Family Centre in Auckland. White was perhaps the more widely influential of the two, and his ideas and practices have had a major impact on family therapy and community work worldwide. Narrative therapy has now moved beyond its original family therapy context as counsellors who work with individuals and couples have discovered it.

The key term 'narrative' refers to those times when self-reinforcing memories, thoughts, images and feelings which make up a person's apprehension of himself/herself and the world, are given expression as narratives (or 'stories') of life. These stories may take the form of a ruminative monologue, or the literal form of everyday conversation with other people. In narrative therapy, persons are encouraged to extend their accounts (stories, narratives) of their problems so as to include previously ignored or un-noticed elements that build to a wider perspective on the problem and on the persons' self-view. These revised, extended, 'enriched' stories, told at length to the therapist in response to questions and then perhaps also told to other people, are closer to the reality of their actual experiences than their more limited initial descriptions, and this wider perspective becomes the foundation for change. How this is achieved will, I hope, become clear in the rest of the book. But how different is narrative therapy from other counselling approaches?

Common ground

Therapies firmly based on believing in, respecting and activating the person's own personal and social resources have many elements in common. Narrative therapy departs in certain aspects from some of the traditional counselling culture's taken-for-granted assumptions, but always as a re-thought enhancement of the person-respecting values it has in common with most other therapies. It shares the assumption that the therapist's role is to assist persons to modify or remove distorted perceptions and other negative influences which have been holding them back from releasing their own skills and capacities, and then assist them to call on these more positive elements to resolve the issues brought to counselling.

All therapies explore persons' narratives, as this is the material presented in counselling. Angus and McLeod, in a book with contributions from therapists representing a range of models including cognitive, person-centred, experiential, relational and psychodynamic, affirm that 'All these writers have identified client narrative expression as the common ground of social discourse in psychotherapy and an essential constituent of client reflexivity and human agency … ' (2004: 367). The concept of 'narrative' is a place where diverse therapeutic minds can meet.

Below, I suggest common ground between narrative therapy and some other approaches (with therapies given in alphabetical order).

Adlerian therapy

Adlerian and narrative therapists emphasize the significance of power relations between individuals, and between social institutions and individuals. In both ways of working, the examination of these interactive power relations, and a concern with the social context of individual distress, is seen as more important than analysing assumed psychological deficits (Carlson 2004: 76).

Cognitive therapy

White was indebted to the psychologist Jerome Bruner for many ideas on the importance of narrative (1995: 32) and Bruner originally identified himself with the 1950s 'cognitive revolution' in psychology (1990: 2–3). Narrative therapy is a cognitive therapy in that it aims to facilitate a revision of existing cognitive habits that are limiting the person's ability to resolve the issues brought to counselling. Perceptual re-formation is the aim of both approaches. The theoretical assumptions of cognitive therapy, as summarized by Moorey, apply equally to narrative therapy:

1. The person is an active agent who interacts with his or her world.
2. This interaction takes place through the interpretations and evaluations the person makes about his or her environment.
3. The results of the 'cognitive' processes are thought to be accessible to consciousness in the form of thoughts and images, and so the person has the potential to change them. (2007: 300)

Both therapies take the person through structured therapeutic sessions with an emphasis on conscious rather than assumed unconscious processes, with an underpinning assumption that the therapist's task is to assist persons to recognize, and escape from, rigid and unproductive ways in which they have been interpreting their lives. Aaron Beck recommends something very like externalizing the problem, which is a core element in narrative therapy: 'the therapist's … role is working with the patient against "it", the patient's problem' (Beck 1989: 220–1).

Gestalt therapy

Gestalt therapy's concept of people as essentially communal and interactive beings rather than bounded within their individual subjective experience, its focus on lived experience and its concept of distress as caused by damaging external factors rather than 'illness' (Parlett and Denham 2007: 230–1) are all paralleled in narrative therapy.

Neuro-linguistic programming

Neuro-linguistic programming and narrative therapists both identify the subtle and unrecognized implications of language usage as central to persons' perceptions, and they both pay close attention to the language used by the therapist as an influential factor in the therapeutic process (Peter Young, personal communication, 2004).

Personal construct psychology

Personal construct psychology matches narrative therapy in its identifying the exploration of persons' constructs of reality as a key starting point for assisting them to escape the limitations of their taken-for-granted perceptions of life and relationships (Fransella et al. 2007: 37–8).

Person-centred therapy

When I came across White's and Epston's work, I recognized similarities between their ideas and those of Rogers (Payne 1993/1996). Both therapies reject a stance of expert, superior knowledge. Neither model attempts to interpret the person's experience, to define problems in medical or psychiatric terms, to teach persons to relate better or to think more logically, to offer advice, or to role-model. Trust in persons' ability to reconnect with temporarily diminished capacities is a core 'given' in narrative therapy as it is in the person-centred approach. Both therapies identify the internalization of others' perspectives as at the root of identity loss, with identity loss seen as a major contributor to confusion, distress and disorientation (Rogers 1951: 498–503; White 2004a: ch. 5. White 2004b: 45–6). It is abundantly clear when watching videos of Michael White at work that he has positive regard for the person or persons consulting him, that he enters into and respects their view of their experience, and that he is being wholly himself – that he relates in the mode Rogers believed to lie at the core of good therapy. In their writings and interviews, both men sometimes demonstrate an endearingly puckish and self-deprecating sense of humour which sits easily with their seriousness of purpose.

Psychodynamic therapies

Common ground between psychodynamic therapies and narrative therapy lies in certain theoretical starting points. According to the psychoanalytic therapist Donald Spence, 'Freud made us aware of the persuasive power of a coherent narrative – in particular, of the way in which an aptly chosen reconstruction can fill the gap between two apparently unrelated events and, in the process, make sense out of nonsense' (1982: 1). This strikingly resembles Michael White's proposal that there are always 'gaps in the text' in the narratives persons tell the therapist, and that these provide the key to processes of perceptual change (2000: ch. 7). Narrative therapists, like Spence, stress that therapists do not address the actual events of a person's life, as these are unknowable in their complexity; the therapist's material is the person's told *account* of his experience, which is inevitably partial, selective, inconsistent and influenced by assumptions and norms of the person's culture and wider society. Spence suggests that therapists themselves bring embedded professional, personal and culturally formed assumptions and interpretative biases to the therapy process, with linguistic forms and conventions adding their own shaping (Spence 1982: 221–37). Narrative therapists would agree with these observations, recognizing in them similarities to the ideas of Gregory Bateson, who was a seminal influence on Michael White's thinking (White 1989: 85–100).

Solution-focused therapy

Narrative therapy and solution-focused therapy are perhaps closer to each other in conception than is either model to any other approach. Both therapies reject the concept of assumed deficiencies or inadequacies in the person, and give time and attention to positive aspects of experience rather than to negative aspects. Therapists of both persuasions invite persons to identify occasions when the problem was absent, which are then explored in detail, and constitute the basis of change (De Shazer 1988: 131–8; White and Epston 1990: 15–6, 55–63). Although narrative therapists do not define their approach as 'brief', like solution-focused therapists they usually hold considerably fewer sessions than traditional therapists.

None of the above implies that narrative therapy is much the same as other ways of working, or that the above approaches are much the same as each other. There are real and important differences. Nevertheless, I hope that this preamble will reassure readers that they are likely to find narrative therapy sympathetic, and that its practices have the potential to form the basis of their work with couples – and also, perhaps, to enrich their other work.

SELF-STORIES

As we live from day to day and year to year, we accumulate a huge store of memories. As with experiences, some memories are trivial, some are significant, some are central to our lives and have powerful emotional meaning. Memory makes up our sense of what life has been, is and might be, providing a kaleidoscope of mental images that define our own unique personal history, our sense of ourselves and our sense of our place in the world.

Recall of memories is selective. In everyday living, memories are restricted and self-censoring. How we remember experiences, and what they mean to us, are powerfully influenced by multiple factors, including social, cultural and relational factors we have internalized. Our identity and self-view is involved in the censorship; we need to think well of ourselves, we need to believe that our lives make sense, we need to posit links between events that might otherwise seem random and meaningless. These factors filter our memories and re-cast them.

How do we define our lives and represent them to ourselves? How do we give *meaning* to our experience? We accrue beliefs, and we interpret our lives in the light of these beliefs. Some beliefs are fully in our awareness – our religion or lack of it, our political positions, our ideas about what makes for a good relationship. But even these consciously held and acknowledged beliefs have been arrived at randomly to some extent, through the accident of our existence in the social and cultural contexts in which we happen to find ourselves, although our beliefs and assumptions seem 'meant' and inevitable once they have been formed. They tend to be self-reinforcing (how many people read a newspaper supporting a different political party than the one they vote for?). Other beliefs and assumptions embed themselves as 'unexamined truths' which are hardly noticed as such, let alone questioned – we have absorbed them as obvious 'realities' and norms according to our socio–cultural context.

Because life is full and complex but memory is selective, there is a potential for telling many contrasting accounts or stories about the events, feelings and thoughts of our past and more recent history.

These stories are told around particular themes (or 'plots') according to the triggers that produce them in interaction with the listener or listeners. They may concern our career, our love life, our giving up smoking, the cars we have owned, our health problems, people we have lost touch with, our last holiday, memories of childhood games, house moves ... the possibilities are endless. Sometimes these themes will intersect (changes in career meaning house moves and losing touch with friends) and sometimes they will be wholly disconnected with other story-strands of our lives. If we are unhappy or worried, the themes we talk about and shape into narratives will reflect this situation, and if we are immensely distressed and confused, any happier themes may seem unimportant or even illusory, and are even less likely to be included.

Memories and their meanings are slippery and transient if they remain restricted to internal monologue, though this does have a part to play in building up our store of life images. However, as social beings, we continually share experiences through dialogue with others, and in so doing we review, consolidate and structure our memories and attribute meaning to them. In buses, shops, queues, restaurants etc., we can hear this process happening all the time:

> 'I went to see her last week and do you know what? She was out – she'd forgotten I was coming. I'd bought a bunch of flowers, and they were wasted. Typical of her, it was just like when I went last month – well, I shan't go any more. Let *her* contact *me*, if she can be bothered to pick up the phone!'

This invented fragment is a little narrative or *story* in itself, and will become part of a longer narrative if the conversation continues. Only selected events are chosen for the narrative, with irrelevant details omitted (the weather, the exact number of flowers, what the speaker was wearing). Significant detail is emphasized (the wasted flowers). The event is set in personal history (last week ... last month) and its meaning projected to the future ('I shan't do it any more'). Meaning is conveyed implicitly – something like, 'I now realize this relationship isn't worth the effort.' A conclusion is drawn about future action, or in this case inaction; the speaker will leave it to the visited person to make contact. Of course, the overall spoken tone of the fragment is not conveyed by bare print; a resigned, humorous and ironic tone of voice will convey something rather different in terms of meaning and intention than if the tone is furious, tense and bitter.

If we were to hear an account of this incident from the viewpoint of the visited person, it might correspond exactly to the visitor's story, but it is more likely that the narrative would be rather different; perhaps the visitor knocked softly, not allowing for the other person's deafness, and just went away again; or perhaps there were previous incidents when the visitor was tactless or offensive, and since she won't take hints that the relationship is unwanted, the only thing to do is not to answer the door. For both people, the act of narrating the incident to other people will structure it, reinforce the meaning they attribute to it, and be a major factor leading to its becoming a fixed account reflecting the teller's apprehension of the truth – unless it is *questioned* tactfully, perhaps by a friend attempting to promote reconciliation, so that both people involved come to see the other's point of view and modify their narratives in the light of this.

Hearing the person's story and encouraging it to be extended and modified

The core of narrative therapy consists of encouraging people to tell their problem-story in detail, then encouraging them by means of carefully chosen questions to 'tell and re-tell' extended versions of the story which include previously neglected, forgotten, undervalued or unnoticed elements. Incorporating these elements produces not just a revised and extended story/narrative in a neutral sense, but makes the new story influential; it changes the person's thinking and feeling, and modifies how she perceives her problem (she becomes 'differently positioned' in relation to it). These cognitive and emotional changes initiate a new progression: typically, from feeling defeated and hopeless to becoming more energized and hopeful, based not on some kind of facile optimism but firmly rooted in the previously unrecognized or forgotten realities revealed by the new perspective.

Here is a simple example from my own practice:

Joyce, an elderly widow, was consumed with guilt. The last words she said to her husband, Fred, just before he unexpectedly died, had been angry and hurtful, because he had soiled the bedclothes. She told me the story of their marriage over the whole of the first session, including how it had ended in Fred's death, and her story was guilt-ridden, permeated with incidents when she had yelled at him furiously or not behaved in kindly or loving ways. It was what White calls a 'problem-saturated' account (White and Epston 1990: 16, 39). Over three further sessions, when I had acknowledged her terrible feelings about how Fred's life had ended, and not in any way tried to suggest any consolation concerning her last words to him, I invited Joyce to tell me more about the history of the marriage, and especially about good times they had enjoyed together. There were plenty of these 'exceptions' and they built to a clear picture of a volatile but very loving relationship where outbursts of temper and quarrelling had been quite common on both sides, but accepted as part of the relationship's liveliness. There had been many occasions when they laughed a lot, enjoyed each other's company, supported each other in hard times, and shared pleasure in their children and grandchildren. These incidents were, with my prompting, reminisced in considerable detail, and fully re-lived in Joyce's imagination, memory and feelings. I gave her photocopies of my notes for the second and third sessions as reinforcing reminders of the good and happy aspects of her marriage which she had described. Towards the end of the fourth session, responding to a question from me, she said that if Fred could be present with us in spirit he would probably tell her impatiently to stop feeling guilty, and to remember all the good times. She still bitterly regretted her last words to him, but now she could recognize it was just very bad luck that he died soon afterwards rather than after a happier incident. She decided she did not need any more counselling.

Session content and sequence

In narrative therapy, the relationship between the counsellor and the person is not in itself seen as the means of bringing about change, but establishing an accepting, honest and non-judgemental atmosphere certainly is an aim. There is a basic sequential framework within which the counsellor tends to organize sessions, and I outline this below, with the caveat that for the purposes of this book, there are simplifications and omissions. Narrative therapy does not follow a rigid and inflexible pattern, as the priority is a sensitive response to the person seeking assistance. Timing of the elements varies, the sequence may be altered, and some practices may be left out altogether. According to the nature of the problem and the circumstances of the person, additional practices may be introduced which are not included in this summary but are described later in this book.

1. The person is invited to describe the problem. The counsellor listens carefully, checks out and summarizes.
2. By means of asking follow-up questions, the counsellor invites the person to extend the problem-story into areas not included in the original account, such as his work, health and sleep, family and other relationships, his sense of self. The aim is to elicit a comprehensive narrative covering the indirect as well as the direct effects of the problem on the person's life and relationships, so that he will feel fully heard and understood, and also to make reversion to problem-description later in counselling less necessary.
3. During the telling of the problem-story, the counsellor notes any elements that seem to offer the possibility of the story's being extended by the addition of aspects that throw a different light on the problem. (Narrative therapists use various different terms for these elements, especially the rather odd-sounding 'unique outcome', but *exceptions* is the simplest, and I have chosen to use this term throughout the book despite its more commonly being associated with solution-focused therapy than with narrative therapy.)

4. A name for the problem is discussed and agreed, often (but not always) a non-medicalized definition which implies *a distinction between the problem and the identity of the person*, such as 'the anxiety attacking you' not 'your anxiety'; 'difficulty in leaving the house' not 'agoraphobia'. This is called 'externalizing the problem' and when used in subsequent therapeutic dialogue, it implicitly separates the problem from the person's sense of who he or she is: 'the person is not the problem. Instead, the problem is the problem' (White 1989: 52).
5. If appropriate, the counsellor invites the person to consider the origins and effects of social, cultural and political factors on the problem, on the person's view of the problem and on the person's view of himself in relation to the problem.
6. Further questions invite the person to describe exceptions in detail, to consider their significance in relation to the problem, and to discuss how the exceptions might throw light on how to address it.
7. As the more complete story emerges, the counsellor may reinforce it by means of 'therapeutic documents'. These are written or other permanent recordings of discovery and progress, and may include taped recordings of sessions, summarizing letters, statements of intention and decision, certificates of achievement and personal writings such as poems and autobiographical fragments.
8. The counsellor may suggest that people significant to the person might like to hear the developing story, and by commenting, contribute to it. Such people may be invited to one or more carefully structured sessions.
9. The above process frees the person to escape from his initial 'problem-saturated' perspective, to see himself differently, to think purposefully and to decide on action.

AN EXAMPLE OF NARRATIVE THERAPY

This is another example of individual therapy rather than therapy with a couple, to enable counsellors accustomed to working with individuals to grasp essentials of the approach more readily at this stage. In my work with Mrs Dobson, not all the elements listed above were called on, but it did follow the general pattern.

Marjorie Dobson, age 70, was referred by her doctor because of 'chronic anxiety'. She was worried all the time about everything, and always had been, she said. She was scared about her slight high blood pressure despite her doctor telling her it was not a threat; frightened when her husband was out; too anxious to use buses; and cycled to her job as a school dinner lady because she was too frightened to walk. She was sleepless, and fretted about minor difficulties. We agreed to call her problem 'intrusive anxiety' and she confirmed she was fed up with it and wanted it to end.

I asked Marjorie when intrusive anxiety had first affected her life, and she talked of her childhood.

At 10 years old, in an impoverished family with nine children, she had been farmed out to her mother's sister and her husband, and brought up by them for six years. There was an atmosphere of severity and fierce discipline deriving from her relative's religious bigotry, and Marjorie developed a continuous nervous alertness, since she was often punished for minor or imagined 'sins' and offences. She was forbidden company of her own age outside school, and made to perform a long list of domestic tasks, with punishment and lectures on sin if she fell short. Occasionally, an older cousin had taken her out for the day – the only happy memories she retained from that time. When aged 15, she met Jed, a young soldier. He was posted away, but they corresponded. Her aunt discovered the lad's letters, and burnt them, screaming about sin and deceit. Marjorie did manage one meeting with him a year later, but the relationship was over. She decided to return to her parents' house to live, but was not made welcome. She got a job in a factory, where she enjoyed mixing with other young people and met Derek, a lively young man who took her out on his motorcycle pillion, and whom she married a few years later. They lived happily with his parents and siblings for a few years. However, when the couple moved to a house of their own, Marjorie became overwhelmed by anxiety, was referred to a psychiatrist, and was prescribed powerful tranquillizers, which she still took. Anxiety retreated for a while but returned with a vengeance when she had a baby, and she became virtually housebound for several years. A different psychiatrist suggested she might take a small job, so she became a school dinner lady, a post she loved and still held, though she was terrified she might lose it because of her heart condition.

I had noted some exceptions, aspects of Marjorie's narrative which appeared to contrast with her problem-saturated description of how unwanted anxiety had dominated her life. I expressed interest in these examples and invited her to describe them in detail. This process took up the last part of the first session and the whole of the second session a fortnight later. In each instance, I mentioned the possible exception then asked questions around it, which led Marjorie to reminisce at length and with animation about some of the key experiences of her life.

- You often defied your uncle and aunt. How was it that they failed to break your spirit despite the unwanted anxiety they introduced into your life?
- You were kept under close supervision yet you managed to meet Jed. How did you do this? How did you manage to meet him several times? I'd love to hear all about this secret romance.
- You must have had great difficulty in corresponding with Jed. How did you get hold of envelopes, stamps and notepaper? How did you smuggle your letters to the post? What ruses did you employ to grab his replies before your aunt and uncle saw his letters? How long did you manage to keep up this correspondence?
- What do all these examples tell you about your ability to stick to your own beliefs and values despite the way you were treated?
- What did the occasional days out with your older cousin do to keep up your spirits?

- What did your cousin's opinion of you do to help you to maintain your sense of who you are, as opposed to the obedient drudge your aunt and uncle wanted you to be? What benefits did your cousin get from her outings with you? What was the effect on *her* life of knowing she was so helpful to you?
- What name could we give to your aunt's action in burning Jed's letters? What thoughts, feelings and decisions did this act lead to on your part?
- You went back to live with your parents even though you weren't welcome. How did you overcome anxiety's attempts to dissuade you from this?
- You enjoyed your factory job. No real anxiety at that time? What actual job did you do? How was it you got on well with the other young people, when you hadn't mixed socially with people of your own age before? You met Derek – and rode pillion! What was it like to ride at some risk but not caring about it, holding tight to the man you were starting to love?
- Anxiety wasn't able to stop you marrying Derek and having a child, even though it did intrude badly at later times. And in later years it didn't stop you from getting a job at the school. How did you manage to get yourself to the interview? How did you stop unwanted anxiety from making you tongue-tied?
- What technique did you use to get yourself to the new job on the first day? Was it like when you went to the factory for the first time all those years ago?
- You ride a bike – a bit slower than riding on a motorbike pillion! But you still have to cope with traffic. How do you manage that? How and when did you learn to ride a bike? What did you do to stop anxiety from preventing this achievement?
- Can you think of more examples of when you defeated anxiety in the past and recently?
- If your cousin was still alive and knew what your life is like now, what would make her proud of you?

In answer to that last question, Marjorie said that her cousin *was* still alive, in her nineties. They often talked about the past. I wondered if the cousin would be interested in hearing Marjorie's discoveries about how she had defied oppression and rejected anxiety's attacks on her happiness? Marjorie said she thought this would make a good topic of conversation, and she would up take this suggestion. We also discussed how she might finally dismiss her dead aunt and uncle from her life, and so diminish the times when their influence still haunted her.

All our sessions were held fortnightly. At the third, Marjorie said that she had been worrying much less than usual. When worries did appear, she had taken practical action to dismiss them by immersing herself in a home decoration project. She shed quiet tears while telling me she had summoned the courage to ask Derek not to be so protective – she wanted him to recognize that this well-meant attitude made her feel worse about herself. She had seen her doctor to discuss a reduction of medication with a view to stopping it. We discussed the significance of these decisions and actions and their continuity with her past successes. I offered to summarize her life-long defiance of anxiety and oppression in a document, and this idea intrigued her.

In the fourth session, which turned out to be the last, Marjorie walked into the room smiling shyly, saying she had some things to tell me. She had gone shopping by bus, twice. She had also walked to her job – 'I just didn't give it a thought'. And she had gone to motor racing with her son, stood in the front row where cars roared past just a couple of metres away, and thoroughly enjoyed it. She liked the draft document of affirmation I had prepared (Figure 2.1), and she agreed without hesitation when I asked for permission to describe her counselling in my teaching and writing.

**THIS AFFIRMS MY PERSISTENCE IN RESISTING *ANXIETY'S*
ATTEMPTS TO CONTROL MY LIFE**

AND

**MY DECISION TO *DISMISS* AS MEMBERS OF MY LIFE THOSE
RESPONSIBLE FOR ANXIETY'S GAINING ITS POWER BY THEIR
EMOTIONAL AND PHYSICAL ABUSE IN MY CHILDHOOD**

- I did not allow separation from my parents at age 10 to destroy my spirit.
- I did not allow my aunt and uncle's deadly joylessness and their repression of my liveliness and happiness to destroy me.
- I took nourishment and hope from my cousin, despite the severe restrictions on her help imposed by my aunt and uncle.
- The abusive restrictions by my aunt and uncle did not suppress my delight in Jed's attentions, and I defied them by corresponding with him.
- I know that their destruction of his letters and cutting me off from him were unforgivable acts of interference and cruelty.
- I was able to rescue myself from their clutches and return to my own family. Anxiety was not strong enough to prevent me doing this.
- I was able to overcome the disappointment of my own family's lack of concern and to take a demanding job where I made friendships. Anxiety had not paralysed me and it had not prevented my taking a new direction.
- I was able to recognise in Derek a man worthy of my love and who loved me, to throw off old habits of doubt by entering into a period of courtship, to begin to experience joy, and to commit myself to him as his wife. Anxiety was powerless to prevent this.
- My relationships with Derek's family conquered anxiety for years.
- When anxiety regained power in my life I sought help, recognised good advice, and followed it by taking a part time job in a school.
- Anxiety was powerless to prevent me from becoming a mother.
- I push anxiety away by being active, and I enjoy going to motor racing.

There are many more examples of my ability to resist anxiety.

I hereby RENOUNCE my uncle and aunt, whose abuse led to anxiety invading my life. I REFUSE to mourn them and I REJECT and DISMISS them from membership in my life.

Signed ....MARJORIE DOBSON
Witnessed by ....MARTIN PAYNE
October 2006

FIGURE 2.1   MARJORIE'S AFFIRMATION DOCUMENT

PART 2
SOCIAL AND CULTURAL INFLUENCES ON COUNSELLORS AND COUPLES

3
CULTURALLY FORMED ATTITUDES TOWARDS COUPLE RELATIONSHIPS

This chapter suggests some precautions to take when working with persons whose ideas, assumptions and norms contrast with the therapist's. Many of the ideas and examples also apply to counselling individuals, but the emphasis is on couple counselling. It is, of course, impossible to cover all possible eventualities, but I hope that by discussing some of the most common pitfalls, the chapter will alert readers to areas where vigilance is particularly important.

TAKEN-FOR-GRANTED 'TRUTHS'

Socialization affects us all. In our own society and its various sub-groups, there exist beliefs, standards and values which permeate our thinking and result in decisions and actions seen as inevitable, normal and universal. Because historically and socially derived, their arbitrary nature mostly goes unrecognized and unexamined. These received ideas, taken-for-granted as truths, and conventional actions based upon them, do become strange and alien to later generations – they become curiosities defining our mental images of the past. Films portraying the past allow us to feel comfortable in our differences from that time, and perhaps rather self-congratulatory. In most of Western society, we no longer fill cinemas with cigarette smoke, force children into restricting clothes, close pubs and shops on Sundays, wear formal clothes to the theatre or assume that women will give up work if they marry. Most people no longer hold to the assumption that the male sex is 'of course' more capable of rational thought and action than the female. Such change is not a neat process. Sub-groups frequently continue to hold to assumed truths when majority groups have abandoned them, and the reverse is also true, with minority groups developing ideas that may gradually permeate into wider society as time passes.

Counsellor awareness of socialization

I suggest that all counsellors should attempt to be aware of their own assumed beliefs and values and how these have been formed, not necessarily to reject them but so as to examine whether they produce positive or negative results in their lives or the lives of others, including people who consult them. We need to bear in mind that in other cultures, including subcultures within the same nation or social group as ourselves, others may hold to different assumed truths. These have become an intrinsic part of their apprehension of the world and of their identity, and this is why others' cultural and social differences need to be respected and taken into account in our work.

Socialized differences are relatively easy to recognize when they are clear and conscious, such as religious or political beliefs, but more subtle assumptions are less easy to identify. An example is therapy itself. How many of us carefully chose training that matched our existing attitudes and beliefs about how people may best be assisted to overcome problems, and how many of us developed those beliefs via our training, taking on assumptions, values and beliefs of the counselling culture in general and of our own particular model? Do those beliefs match the cultural expectations of couples who come to us for help? Do these persons really want an opportunity to address their problems through encouragement of their own capacities, or are they seeking clear expert advice such as that given by doctors, or by respected leaders in their own society? Do they see the relevance of questions about childhood family relationships when they are distressed by their inability to keep their marriage together? Do they come from a culture where sorting out your own problems, or putting up with them, has high value? Do they have a degree of unspoken resentment at attempts to improve the logic of their thinking when their sub-culture primarily values feelings and emotions?

When counselling couples, attempting to be aware of their *and our own* assumed truths is not just valuable, it is necessary for good practice. Do we assume that heterosexual couples are the norm and gay/lesbian couples a deviation? Do we assume that marriage should be the goal of heterosexual couples, that lesbian and gay marriage is less real than heterosexual marriage, or that people living together are less committed to each other than married couples? Do we see certain sexual behaviours as normal/OK and others as abnormal/wrong? If a couple do not want to have children, do we see this as selfish? If a couple rent rather than take out a mortgage, and spend most of their income on expensive holidays and other luxuries, do we feel censorious? If the choice of married partners has been arranged by their parents rather than by themselves, do we assume this is wrong? If there is a large age gap between the two people, do we secretly disapprove? If the woman is the older, do we disapprove more than if the man were the senior of the two? What other assumed-normal ways of being a couple have we absorbed from our background and bring to this work?

None of this implies that all assumed truths are wrong, mistaken or dangerous. Nor does it imply that we are irretrievably conditioned by socialization; we are capable of identifying and examining our assumed truths, and we can then accept, modify or reject them. The point is that some assumed truths remain unacknowledged as such, and may be contributing unawares to problems and to attempts to resolve those problems.

Awareness of assumed norms is particularly important because in couple counselling, there is an additional complication not present in individual counselling: differences may exist not just between the therapist and one person, but between the therapist and two persons, sometimes with the pair differing between themselves as well!

> I counselled Simon and Leila, a husband and wife who were unable to agree on how they should help their unmarried son, who appeared wilfully to be throwing away his career prospects. Simon strongly believed they should take a firm stance and tell the young man in no uncertain terms to get his act together and take his responsibilities seriously, whereas Leila believed that she herself was responsible for her son's unsatisfactory behaviour and was so affected by depression, and consumed with guilt and distress, that according to her doctor she was in danger of emotional breakdown. I privately thought Simon was too harsh, too affected by a patriarchal culture of 'men know best', both in his opinions and in the way he delivered them. I could not grasp Leila's attitude at all. Their son was over 30 years old, lived in another country and was surely at a stage when he was in charge of his own life – why on earth was his mother feeling such debilitating guilt at the situation? What I have left out of this account is that Simon was English and Leila from a country where, as she told me later, there is a historically embedded cultural assumption that all children remain their parents' responsibility right up to the day they marry, no matter what the child's age. Failure to enquire into Leila's taken-for-granted beliefs, and also a failure to examine my own assumptions (including jumping to a stereotyped conclusion of male insensitivity), sabotaged my work with this couple, and counselling only continued for one further session. I had not understood how profoundly and understandably frustrated Simon had become by the conflict between his cultural beliefs and Leila's, and I had failed to understand how, for her, this divergence had combined with a sense of helplessness to produce suicidal despair.

If I had been more skilful in my counselling with Simon and Leila, I would from a much earlier point have suspected and verified the cultural differences underpinning the problem. Although Leila's culturally derived attitude to her son's independent status was very different from mine towards my own adult children, I would have respected her beliefs and would have conveyed this clearly. As it was, I suspect that my incomprehension allied me in her eyes with Simon, and added to her despair.

Eliciting and respecting persons' taken-for-granted values and beliefs does not mean that we should assume an anything-goes attitude; for example, when counselling people whose sub-culture's norms have encouraged them to be predatory and disrespectful towards others, I do not mentally shrug my shoulders and respect that sub-culture's values; I oppose this attitude, and this opposition permeates my counselling. (This point is discussed further in Chapter 4.)

Status of 'the couple'

Hotels charge lone guests more per head than couples, novels and films frequently feature the search for couple-love and its vicissitudes, most pop songs feature heterosexual love, advertisements often portray couples as idealized consumers of their products, and the very word 'couple' usually implies a one-to-one chosen and committed relationship, unless a different context is given. Being in a couple carries much status and assumed normality in Western society, and this sometimes negatively affects attitudes towards people who have no partner. 'Coupleism' being rife, it is usually unrecognized as an assumed norm and is therefore largely unexamined. It produces huge social pressures for people to choose partners, and once these are chosen, it produces an expectation for the partnership to result in happiness and fulfilment. The commercialization of marriage and the large sums frequently spent on ceremony, reception and honeymoon all play their part (Falcof 2007: 68–99).

Coupleism can produce intense distress, longings and identity crisis on the part of persons who have not achieved couple status. Established couples whose relationship becomes threatened may find their uncertainties, disillusion and unhappiness increased by social disapproval, especially if the nature of the relationship deviates from socially approved norms, such as unmarried heterosexual persons living together, or same-sex relationships. Friends and relatives may directly or indirectly convey judgemental attitudes ('We knew it couldn't last', 'I told you it would end in tears', 'Perhaps it's just as well, really'). And the person's own identity, bound up with being a member of a couple, may feel threatened at the prospect of ending the relationship.

Heterosexism

It is all too easy for counsellors to feel proud of their acceptance of lesbian and gay persons' sexuality, and not to recognize that we are all to an extent the victims of homophobic socialization which is lurking and ready to affect our work.

Did that sentence seem liberal, well expressed, properly pointing out a possibly unrecognized danger? It was actually riddled with heterosexism, which I define as an assumption that heterosexual relationships are the approved norm – in other words, with subtle homophobia. The words 'we' and 'our' particularly give it away. The sentence addresses the reader with an unstated assumption that she/he is heterosexual, implicitly sidelining gay and lesbian counsellors. By implying that I am heterosexual too, it invites a warm feeling that 'we' belong to the approved majority who, while apparently inviting self-examination, in reality, share condescending feelings of self-congratulation at 'accepting' the sexuality of others.

I invite the reader to re-write the sentence in wording that eliminates these elements. I also invite the reader to take the point that heterosexism can be a dangerous and subtly expressed element of heterosexual counsellors' socialization, a suspect element when counselling not only gay or lesbian couples but at work when counselling heterosexual couples too, where its effects can be to validate and reinforce homophobia if these persons' attitudes include this. Heterosexual counsellors need to monitor their use of language carefully and to make conscious efforts to eliminate apparently neutral, but actually homophobic, phrasing. Even if homophobia is not an overt element in the couple's problems, it is ethically unacceptable and socially irresponsible for counsellors to validate it, no matter how subtly, for example by using words and concepts implying heterosexuality is the valued norm.

Gender socialization and stereotyping

Gender socialization should always be taken into account, especially when counselling heterosexual couples. In certain societies and social groups, it is still considered normal for the man to be the dominant partner, and a woman who (for example) takes a full-time job before her children are of school age may face not only the resistance of her partner but the disapproval of those close to her. For the counsellor, it is not just a question of being aware of the norm of male power in heterosexual relationships, crucially important though this is, but of recognizing how women can internalize this situation even though they may resent or react against it, and how, arising from their own socialization, they may feel guilt at countering their society's assumed norms. I have lost count of the number of women who have expressed resentment of their male partner to me in the form of 'I hate it that he won't let me take a job/see my friends/wear sexy clothes/go to the tennis club without him' etc., where their resentment is not so much against the male assumption of ownership and control, but against *not being given permission*. In these instances, the woman can benefit from the counsellor's gently inviting her to consider the implications of her phrasing.

Counsellors should also beware of their own tendency to stereotype. In my work, I have come across instances of male violence to women partners, and I know of statistics indicating that domestic violence is predominantly male. I have read books on, and am wholly sympathetic to, the women's liberation movement. This predisposes me to a prejudiced view that domestic violence is always a male phenomenon. I once counselled a man, however, who was very cynical about counselling, and who in our third session told me that his diminutive wife was habitually physically violent towards him, occasionally causing injury. He said bitterly that he had not previously told anyone else of this, let alone seen a counsellor, because he knew they would not believe him, and would probably assume that his story was a cover for his own unadmitted violence. My accepting his account was a great relief to him, and enabled our counselling to be fruitful.

As a male therapist, I always try to be aware of how my own gender socialization is active when I counsel individuals. There is an ever-present danger of my either over-identifying with men, or being so aware of this danger that I go too far in the other direction. Also, my own male habits of stance, gesture, tendency to dominate conversation, and assumption of superior knowledge are elements lurking ready to reveal themselves and to affect my work negatively. So, when counselling a heterosexual couple, I need to be aware that the woman may feel outnumbered and the man may feel automatically supported. Female therapists face a different danger when counselling a heterosexual couple; the female partner may feel more comfortable with her than the male partner, but the man may try to assert his habitual male dominance over both the counsellor and his partner.

Modes of couple relationships

At least in Western society, many modes of couple relating and commitment have evolved over the past 50 years or so, and counsellors need to be alert to the danger of their own preconceptions triggering negative judgements when counselling persons whose union embodies unconventional elements. There can be a temptation to attribute couples' difficulties to their chosen mode of relating rather than wholly to accept it as one of a rich variety, in some instances not perhaps to the counsellor's personal taste but legitimate for the persons themselves. I suggest below some possibly problematic forms of relating which couple counsellors may encounter.

The 'conventional' couple

In my experience, counsellors tend to be among the more progressive and liberal members of society. I have never met a woman counsellor who claimed that a woman's role should be subordinate to a male partner and limited to the domestic, or a male counsellor who has admitted to such beliefs. I myself think that such attitudes are outdated and harmful. But what about when a married, heterosexual couple comes to counselling and, whatever other problems they are experiencing, neither party appears at all unhappy with the man going to work and the woman staying at home, cooking and cleaning and looking after the children? Certainly, a different and previously unadmitted situation may emerge through the counselling process, with the apparent domestic harmony an illusion, but what if it does not? I suggest that even though this may go against the grain of progressive thinking, there are many couples who are genuinely satisfied with this conventional way of organizing their lives together and that a counsellor who too swiftly assumes it to be suspect can swiftly alienate the couple.

Unmarried couples living together

This is such a common situation, at least in the West, that I hesitate to include it. The time is long past when hotels asked for proof of marriage, or when heterosexual couples had to be married in order to get a mortgage, and use of the term 'partner' is widespread with a meaning beyond its original connotations. Many couples who live together intend to marry but many others do not, and counsellors need to be clear on two contrasting points. They should not assume that partners engaged to be married are so conditioned by the expectations of relatives and wider society that they are mindlessly bound by convention and heading for a fall.

On the other hand, they should not assume that those who have no plans to marry are less certain of each other, or less wholeheartedly committed to their relationship, than the other group.

Couples who do not have children

Counsellors need to avoid bringing assumed–truth attitudes to bear when counselling couples who do not have children, particularly when the issue is not raised by the couple themselves. There are linguistic traps for the counsellor similar to those suggested above concerning heterosexism, which can spring even in the first moments of asking the couple about themselves – the very term 'childless', for example, implies that parenthood is the norm. If it were a neutral term, there would also be an accepted word meaning the limitations on life brought about by parenthood – 'child-burdened' perhaps? The language lacks such a word, as far as I know, which is perhaps significant in itself.

This is not, of course, to deny that for many couples there can be a damaging division if one partner wants children and the other either does not or is uncertain, and for lesbian and heterosexual couples this can be compounded and made more urgent if the age limit for conceiving is approaching. There are different but equally problematic and distressing conflicts for couples who have come to counselling because they want children but are physically unable to have children of their own, cannot come to terms with this situation, and perhaps have doubts or other difficulties about fostering or adoption.

A therapist who implies that having children is the desired norm will bring to bear a powerful and value-laden assumption with all the force of wider society's approval, possibly to the detriment of sensitivity to the couple's own wishes and values. I narrowly avoided this mistake with Joanna and Will, whose doctor's referral indicated that Joanna's problem was connected with not having children.

I asked Joanna if she and Will had had fertility tests, and she said they had not. I was about to ask her whether considering such tests might be a good idea when Will told me that they each had a demanding but rewarding job, were in a happy relationship, and that neither of them wanted to be parents. Joanna liked children and enjoyed being a 'good aunt' to her brother's two little girls, but did not want her satisfying life to be altered. The problem was that their parents were 'heartbroken' at this decision. They were pressurizing the couple to change their minds, saying that Will and Joanna would regret their lack of children, that Joanna would feel unfulfilled as a woman, that in the end this would cause conflict between them, and that in any case they were being selfish by denying their parents the pleasures of being grandparents. This pressure was so immense, reinforced by some friends who were parents themselves that, despite herself, Joanna was having agonizing doubts. Yet every time she imagined how pregnancy and parenthood would shatter her life, she could not bear the thought of reversing the decision.

Counselling took the form of assisting Joanna and Will to re-engage with and reinforce their knowledge of what was right for them, and to resist the attempts of others to persuade them otherwise.

Unconventional organization of the relationship

Engagement followed by marriage is society's approved norm for heterosexual couples, though the presumption of not having sex before marriage no longer carries weight except among a minority. Living together is fast becoming equal to marriage in popularity and acceptance. Civil partnerships and same-sex marriages, though by no means universal internationally, give gay and lesbian couples the opportunity to form a legally binding and publicly witnessed ceremony of commitment.

However, counsellors are likely to come across couples whose organization of their circumstances is contrary to socially approved norms, and again, it is important to recognize the danger of value judgements based on the counsellor's own socialization. Writing about Joanna and Will reminded me of Sarah and her boyfriend, Joe.

Sarah and Joe were having uncertainties about their relationship. For several years, they had put off living together, then eventually decided to take this step, so Joe had given up his bedsit and moved into Sarah's flat. To their dismay this had not worked – Joe felt awkward and out of place, and Sarah resented the ending of her privacy and her routines being upset. After many escalating quarrels, they decided to end the relationship, and Joe moved into a flat of his own, whereupon both realized they missed the other terribly, and after a while they took up again. A few months before they came to counselling, Joe had once again moved in with Sarah – her flat was larger and better furnished than his – but the old stresses had returned and both had started to wonder if the relationship was doomed. Did they really love each other? If they did, surely they wouldn't have those quarrels and those negative reactions? Sarah was seriously thinking of asking Joe to move out yet again but was worried that he might see this as a final rejection. Through counselling, the couple decided that conventional social expectations, absorbed as assumed truths, had affected their confidence in their own experience. They decided that they could live separately and still be fully committed to each other, and their pleasure at this decision was reinforced by my quoting examples of several famous couples who had found such a solution satisfactory.

Sexuality

Sexuality is an important issue in couple counselling and I address it in Chapter 4. Perhaps it is enough at this point to suggest that a heterosexual therapist counselling a lesbian or gay couple, or a gay or lesbian therapist counselling a heterosexual couple, needs to consider certain issues that are not present when the therapist is working with a couple of his or her own sexuality.

Variants of sexual behaviour

There is a great variety of ways in which individuals and couples practise sex, and the unwary counsellor can find himself at a disadvantage if persons' choices clash with his own taken-for-granted values and he consciously or unintentionally transmits his distaste to the couple. As with all the variants presented in this chapter, there can be a temptation to make value judgements and to rationalize these as insights into what is wrong with the couple's relationship, when in actuality they find the practices perfectly acceptable. This is quite a different matter from discovering that a couple disagrees about how often they should have sex, or that one partner wishes to impose certain practices on the other. Group sex, partner-swapping, sado-masochistic play, fantasy dressing, cross-dressing, heterosexual anal intercourse, watching pornography, and filming themselves having intercourse are some practices the couple counsellor may well encounter.

> John and Lynn were worried about John's irrational jealousy. Both said firmly that in reality they trusted the other, and that sex together was frequent and enjoyable, but sometimes when John saw Lynn talking to an attractive man, he started to feel angry and could not stop himself from wondering if anything was going on. This led to his becoming silent and moody, followed by accusations and quarrels, and the couple were becoming afraid for their relationship. They belonged to a group of couples who for several years had met regularly to exchange sexual partners for the evening. In this setting, John did not have jealous reactions, though at times he felt uneasy when Lynn's temporary partner was particularly attractive, or a man he didn't very much like.

On hearing John and Lynn's story, I immediately started silently to hypothesize that the partner-swapping was at the root of the problem, and even as I write this account, I can still feel the temptation making its presence felt, so deep-rooted and different are my own attitudes. However, it transpired that John's first wife had been serially unfaithful and that he had developed a reflex reaction of suspicion when anything reminded him of how she flirted with strange men.

The exceptions which emerged from my questions, and which were instrumental in extending the original problem-story to a wider perspective, were around the differences between Lynn and his first wife: the different qualities Lynn brought to their marriage; the meaning of times when they were happy together. The jealousy that had invaded John's view of his marriage never quite disappeared but did retreat to a manageable distance, and there was never any need for us to address their unconventional social life.

DISCUSSION POINTS

Consider these points, if possible in discussion with a colleague:

1. Can you recall an occasion when you found your own assumed truths were different from those of the person you were counselling? How far were you able to recognize that both sets of beliefs owed much to socialization?
2. From what contrasting sources did your assumed truth, and the person's, originate?
3. Discuss at what point you recognized this, if it hindered your counselling, and if so, how you dealt with this.
4. With hindsight, do you have any ideas as to how you might have addressed the situation differently?
5. Identify additional examples of your own assumed truths that might clash with those of persons you may counsel.

4

COUNSELLING COUPLES OF A DIFFERENT SEXUALITY, AGE OR CULTURAL BACKGROUND FROM THE COUNSELLOR

As I suggested in Chapter 2, counsellors who work with individuals will bring assumed and familiar ethical assumptions to couple counselling. It would be patronizing, and surely superfluous, for this book to argue the case for accepting persons for counselling no matter what their sexuality, age, ethnicity, culture or personal beliefs. In their work with individuals, counsellors will already have developed sensitivity to when their own culture's norms might clash with the norms of persons who consult them; for example, male counsellors are unlikely to offer to shake an Indian woman's hand, and a Western woman counsellor is unlikely to wear a dress revealing her arms when counselling an orthodox Muslim. This short chapter identifies some situations in couple counselling, as distinct from individual counselling, where cultural or other differences between the counsellor and the couple, or between the partners, may be factors that should be particularly borne in mind.

DIFFERENCE OF SEXUALITY

This section is addressed to heterosexual counsellors. I am sure there must be important issues around difference in sexuality for gay or lesbian counsellors when they counsel heterosexual couples, but as a heterosexual man, I am unable to envisage or discuss these with any kind of validity. I have also been unsuccessful in my search for books or articles addressing the issue – is this, perhaps, an aspect of heterocentrism in the counselling culture? I have counselled gay and lesbian individuals, but no same-sex couples, possibly because where I live there is a well-publicized counselling service run

by and for gay men and lesbians. I therefore share Freedman and Combs' 'reluctance ...
as [a heterosexual therapist] to write about the lives and relationships of lesbian and gay
couples' (2002: 11). The ideas below come from the narrative therapy literature, and
from contributions made by gay and lesbian participants in my workshops.

Ambience

It is important to consider the ambience of the waiting room and the counselling
room. Heterosexual counsellors should not display photographs of themselves and
their partners and children, or notices that portray only heterosexual couples. Persons
who have chosen to live alone, sole parents, divorced or separated persons, widows
and widowers might also feel that pictures portraying couples (of whatever sexuality)
implicitly marginalize them.

Ignore or acknowledge?

An immediate dilemma for a heterosexual counsellor working with a gay or lesbian
couple is whether to acknowledge the couple's sexuality. Ignoring it might be taken
as a respectful assumption that this is not intrinsically problematic, but might also be
seen as an embarrassed avoidance of the issue. On the other hand, acknowledging the
couple's sexuality could be interpreted either as a sensitive awareness of the homophobic disapproval likely to have been encountered by the couple, or as a patronizing
attempt by the counsellor to convey his acceptance of their sexuality.

From discussions with gay and lesbian counsellors about dilemmas such as the
above, I conclude that there is frequently an element of *balancing choices* for a heterosexual counsellor seeing a gay or lesbian couple. Good practice involves trying to be
sensitive to which way the scales should tip when assisting this couple to address their
particular situation.

Heterosexual counsellors should:

- avoid defining couples wholly by their sexuality, *but* be prepared to acknowledge
  the differences in social experiences of lesbian and gay couples when compared
  with heterosexual couples
- avoid assuming that issues widely identified with gay or lesbian couples are affecting
  their relationship, *but* be alert to this possibility (for example, uninformed attitudes
  of family, acquaintances, workmates, professionals; coming out, especially if only one
  partner has done so; parenthood)
- avoid defining the couple's relationship by heterosexual norms, *but* also recognize
  common ground between all committed couples
- avoid assuming that the couple would prefer a therapist of their own gender or
  sexuality, *but* bear this in mind as a legitimate possibility
- check the couple's preference for counsellor sexuality and gender and, if possible, offer
  a choice, *but* if no choice is available be open about the counsellor's own sexuality

- monitor reactions to the couple in recognition that despite consciously developed beliefs, socialization will have tainted the counsellor with some degree of homophobia
- avoid patronizing attempts to demonstrate acceptance of the couple's sexuality
- firmly and consistently bear in mind that being gay or lesbian is not the problem, but that social attitudes to sexuality often are.

Overall, the counsellor should:

- elicit, acknowledge, validate and focus on the couple's own view of their problem and on their knowledge, meanings and values.

AGE DIFFERENCE

Beth and Roger, a couple in their late seventies, walked into my counselling room hand in hand, and it was as if the sun had suddenly come out, so clear was their love for each other. But as the session got under way, I became more and more puzzled. Beth and Roger said they had known each other many years ago, and had been attracted to each other, but nothing came of it at that time. Beth then met Jim, who was to be her husband, and she and Roger lost touch with each other. Over time, Beth's marriage became very unhappy, as Jim's behaviour became increasingly selfish, erratic and threatening. He now had a generous pension, spending a great deal on his hobbies of internet gambling and financial speculation, but Beth had to ask him for money every time she needed necessities such as clothes for herself and replacement items for the home. The housekeeping money Jim allowed her was inadequate, but he continually blamed her for not managing it well enough. Recently, Jim had become verbally and physically violent, insulting her grossly and hitting her. Then Roger unexpectedly came back into her life, a widower now; their old affection renewed and blossomed, and he had asked her to divorce Jim and marry him.

So, I wondered, where was the problem in this moving story of loss and rediscovery? Beth explained that she could not leave Jim, let alone divorce him, and she and Roger were distraught at their impossible situation. If they stopped seeing each other, this would break their hearts. I was still puzzled. Was Jim dependent on her – perhaps handicapped, or very ill? No, he was in good health, and active, Beth said. There was nothing for it but to be direct, so I asked Beth why she couldn't leave her marriage. She looked at me, astonished, and said firmly, 'My marriage vows'.

This example incorporates several elements of unrecognized prejudice on my part deriving from my own socialization. Certainly, many couples see their marriage vows as a permanent and indissoluble commitment, but in my social circle this is not the case, and I was bringing my own assumptions to bear rather than thinking beyond them. There was perhaps an additional element of not being sensitive to generational difference, by my interpreting the couple's situation with reference to values more generally held by my own age group than by an older generation.

Insensitivity to age difference can also take the form of people belonging to a particular age group projecting ageist stereotypes onto those whose age is different. In the West at least, people are living longer, due to better diet and advances in medicine, and in some cases, they also have adequate or even generous pensions. They can extend their active lives in ways impossible for people of their age in the past. Counsellors who unthinkingly bring stereotyping expectations to their work with older couples risk offending them, and may also miss opportunities to follow lines of enquiry that may turn out to be relevant.

When there is a considerable discrepancy in age between the counsellor and the couple, the counsellor needs to take into account possible ageist stereotyping by himself *and* by the couple.

> Pat and Arthur, a couple in their mid-sixties, said they had come to counselling because they had begun quarrelling over trivial matters. I was their second therapist, since their first had been very young, which made them uneasy about revealing intimate problems. I discovered that they were worried about their sex life, as Arthur no longer had strong erections. His doctor told him this was inevitable in old age and he just had to accept it (an example of ageism by an authority figure whose attitude compounded the problem). A combination of discussion about variants of sexual activity, and monitoring their progress over several sessions, produced considerable improvement in their sex life and a better atmosphere between them.

Not only had Pat and Arthur's young counsellor missed the possibility of sexual difficulties in the couple's deteriorating relationship, perhaps because she thought this irrelevant to people 40 years older than she was, but Pat and Arthur themselves had not revealed these problems because they stereotyped this young counsellor as unlikely to deal sensitively with the sexual problems of older people.

A contrast to Pat and Arthur's difficulty in being frank with their first counsellor can occur when a young couple see an older counsellor, whom they may assume will be embarrassed or offended by their problem, or not understand it. Counsellors who are not themselves young need to be alert to this possibility, pick up clues from what is said, and reassure the couple that it's OK to raise these problems. A frank and open acknowledgement of the counsellor's possible age-stereotyping can be useful when counselling younger persons. The counsellor can do this by saying something like, 'I know there's a danger of people of my age assuming that all you young people are into drugs, so forgive me if I'm falling into this trap, but what you both say about Jerry being forgetful, spending most of the day sleeping, and having bursts of temper, makes me wonder if there might be a drug issue here?'

Increases in divorce and remarriage mean that many older people are in second or third committed relationships. This, together with the growth in the number of people who choose not to have children, can mean that an apparently simple and straightforward question to an older, heterosexual couple can unwittingly be fraught with stereotyped assumptions. Questions such as, 'How old are your children now?', 'Do you have any grandchildren?' or even 'How many grandchildren do you have?' might have been easily and quickly answered by most heterosexual couples some 50 years ago, but today a reply can be complicated, and possibly embarrassing. Time can be wasted as a couple try to explain the complications of their family structure when this has nothing to do with why they have come to counselling. One partner may have children from a previous relationship and the other none; perhaps neither has children or grandchildren; some couples may now be in a third relationship and have children from both previous relationships; many other possibilities exist. It is also easy for the counsellor to assume that an older couple are married when in fact they live together, so even an apparently straightforward initial greeting can get things off on a wrong footing ('Hello, Mr and Mrs Bowden!' 'Er, actually my surname is Bowden, and his is Taplow … '). A few minutes spent asking questions about couples' lives at the very start of counselling can be helpful to them and to the counsellor (as described in Chapter 5) but the questions need to be general and open-ended.

CULTURAL DIFFERENCES

Gaining detailed knowledge of other people's cultures is difficult when there is no ready source of information available, but the problem can partly be overcome by the counsellor's being frank about the limitations of her knowledge and enlisting the help of the couple, rather as in the example I gave earlier in this chapter for when an older counsellor works with younger people. Early in the first session, the counsellor can say (for example) that as a white woman brought up in an area where there were no Chinese families, she has a rather limited understanding of their beliefs and customs around marriage and other forms of committed relationships, so if she says anything that reveals this lack of understanding, she would be really grateful for the couple to tell her. Not all mistakes will be avoided, but a couple will feel more comfortable and forgiving of these errors if the counsellor has genuinely consulted them.

Religious and political differences

Respecting couples' views

Therapists may have strong beliefs around religion and party politics, but they will be more consciously aware of their own positions on these topics than of the assumed truths more subtly developed through their socialization, and therefore more alert to guard against their known beliefs inappropriately affecting their work. A determination to respect others' beliefs can nevertheless be subtly undermined in subtle and unrecognized ways. I know of a Christian counselling centre which has always had a clear and stated policy of accepting 'clients' no matter what their religious affiliations, and of not introducing a religious element to counselling unless this is specifically requested. Despite this policy, the centre's information leaflet and notepaper used to have a heading incorporating a formalized cross, which I think might have made non-Christian couples feel devalued or excluded. Couples who live together might have avoided going to this centre for counselling in the belief that their not being married might be met with disapproval. The logo has been abandoned recently in favour of a neutral design, but the Centre's publicity has never specifically stated that gay or lesbian couples are welcome, so same-sex couples might still avoid going to the Centre, given the various Churches' present confused and ambivalent attitudes to homosexuality.

Couples with different beliefs from each other

When partners have different political or religious beliefs, they have probably learned to tolerate these during the good times of their relationship. When things go wrong and tension mounts, *any* differences of opinion can become triggers for explosive quarrels and a further deterioration of the relationship. The couple counsellor needs to put his or her own religious or political opinions firmly aside so as to avoid the development of a counterproductive sense of solidarity with, or by, the partner who happens to share those views. And if the couple is heterosexual, the person with different political or religious views from the counsellor will feel even worse if the counsellor is the same gender as their partner.

Taking a stand against harmful beliefs

The conventional view that it's best to avoid religion and politics in conversation cannot always apply to counselling, because these areas reflect and confirm persons' identities and permeate their views of life and the world. In most instances, counsellors will respect persons' views, and draw on the meaning of these views for the person as part of counselling, but there are times when this is inappropriate. When persons hold beliefs that are actually or potentially harmful to themselves and/or others, including beliefs that are 'political' in the wider sense of embodying the enforcement of interpersonal power, neutrality or tolerance in couple counselling are not ethical stances but a stepping out of professional, personal and social responsibility.

There can be confusion here arising from a clash between the counsellor's own views and her wish to respect another culture's contrasting beliefs, especially when couples from the other culture might interpret her stance as racist. However, as Michael White pointed out in his training courses, there are always minorities who actively oppose their own culture's more damaging and outdated religious and political beliefs, often at considerable risk to themselves, and by identifying with these brave people, the counsellor demonstrates support for the best elements of those cultures. Counsellors should not hesitate to hold fast to their own values in these circumstances and they should bring these values into play in their counselling by asking questions designed to assist persons to see the real results of their views and, by implication, to reconsider them. It may also be necessary for the counsellor to make her own position clear, especially if she is directly challenged.

Addressing harmful religious and political attitudes held by one or both partners may not change or even modify those views, as they are likely to be emotionally charged, entrenched and habitually rationalized, but there are good reasons for the attempt. Well-conducted sessions where damaging opinions are laid open to question *may* produce some change. Even if this does not happen, a seed of doubt may be sown, possibly to blossom later. Should none of these possibilities come to fruition, the counsellor has at least witnessed to her own ethical positions.

In couple counselling where either or both of the partners are influenced by harmful religious ideas, the counsellor's refusal to validate those beliefs will be important to those whose lives are adversely affected. A woman who is a victim of bigotry in a fundamentalist sect that believes women are destined by the deity for a wholly domestic role will gain a sense of support for her hard-won opposition to her husband's and her culture's sexism. A gay couple whose relationship difficulties are made worse by their church's disapproval of their sexuality will feel validated and supported by a counsellor who expresses clear disagreement with the church's stance.

The following illustrative account of counselling a couple with political beliefs very different from my own conflates several actual examples.

Robert and his pregnant wife, Joan, were living in a very cramped and damp bedsit. Joan had become depressed, and her doctor had referred her to a psychiatrist, who had just begun to see her. Robert and Joan's relationship had started to deteriorate through the stress and worry of this situation. They had applied to the local council for a flat, but there was a long waiting list. Robert mentioned that they supported the British National Party as 'the blacks and Pakis always get priority for council flats'.

I did not take up the theme of the couple's relationship stresses as it appeared clear that these would be alleviated if their accommodation problem could be solved. The priority was to help them maximize their chances of moving. I was taken aback and dismayed by what Robert said about immigration and housing allocation, but if I had immediately challenged these ideas and attitudes, we might all three have got into an argument, which would have jeopardized the counselling; on the other hand, I had a professional and ethical duty not to ignore (and thereby indirectly validate) the misinformation and racism in Robert's narrative.

So I invited the couple to describe the shortcomings of their accommodation in detail, and to tell me the effects it was having on their lives. We then looked at the steps they had taken to improve their chances of a council house. This took up most of the session. I suggested they might get help from the Citizens' Advice Bureau, and we discussed whether Joan might ask her psychiatrist or doctor to write a letter to the council supporting their application on medical grounds. By these means, I showed that I took their problem seriously and had practical suggestions to offer.

They had not thought of these possibilities, and appeared heartened at the thought that there might still be hope.

At the end of the session, I asked if I could mention some ideas about immigration and council housing which they might find interesting. They agreed, so I read the section 'They get to jump the queue for nice council flats' from the booklet *Mobiles, Money and Mayhem: The Facts about Asylum* published by Refugee Action. Robert did not respond and I had the impression that the information made little or no impact, and Joan looked equally impassive, but I thanked them for listening and we made an appointment for five weeks' time, by which time Robert would have consulted the CAB and Joan would have seen her doctor. Four weeks later, Robert phoned to cancel the appointment, saying that the doctor had written to the housing department, and that they had seen an official there who told them they were very likely to be moved up the waiting list. I was left with an uneasy feeling that my reading them a text directly contradicting their opinions might have helped them decide not to continue to see me, but I also knew that I had addressed their presenting problem, been instrumental in its potential solution, and had not ducked the professional and ethical challenge of presenting evidence against the racism which had infected them.

Culturally formed gender attitudes

Habitual male behaviours

When counselling heterosexual couples, I frequently find that the man assumes a dominant role that the woman finds hard to counter. He may talk more emphatically than her, make authoritative-sounding statements, try to 'hold the floor' to lecture, and be dismissive of her contributions, sometimes in an apparently good-natured and humorous way which nevertheless implies superiority. Women often make firm rejoinders and disclaimers, but I frequently detect an attempt by the man to recruit me as an ally against the woman, not usually openly but by means such as head-shaking, sideways glances, lifting of the eyes and knowing, pseudo-tolerant smiles. I try to remain unresponsive to such invitations but as I myself am a member of the male culture, this stepping back from collusion has to be done by means of continuous alertness, and never taken for granted.

As a man subject to many years of male peer-group and cultural socialization, I have to make a conscious effort not to validate this way of behaving and to ensure the other partner is able to make an equal contribution to the session, even if this means interrupting the dominant partner in full flow or asking him to hold back comments to allow his partner time to speak.

Women colleagues tell me that experiencing patriarchal behaviour when counselling heterosexual couples makes them very uncomfortable, and that (in a way that mirrors my own danger of sliding into patriarchal responses) they sometimes have to resist their own socialized tendency to defer to the man. Inappropriate gender-based responses by the counsellor can, of course, be a lurking danger in work with individuals but in couple counselling, they pose an even more toxic threat as the dynamic of the three-way relationship may be adversely affected through the implicit two-against-one marginalization of one partner.

To add a complication: I have sometimes counselled spirited women who have rebelled against dominant behaviour by men but who reproduce it themselves, by assuming a leading role that puts their partners in an inferior position. For a male counsellor, this is particularly tricky as it is a double bind (no-win) situation. If I allow the woman's dominant behaviour to continue, I am complicit in it. If I attempt to counter it, I may be seen by the woman as behaving in a patriarchal and controlling way, and by the man as demonstrating male solidarity by putting the woman in her place. Either action will be counterproductive to my work with the couple. My practice is to choose what I believe to be the most important option – to promote the equality of the partners by ensuring that the more silent partner is given ample opportunity to contribute, and to do this as tactfully as possible. I warmly thank the woman for her engagement with the issues, then say I would like to hear her partner's ideas. I invite him to comment on what he has heard and firmly signal that it is his turn by slightly swivelling my body towards him and perhaps even turning my chair a little. Usually, this is enough, but if the woman interrupts, I have no alternative but to ask her to wait; when the man has finished speaking, I turn towards her and give her my full attention.

This is another, important example of the difference between individual and couple counselling. It illustrates the crucial, general point that always, when addressing one partner, the counsellor needs to bear in mind the possible impact of his questions, comments and statements on the other partner. He should continually bear in mind: 'What effect might my saying this to A have on B; so how should this shape what I say to A, and how I say it?'

Stereotyping of gender language and sensibility

When a woman colleague and I counselled in the same GP surgery, we requested the referring doctors to ask persons which one of us they would prefer to see, so that people could choose a counsellor of their own gender if they had a preference. I soon had gaps in my appointment schedule whereas my female colleague had a waiting list. The doctors said that people asked to see her because they thought women were better listeners, with more human understanding, than men. At our suggestion, the doctors then asked about preference of counsellor gender only if the person's problem seemed particularly appropriate for this, and our waiting lists equalized.

Many people hold to the idea that whereas women are good at feelings and talking, men's limitation of language makes them less competent in these areas. Therapists need to be alert to these myths when they arise in heterosexual counselling, for example when a man says that 'failure of communication' is the basis of the couple's problems, or when a woman excuses her partner for not attending a session because he finds talking about relationships difficult. People becoming so angry with each other that they cannot discuss their differences is not 'failure of communication' based on some kind of gender-based, innate barrier, and avoiding cooperation in resolving emotionally charged issues is not the same as some kind of blockage of ability based on innate masculine limitations. These are rationalizations, and the therapist should not be a party to them, but subject them to persistent clarifying questions that undermine them.

DISCUSSION POINTS

Consider these points, if possible in discussion with a colleague:

1. When in your work or your everyday life have you experienced one or more examples of: homophobia; age stereotyping; cultural misunderstanding; harmful religious assumptions; a clash of basic beliefs? How might your awareness of these occasions contribute to your work with couples?
2. When have you yourself demonstrated one or more of the above? How might your awareness of those occasions contribute to your work with couples?
3. How far is it ever possible to escape the influence of socialization-originated biases? What biases of your own do you need to beware of when counselling couples?
4. Was my way of dealing with Robert's and Joan's racism well judged, or not? If not, what else might I have done that would have been preferable?
5. Is it ever legitimate to refuse counselling to people whose opinions the counsellor finds offensive?

PART 3
SESSION ORGANIZATION

In the following chapters, I offer a detailed framework for counselling sessions with couples in the belief that by following these sequences the counsellor new to this work will at the least avoid serious errors and at best will perform useful couple counselling from the start. With practice and experience, including recognizing times when sessions or parts of sessions have not gone too well and discussing these in supervision, as well as discussing and evaluating times when sessions have appeared to be effective, previous counselling experience and the framework will merge, as the counsellor develops modifications and personal touches that come to constitute his or her own unique style.

In Chapter 5, I give a detailed framework for a first session, followed in Chapters 6 and 7 by frameworks for subsequent joint and individual sessions. For the reader who has achieved familiarity with these session frameworks, I describe some more advanced narrative therapy practices in Chapter 8.

The session frameworks largely consist of an adaptation and amalgamation of Michael White's Externalizing Conversations Map and Statement of Position Map (2007: 38–58, 233–49) and I have also included some practices from solution-focused therapy which complement and enhance these narrative therapy elements. I describe each stage of therapy in some detail, illustrating them over the three chapters with a continuing example of my own work with a couple. There are 'memory-jog' pages, which the reader might like to copy and have at hand for reference when taking part in the suggested learning exercises and when counselling actual couples.

To learn any new skill – tennis, driving a car, playing the piano, couple counselling – it is helpful (a) to have some prior experience of a related activity, (b) to learn and follow a logical sequence that forms a framework for performance, (c) to refine and modify technique through practice and experience and (d) to transfer it to different situations, adapting and modifying it as experience accumulates. Counsellors experienced in work with individuals already have experience directly related to this new area; the session frameworks will provide a transferable template for couple counselling; further practice and experience will enable them to use the frameworks flexibly and creatively.

Throughout, I refer to heterosexual couples as a means of avoiding excessive and awkward 'her/him' phrasing and to assist the reader to distinguish one partner from the other. Although the detailed example is of work with a heterosexual married couple, the framework applies to counselling couples whatever their sexuality or marital status.

5
THE FIRST JOINT
SESSION FRAMEWORK

This chapter presents a framework for the first session with a couple presenting for counselling. It uses examples from my counselling of one couple, Melanie and Neville, to illustrate the sequence.

INITIAL CONTACT

In some counselling organizations, the first contact with persons, and making arrangements for the first session, are by people other than the counsellor such as administrative staff. For the purposes of this chapter, however, I am assuming that a person will contact the counsellor direct, probably by phone, even if (as with some counselling centres) there has been a previous meeting with a team or individual with the aim of allocating the most appropriate counsellor.

Initial contact launches the couple counselling process even before the counsellor and persons have met face to face. Counsellors who work with individuals will already be familiar with taking into account persons' possible nervousness at contacting a stranger who is probably going to hear some of their most personal, private and possibly embarrassing confidences. When the contact is made for couple counselling, there are additional considerations. Obviously, two people cannot contact the counsellor simultaneously, and it is usually the partner who is most concerned at the difficulties the couple are facing who makes the first contact. Sometimes a person will attempt to arrange a joint appointment without consulting her partner, so as to face him with a fait accompli as a means of pressurizing him to attend. If he does come to counselling, he will feel manipulated and resentful, and is likely to be hostile to the counsellor. My practice is always to ask whether the partner knows of the counselling request and if he does not, I ask the contacting person to inform him as soon as possible and to ask him to phone me. He can then confirm he wishes to come and, since he has also spoken with me, will not feel at a disadvantage when we meet.

I always divert any attempt to talk at length about the couple's problems at the contact stage, though it is sometimes hard, tactfully, to stop the outpourings of an unhappy person who has been holding back worries and powerful feelings. I suggest that it will be best to leave the problem until the session so that both partners can have an equal chance to explain their concerns. I have always found that this is accepted without demur, and sometimes with relief.

Couple counselling can arise out of individual counselling already taking place. An individual who is unhappy in his relationship and sees himself as the source of the problem may come to counselling for help in overcoming his imputed faults and, he hopes, to be told how to make his partner love him again. Sometimes his partner will have persuaded him to have counselling and sort himself out, thereby absolving herself from any responsibility for the deteriorating relationship or for putting it right. Certainly, there are times when the reasons for deterioration in the relationship lie much more with one partner than the other – it's *not* always 50/50 – but in perhaps the majority of instances, both will to some extent have contributed to the development of a harmful pattern of interaction that has got out of hand. This pattern is best addressed by both partners to maximize the possibility of change for the better, so unless there are issues of violence or abuse, I always suggest joint counselling at a point in individual counselling when this seems appropriate, often in the second or third session.

Some people assume that I must be competent, even though they may know very little about me! During initial contact, as well as giving the person a chance to ask about my counselling qualifications and experience, I confirm that I have worked with couples as well as individuals.

I also state my fee, when it is to be paid, how long sessions will last, the approximate number of sessions I usually find is needed (about 6–12 for couples), and of course, arrange the date, time and place of the first session. I do not assume that regular weekly sessions will be necessary, but prefer flexibility according to the development of the counselling, so I try to make sure the person understands this. I also take address and telephone number in case I have to alter arrangements unexpectedly. These details are particularly important since some couples live at different addresses, which may not be mentioned by the contact person. I immediately follow up with a confirming letter (or letters if the couple live apart), since it is easy for the contact person to forget or be unsure of the arrangements, especially if they have found the conversation rather stressful. If the partners are living in the same household, I address the letter to both, to convey an unstated message that they have equal status in my eyes, and joint responsibility for taking part.

Melanie rang to request an appointment for herself and her husband Neville. I had been recommended to her by a friend who had seen me for counselling. She said she had become very unhappy in her marriage and was thinking of leaving Neville. I asked if Neville knew she was asking for joint counselling and she said he did, and was keen. Melanie started to say how difficult she found Neville at the moment but I suggested we wait until the session for details of the couple's problems as Neville would also want to tell me his side, and she agreed. She did not need to ask my qualifications, she said, as her friend had passed on my leaflet, which they had both read (this leaflet also explains the number, length and timing of sessions). We arranged an appointment for a few days' time and I gave her directions, then took down her address and phone number.

THE FIRST JOINT SESSION FRAMEWORK (70 MINUTES)

1. Opening moments (about 10 minutes)

I begin by indicating where the couple might sit, as with three chairs in the room they can feel uneasy and disorientated unless I do this. The chairs are placed so that the couple are sitting a little closer together than either is to me. I ask each how they would like to be addressed – by their first names, or as Mr/Mrs/Miss/Ms? Usually, they suggest using first names, and I reciprocate by suggesting they call me by mine.

If there has been phone contact, I briefly repeat the information I have already given to one of them, or if this session is the first contact for both, I give the information now. This is to ensure that both partners have an equal awareness of my qualifications and experience, my way of working, and the length, frequency and likely number of appointments. I say that there will probably be both individual and joint sessions, and that we will make decisions on this as counselling progresses. I ensure they are aware of confidentiality, and of its limits concerning illegality or danger, and I stress that I shall not reveal to the other partner what is said in individual sessions; nor should they feel they have a right to ask their partner for this information. Because the start to the session is practical and neutral, it gives the couple time to settle in and relax a little.

Next, I suggest the couple tell me a little about themselves, explaining that it will be helpful to me to gain a rough picture of their lives. I make sure this part of the session is also brief, as usually persons have keyed themselves up to talk about their problems and can be disconcerted by too much everyday conversation. I also have to phrase my invitation carefully or the response may be an immediate jump into problem description, so I make it clear that I am referring to general details such as when and how they met, how long they have been together, and about any family and employment. By this means, in these opening moments, the couple are briefly removed from their problems and reconnected with the normal everyday elements of their lives, a calming influence in an unfamiliar and stressful situation. If, despite my precautions, one of the couple does start to talk about their difficulties, I ask them to hold on a moment, and then continue the session, looking later for an opportunity to ask about more general details if these do not emerge.

An unfamiliar element for readers who have not used narrative or solution-focused approaches is that as well as giving me a general idea of the couple's circumstances, their account may also give me clues to 'exceptions' to the problem which I may be able to draw on in working with them (see Chapter 2: 25–8). It is crucial that from the very first moment of counselling, I try to be alert to clues to exceptions, a skill the couple counsellor unfamiliar with narrative or solution-focused therapies will need to develop. Clues to exceptions can appear even before the problem has been revealed: if the couple have been together a long time, this means they must have found ways of maintaining their relationship. If they have children they must have shared the ups and downs of parenthood, unless one of them refused all responsibility. Sometimes, when describing how they met, a look of affectionate reminiscence will pass between them, an indication that no matter what their present problems, a precious memory is still alive and significant. The fact of their coming to counselling is in itself an exception, as many couples in difficulties do not try to face their problems together.

I always have a notepad to hand during counselling sessions and once I have checked with the couple that my taking notes is acceptable, and assured them that that they can see the notes at any time, I jot notes using the pattern-note method of Tony Buzan. This method, a little like mobile phone texting, incorporates abbreviations and short phrases or symbols rather than using extended phrases or sentences, and upper case lettering is used because of its legibility (Buzan and Buzan 2006). This allows notes to be taken swiftly and unobtrusively, with my eyes lowering only momentarily. Taking notes is particularly useful when counselling couples, when the amount of information to keep track of is usually more complex than with individuals. I indicate possible exceptions by putting a little 'smiley' symbol by my note, so I can identify, check and if appropriate draw on the exception later in the counselling. At a later stage, it can be useful to show the notes and symbols to the couple to demonstrate their progress, as the typical pattern is for few or no exceptions to appear in the first sessions but for them gradually to increase as the couple resolve their differences.

S/T *[= sometimes]* QUARRELS SOON MADE UP ☺
S/T OK LOVEMAKING ☺
ENJOY TV TOGETHER ☺

Melanie and Neville arrived on time and together. Once they were seated, I found it was acceptable to use first names, then spent a few minutes confirming information about confidentiality, session length etc. I asked for a few details about their history and everyday circumstances. Melanie said they met through mutual friends, had been married for eight years, and had two girls aged seven and six. Neville grinned and said, 'They're quite a handful,' at which point Melanie looked at me, nodded and smiled. Neville said he managed a chain of stores, and Melanie was a nurse working part-time in the local health centre. Both sets of parents were alive but the couple saw more of Melanie's parents than Neville's.

As well as their length of marriage, family details and jobs, I noted two clues to exceptions on my pad. Melanie and Neville appeared to have a similar attitude to their children, loving but unsentimental, and when responding to my questions, they took turns without any sense of rivalry or tension:

MGE 8 YRS
2 DTRS 7/6
N = MANGR
M = NRSE P/T
PRNTS ALIVE/SEE M's MORE
M&N LOVING/UNSENTMNTL
OK SHARING STORY

I shall not continue to give examples of abbreviated note-taking as those above are enough to convey the general idea.

Once preliminaries are over, I ask if there are any issues that must be addressed immediately. This is not often the case, but couples with very urgent problems would find the slower-paced and exploratory nature of the usual first session framework inappropriate – they would need a more solution-oriented and intensive session. I give them examples of the kind of situation I mean: if I was seeing a married couple where the woman had an appointment with her solicitor for the following day to start divorce proceedings, and her husband had brought her to counselling in a last desperate attempt to prevent this, there would be an immediate need to negotiate whether she would be willing to postpone her solicitor's appointment and join him in a final attempt to make the marriage work. Another example would be if a couple needed to decide whether the woman would have an abortion, with the legal limit a few days away. Again, if one partner was due in court in the coming week, which could lead to a custodial sentence, it might be necessary to give urgent attention to how they could keep their relationship alive during the term of imprisonment.

2. If necessary, address immediate urgent issues (whole session, 60 minutes)

On the rare occasions when there is genuine urgency, I largely abandon the first session framework, and spend the whole session assisting the couple to discuss possible actions and weigh their likely outcomes, encouraging each person to listen to the other without interruption, and trying to create a thoughtful and objective atmosphere. This kind of concentrated session may turn out to be a one-off, as sometimes the couple reach a decision in the session. Even if they do not, they may find their minds have cleared, so that conversation at home becomes easier and leads to an agreed conclusion about how to deal with the immediate dilemma or problem. If further appointments are held, I follow the usual pattern of first and subsequent sessions as outlined below, adapting the next session slightly to take account of how the couple's situation has developed since their 'emergency' appointment.

I asked Melanie and Neville if there were any problems that were so urgent that they could not be discussed over a period of time but must be sorted out today, and I gave examples. They looked at each other and hesitated, then Neville said that their problems did seem pretty urgent to him but that he could understand the distinction, and would rather not hurry the process. Melanie said she agreed.

If there are no urgent issues—

3. Set up the first-session structure (about 5 minutes)

A characteristic of narrative therapy is *transparency*, which among other things means demystifying counselling by explaining at every stage what the counsellor wishes to do, giving the rationale for this, and gaining agreement. The ethical reason for this is to respect persons as equals capable of partaking in a cooperative venture. It also has practical benefits, as persons enter more fully and confidently into the various stages of the process than if they were treated as uninformed people to whom counselling is 'applied'.

At this point, I introduce a practice which by the very nature of the context could not be used in individual counselling. Nevertheless, the skills of the individual-trained counsellor will be relevant, and are called on at this point. I explain to the couple that, if they agree, I would like to organize the first part of the session in a way that might surprise them. Instead of encouraging them to discuss their problem together, with my help, or jointly to discuss it with me, I would like to 'interview' each of them in turn for about 15 to 20 minutes while the other listens without interrupting, knowing that their turn will come. I will give them notepads and pencils so that they can make notes as their partner is speaking. I explain that the idea behind this is to get away from the usual mode of interchange between two people who have disagreements or are in conflict, when each is probably so eager to put their point of view that they only half listen to the other partner, may jump in prematurely, and usually feel they have to hold so fast to their own opinions that they are blocked from really understanding what their partner has said. I point out that this method of trying to sort things out usually fails, as tempers rise and both come to think the other is stubborn and unreasonable.

There are often nods of recognition, with the partners exchanging rueful glances. Possibly because they see the logic of trying a different way of communicating their concerns, I have never known a couple to question or refuse the suggestion of beginning by talking to me separately. I ask who would like to have the first turn, or if despite my precautions one partner has talked about the problem already, in the phone call making the appointment, I invite the other partner to be first. I give each a notepad and pencil, and gain their agreement not to interrupt while the other is speaking but to wait for their own turn. I then turn my chair to face the partner who is to be interviewed first.

Melanie and Neville readily agreed to my suggestion of individual 'interviews' to start with, and after a little hesitation, Melanie offered to have the first turn. I gave them each a notepad and pencil, then faced Melanie and invited her to tell me what had brought her and Neville to counselling.

4. Talk with one partner while the other listens (about 15 minutes)

For the next 15 minutes or so, I listen to the first person's account of the problem, using basic counselling skills of reflecting back, summarizing and clarifying. My original person-centred training serves me well here. I also ask clarifying and extending questions. By means of the detailed problem-narrative this produces, both I and the other partner gain a clear picture of how this person experiences the relationship now that things have gone awry. I have known many occasions when the listening partner fully grasps for the first time the nature and meaning for his partner of things which he has often heard or half-heard her say, but which he has ignored, dismissed or distorted in memory, and when this new realization occurs, it often begins a shift in his attitude.

I continue to keep alert to clues to exceptions, and I note down anything, no matter how apparently trivial, that does not quite fit with the overall pessimism of the story, and that might be drawn on later when encouraging the couple to reconsider the image they have of their relationship and to identify, and enhance, its hopeful or positive elements. If no exceptions emerge, however, this is nothing to worry about − at this early point of counselling, the power of the problem is at its height. A problem-saturated description by both partners is to be expected, and indeed should be drawn out in detail through questions that 'identify the effect of the problem across various interfaces − between the problem and various persons, and between the problem and various relationships' (White and Epston, 1990: 42–3). Each person is likely to want to convince both me and their partner that they are having a bad time, and perhaps to demonstrate that this is largely their partner's fault. If necessary, I can tease out exceptions later in the session; here I am primarily concerned to discover exactly how the problem affects each of them, in their relationship of course but also in other areas such as their health, their sleep patterns, their concentration at work. I am also interested in the knock-on effects of the problem on others, such as children, relatives, friends and workmates. Although 15 minutes each is not very much time for accounts of the problem, the timescale does encourage brevity and focus. I ask specific questions as well as giving each person an opportunity to say what is on their mind, so I need to balance these two elements both sensitively and purposefully.

I keep a careful eye on the time and try to ensure that this first 'interview' ends after 15 minutes. I then thank the person, remind her of the agreement not to interrupt and turn my chair to face the other partner.

Melanie said that lots of things Neville did, or didn't do, made her feel unsupported and unloved, and that when she tried to make him understand her feelings, he just got angry and said she was imagining things or exaggerating. I asked for an example, and she said that one problem was his parents, who had never liked or accepted her and whose side he always took. At this point, Neville started to shift uncomfortably in his chair and seemed about to say something, so I turned briefly to him and shook my head with a smile, and he subsided. What did she mean about Neville's parents, I asked – could she give more details? His mother was always hinting about how Melanie should bring up the children differently, she said, and his mother interfered in other ways, such as bringing them huge casseroles she had cooked, saying Neville needed feeding up as he was too thin. When Melanie had been ill in hospital for a week, Neville's parents had only visited once and had made an excuse to get away quickly, but all Neville could do was thank them effusively for coming. He'd helped her to write a letter of complaint when she'd been incompetently treated in hospital, but he'd grumbled endlessly when she asked him to come with her to see their Member of Parliament about it, and had only done so under protest. He spoilt the girls, and undermined her when she tried to be strict but fair when they were naughty. How did this affect them? I asked. They always went to him when they wanted anything, said Melanie, even if she'd already said no, and he usually gave them what they wanted. They had started to ignore her and to be more and more out of her control; she was the bad parent and he was the good parent in their eyes. Sometimes Neville had to leave for work early and he never told her in advance, so on these occasions, she had to rush all the work of cooking breakfast, preparing the children for school, and taking them, without his help.

I wondered what the effect was of all this on her life. She said she felt angry and tense all the time, slept badly, had stomach cramps and was sometimes short tempered with patients at the health centre, which made her ashamed afterwards. Neville had stopped showing her any affection and they never had sex. The family had not had a proper holiday for several years. He was always accusing her of nagging, such as when she tried to face him with the need to sort out their credit card debt. Her self-confidence was at rock bottom and she didn't know how much longer she could stand the situation.

Although Melanie's narrative was problem-saturated, I detected three clues to exceptions, which indicated that it might be possible, with encouragement, for her to tell an enriched story which would more fully represent her experience of her marriage. Neville had helped her with her letter of complaint, he had gone to see her MP with her despite his doubts about this, and on mornings when he didn't have to go to work early he took his share of the family's morning preparations – something which not all family men would do. She had presented these factors in a negative light but they had a positive 'flip side' which I felt might have potential for use later in the counselling.

Fifteen minutes had elapsed, so I thanked Melanie for her frankness, reminded her not to interrupt when I talked with Neville, and turned to face him.

5. Talk with the other partner, while the first one to speak listens (about 15 minutes)

I invite the partner who has been listening to comment on what he has just heard, referring to his notes if this helps, and then to give his own account of the problem. I assist him in this by reflecting back, summarizing and asking questions; and as with the first person interviewed, I jot brief notes and stay alert to possible exceptions, adding the smiley 'exception' symbol if these emerge.

> Neville said that in the life of the family, he was left to be responsible for almost everything, and that he was tired of this – literally exhausted, as he had a very demanding job with long hours. Melanie had not gone back to full-time nursing since the children started school, and he was the main breadwinner, with a large mortgage and other debts to account for as well as family expenses. Affording a holiday was out of the question. It was part of his job to work long hours at short notice, and Melanie knew this, yet she nagged him endlessly for not being more available to her and the girls, and more or less ordered him about when he was at home. He found her irritable and unreasonable, with a tendency to be far too strict with the girls over trivial matters. He agreed that their sex life had deteriorated, and said he was unhappy about this, but he was surprised to hear that Melanie was unhappy about it too as he had assumed she just didn't want intimacy any more. He thought they had become so tense and annoyed with each other that any sexual approach would feel artificial and over-deliberate, and on the occasions when he wanted to make such an approach, he had been too apprehensive to try. She had always been distant and indifferent to his parents, and she never made allowances for the fact that they were both quite frail – it had been a real effort for them to visit her in hospital, especially as his mother was herself unwell at the time. His mother had brought round a casserole as a genuinely kind gesture but this had been met with a cold indifference on Melanie's part which hurt his mother, and infuriated him. He was fed up with the whole situation and was sceptical that counselling could help.

This is a typical situation at this point of couple counselling, with the same events interpreted and portrayed differently by each person. I began to suspect a pattern of differences building up and leading to increasing resentment as each internalized their own perception of the other's 'unreasonable' behaviour. These perceptions had solidified, and over time the fixed stories had become so powerful that they fed back into their perceptions, confirming and reinforcing them, and exacerbating the couple's sense of their relationship's deterioration – and of this deterioration being brought about largely through the other's refusal to see reason.

The task of counselling is not 'investigative' in the sense of trying to weigh evidence and to uncover 'the truth,' as this would be doubly futile. There was no way an objective assessment could be made of all the multiple interactions that had led to Melanie and Neville's crisis, since these factors were past, unrecorded, complex and subject to the distortions of memory. Each person's story was so embedded that they would in any case continue to interpret the evidence according to their preconceptions. Therapy's task is to investigate *alternative* stories; to encourage Neville and Melanie gradually to tell an amended, agreed version of their relationship which would undermine the power of their individual dominant stories, and reconnect the couple with aspects of their history that had been distorted, forgotten, sidelined, undervalued or misrepresented in memory. To this end, I noted further exceptions: Neville worked hard for his wife and family, was responsible about money and wished to resume his and Melanie's sex life.

I ask the first person to respond briefly to what her partner has said, referring to her notes if she finds this helpful, but limit this to about five minutes.

> Melanie made it clear she disagreed with most of Neville's points. However, his saying his mother was ill at the time she herself was in hospital had given her pause, as she had since forgotten this. She was also surprised that he wanted to make love sometimes, as she assumed he had completely lost interest in her as a sexual being.

6. Summarize, and name the problem (5 minutes)

Despite noting clues to exceptions, it is important not to rush into sharing them with the couple, perhaps with remarks such as 'Look, you've said things which show the relationship is OK really, such as …'. My notes only refer to clues – they have not been confirmed as significant by the couple and they are therefore tentative and provisional. Also, too swift an emphasis on exceptions will seem like trying to deny the partners' (divergent) experience of difficulty and pain, and they may think I am trying in a superficial way to cheer them up by looking on the bright side or being over-optimistic, which will clash with their actual feelings and thoughts. My next task is to demonstrate that I have 'heard' their stories, believe them and take them seriously.

I do this by offering a brief summary of what each person has told me, using their words as far as possible rather than mine. I sometimes fail to get this quite right, so I ask them to correct me until they are satisfied I have done justice to their accounts. Apart from helping me to ensure I have grasped their stories, this also enables each person to hear the other's points a second time, now voiced by myself. As I am an impartial counsellor, not an emotionally involved partner, the other's viewpoint is even more likely to be understood than when listening to their previous narrative.

I then invite the couple to agree on a definition of the problem: 'What shall we call this problem? Can we agree on a name for it?' Usually, the couple hesitate, or say they don't know, but if one of them suggests something that implies blame ('his bloody-mindedness', 'her unreasonableness'), I say that this is unsuitable as it clearly won't be acceptable to the other person. If one partner suggests a definition that is general, non-blaming and (preferably) non-medical, such as 'shared worries', I check with the other partner and if he agrees, suggest we use this term at least for the moment. If no suggestions are forthcoming, I offer ideas myself.

White's Statement of Position Map locates naming the problem at an earlier stage, before inviting a full account of the problem (2007: 40). I prefer to invite naming at this later stage, so that the definition is related to the persons' accounts rather than more loosely formulated in advance of them.

The most useful definitions, because they can subtly contribute to beginning a process of stepping out of mutual blaming, are those that imply the problem does not arise out of *inherent* characteristics imputed to either of the couple or to their relationship, but from factors interfering with and *affecting* the relationship. If impersonal, reciprocal processes are also implied, so much the better. In narrative therapy, this is called 'externalizing the problem' (White and Epston 1990: 16, 38–76; White 2007: 9, 24–7). 'Habits of quarrelling' is preferable to 'our quarrels', 'a vicious circle of misunderstandings' is preferable to 'inability to understand each other', 'losing sight of our love' is better than 'our disillusion with each other'. Medical definitions or those embodying psychological concepts are usually inappropriate as they carry negative overtones and also imply so-called superior, expert knowledge on the part of the person who suggests them. Examples of ill-chosen names would be 'repressed feelings', 'dysfunctional relationship', 'denial'. In some instances, there may be a genuine medical or psychological element contributing to the couple's difficulties, and here it may be appropriate to acknowledge this factor by using the term in an externalizing way for at least some of the time: 'the depression affecting him' rather than 'his depression', 'the agoraphobia interfering with her life' rather than 'her agoraphobia'. Sometimes it is hard or impossible to find an accurate yet inclusive definition, especially when difficulties are many and complicated, and in this case I do not spend a lot of time on it but suggest a simple, externalized generalization like 'trouble' or 'conflict'.

The dialogue with Melanie and Neville went something like this, which I have recreated from my notes:

Martin: I'd like to try to sum up what each of you said, and please don't hesitate to correct me if I get it wrong. Melanie: you said that you feel angry and tense all the time. Neville doesn't support you with the girls' discipline and this makes you feel he doesn't love you, and that the girls prefer him to you. His parents don't accept you and he takes sides with them. Your self-confidence has been affected. There's no sex and no holidays, and you're often left coping alone with the morning rush …

Melanie: No, not often, just sometimes, when he has to go to work early and doesn't tell me so we can get up a bit earlier.

Martin: OK, right. The other thing is that when he does help you, it's grudging.

Melanie: He was OK about the letter though.

Martin: Is that an accurate summary otherwise?

Melanie: Yes, that's fair enough.

Martin: Neville: you feel put on and unappreciated. You work very hard in your job and at home, and are fed up and exhausted. You see Melanie as over-critical and inclined to nag and give you orders. You think she's too harsh with the girls and unsympathetic to your parents, and you're inhibited about initiating sex because you may be rejected ...

Neville: Not so much that, more that I just don't think she will want it.

Martin: Not to impose ...

Neville: Yeah.

Martin: And you have to be careful with money, so no holidays. Anything I've forgotten?

Neville: No, that's about it.

When we tried to think of a name for the problem, it turned out to be difficult, so we settled for 'unwanted tensions'.

7. Normalize the problem, and establish commitment to address it (about 5 minutes)

Glib optimism has no place in counselling, and narrative couple therapy is no exception. If a couple's difficulties are complex, multi-faceted, severe, longstanding and bitter (or any combination of these), it would be cruel, unrealistic and unethical to give immediate reassurance that they have no need to worry. Ray and Anger-Diaz describe an instance when John Weakland, a pioneering family therapist, does 'the opposite of what many family therapists ... would do ... he encourages [the person] to lower his expectations ... to preempt the possibility of further disappointment, thus allowing the possibility for [him] to experience improvement should it occur' (2004: 219).

Nevertheless, there are times when hope breeds hope, and when renewed hope provides the best condition for movement towards positive change. Many couples – perhaps most – come to counselling with problems which, although genuine and extremely distressing for them, could be placed around the middle of a range from relatively trivial and everyday (in which case they would not be having counselling anyway) to extremely severe and possibly intractable. The couple themselves, absorbed in their own unhappiness, will not have this perspective and it can be helpful for them to know that other couples have faced similar issues and have eventually resolved them satisfactorily. Normalizing their situation, if done in a provisional and tentative way, can bring the couple some relief and add to their motivation. I say something like 'I can see how hard things are for you, and there's no way I want to give you any kind of premature reassurance, but it just might be helpful for you to hear that I know of couples with problems rather like yours who have managed to deal with them and come out the other side'. The therapist who has read this book, perhaps new to couple counselling, in saying this could have in mind the examples I use in this text.

It might be thought obvious that when persons request counselling, they are, by definition, so dissatisfied with their situation that they want things to improve, or why else would they be there? Michael White suggests that it is still useful, even essential, for the therapist to invite persons to affirm whether or not this is what they want – to 'take a position' on the problem. At this point in counselling, the situation has considerably moved on from when the couple walked into the consulting room. They have each gained a clearer idea of how their partner views the problem, and by the act of telling their own version of the story to a neutral counsellor, they have perhaps gained a more complete view of their own experience. They have discovered that the problems can be talked about without either of them lapsing into uncontrollable anger or incoherent despair. Now that the problems and their results have been fully exposed, the next step looms. Do they wish to take the counselling process further, or do they have doubts about this? Has full exposure to the problem unnerved them and made them want to back off for the moment, or conversely, has it made the problem appear less threatening and something they could live with, or sort out without my help? Consulting the couple on how they assess the effect of the problem on their lives, and asking whether or not they wish to address it, decentres the therapist and avoids his assuming a top-down, pseudo-authoritative role and stance (White 2007: 42–5).

I ask the persons in turn whether they feel it's OK to carry on with life as it is now, or whether they would prefer things to be different. This is a genuine query, not a device to ensure cooperation, and should the couple decide to end or postpone counselling, I would readily agree. If they decide that the problem must be dealt with, this constitutes a conscious choice and a commitment to work towards change, and since it is said with and to the partner, it is a *joint* commitment and sets the scene for what is to come.

I thanked Melanie and Neville for the full and frank way they had talked in their individual interviews, and for deciding on a name for their problem. I said that unwanted tensions could be clever and powerful enemies with a capacity to spark off more and more stress between couples, and I didn't underestimate how difficult maintaining their relationship had become or how hard they were finding it to live with the tensions' attempts to undermine their marriage. However, they might find it interesting that I had known a number of couples with similar tensions affecting them who had managed to re-build their relationship. I continued:

'Neville, are you OK to let things run on as they are or would you prefer things to be different?'

'No. Things have got to change.'

'What about you, Melanie? Would you prefer to leave things as they are, or ...'

'Oh no, we can't carry on like this.'

'Thank you. You've both decided to persist with addressing the unwanted tensions that have invaded your marriage, so let's continue.'

8. Explore either one, or two, exceptions (about 15 minutes)

The obvious, common-sense thing to do next would be to focus on the problems outlined by the couple, and to initiate discussion on what changes they might put into place to make things better. I am sure that this approach often succeeds, and that many couples owe a debt of gratitude to a counsellor who has assisted them to look objectively and systematically at their concerns and decide what to do about them, and has monitored their progress with them.

However, this way of addressing the issues has two limitations that narrative therapy attempts to avoid. Firstly, because this approach focuses on the problems themselves, it does not openly and specifically call on more hopeful and rooted aspects of the relationship which have been forgotten or ignored by the couple, or made invisible by the power of the problem. Certainly, many counselling approaches assume that persons themselves have the capacity to overcome their problems and that the therapist's role is to facilitate this process – it is, for example, the basis of person-centred therapy. But with the exception of de Shazer's solution-focused therapy, which has much in common with narrative therapy in this respect, most approaches do not *explicitly* assist persons to identify, affirm, embed and make conscious use of these previously sidelined elements, which means that an opportunity for enrichment of the therapeutic process (and also for legitimately speeding it up) is lost.

Secondly, immediately veering into discussion of how to bring about change is likely to rely fairly heavily on the counsellor's ideas rather than the couple's. After all, the persons have come to counselling because they are stuck – they have already tried to sort out the problem themselves and have failed to do so to their satisfaction, and they may be expecting 'expert' advice such as that presented in TV programmes or dramas that feature all-wise therapists. A counsellor who responds to this un-stated invitation to play the knowing expert, and assumes he can bring psychological perceptions to bear that are beyond the reach of the persons, is imposing his own agenda and centring himself rather than decentring himself and respecting the couple's own skills and knowledge.

> therapists are quite susceptible to taking a position on the people's problems and to acting on this position unilaterally ... This privileges the therapist's voice in attributing meaning to people's problems, imposes the therapist's own understanding about the consequences of the problem, prompts the therapist to take a position on these consequences on behalf of the people seeking consultation, and justifies the therapist's position in terms of what he or she assumes is important to these people ... (White 2007: 39–40)

What is the alternative? Sessions where the counsellor listens respectfully, clarifies through basic counselling techniques, establishes a cooperative and safe atmosphere, and metaphorically stands back to give space and time for the couple to re-examine the problem, may be more effective than the couple's own attempts at resolution in the fraught and resentful atmosphere of their home – as long as the counsellor can prevent arguments breaking out, or tactfully interrupt them when they do! But the counsellor is calling on the couple to break out of their impasse and find solutions from a starting point of disagreement and hostility, at a point when they have not yet begun to develop a balancing awareness of the positive possibilities inherent in their relationship. In addition, few couples know much about counselling theory and they may find the counsellor's lack of direct feedback frustrating, or even interpret it as indifference to their plight.

I explain to the couple that having heard their full and detailed descriptions of the problems and difficulties they are facing, I would like to ask about some aspects of their relationship which I find intriguing. Is that OK with them? If I receive permission for this (and it has never been refused), I explore either one or two of the exceptions I have noted, or if the problem-saturated accounts have been so negative that no exceptions have emerged, I ask questions to bring one forth. If the couple cannot think of a single exception, I fall back on the one example that is always there: they have come to counselling.

I prefer to use exceptions that have been implicit in the persons' narratives, but when questions are needed, I put them 'down the middle' to both persons. This moves the session from individual interviews to a cooperative effort – and, importantly, this effort is focused on areas of the relationship that are *not* problematic. Questions can refer to thoughts and feelings, or actions, or preferably move between both.

Setting aside my account of counselling Neville and Melanie for a moment – my questions when no exception has emerged from the initial accounts are worded something like this:

- Can you think of an example of when Jo was able to resist jealousy a little?
- Have there been any times when Sam's walking away from Jo has been a device to avoid conflict rather than a refusal to discuss things with her?
- You say you are always on edge, Jo. Have either of you noticed any times in say, the past month, when Jo seemed a little more relaxed than usual?
- If disillusion has led to your losing all loving feelings for each other, are you also indifferent to each other's future happiness?
- Jo and Sam, you are really letting me know how very difficult things are between you at the moment. Neither of you can think of any times when the jealousy has retreated or when disillusion has lessened. However, you have come to see me for help in sorting out your problems, and I wonder what that might mean about how you still value your relationship?

What do I mean by 'exploring' exceptions? It is not enough just to assist the couple to make exceptions visible, or the exceptions will soon be subjugated by the couple's dominant stories and slip out of their memory, making little difference to how they conceptualize their relationship. I explore the exception in three ways once it has been identified:

1. I elicit a more complete and detailed description of the exception.
2. I discover its effect in the couple's life.
3. I ask the couple for their feelings and thoughts about it, and in particular whether they see it as positive or negative.

This exploratory conversation has the aim of embedding the exception and contributing to what White calls 're-authoring' (2007: 61–128), which means encouraging the couple to modify the problem-saturated narratives they have told themselves, each other and the counsellor by taking on a wider perspective that incorporates hopeful, positive and encouraging elements. It is not an attempt to deny their distress and confusion – it is an enrichment of their stories, based on their 'telling' a more accurate and inclusive portrayal. It allows for aspects of their relationship that have become obscured or sidelined to become re-activated, and this wider perspective releases them from the entrapment and paralysis of their problem-saturated narratives. A considerable amount of time will be given to various forms of re-authoring conversations in their future sessions, but in the first session of couple counselling, there is only about 15 minutes for this practice, so only one, or at most two, exceptions can be explored.

RESISTING THE TEMPTATION TO EXPLORE EXCEPTIONS PREMATURELY

Counsellors new to identifying and working with exceptions can become rather intoxicated by this practice once they see how effective it can be. There is a consequent danger that the counsellor may too eagerly seize on clues to exceptions and get carried away by them, rather than carefully checking out with the person or couple that the exceptions have resonance for *them*, and then exploring the exceptions in detail. Even if an exception does have meaning for the person, it can be 'left hanging' and then fade unless it is integrated into a detailed, told narrative or story of the person's past, present and possible future. I have fallen into this trap more frequently than I like to admit. This was especially true when I was first discovering narrative therapy but had a tenuous grasp of its practice. A particularly instructive example was my counselling with Jane, 31 years old, who lived with her husband and two small children in a remote country cottage. Before marrying, Jane had lived in the city. Her doctor referred her because she had become affected by depression, which she attributed to a decision by her brother and his family, of whom she was very fond, to move to Australia. This had added to her already acute sense of isolation, made even more difficult by what she perceived as her husband's inability to understand her sad feelings. In my eagerness to identify exceptions, I remarked, over several sessions, on almost anything in her account which appeared to me to form any kind of alternative story to the dulling effects of depression. She took her children to the local primary school even though she had doubts about its standards; she could be frank with her parents about some aspects of their attitude to her marriage rather than ignoring this; she coped when her husband's noisy friends called rather than retreating upstairs; she and her husband had a rather tense relationship but they usually managed to talk about their differences. I identified many other examples. Not all of these possible exceptions

(Continued)

(Continued)

were necessarily misjudged on my part, but I threw too many of them at Jane, and had not yet learned the skills of taking my time, checking clues to exceptions with the person, encouraging detailed description if they struck a chord, and patiently exploring their possible significance. Depression continued to affect Jane and she decided to end counselling.

I told Melanie and Neville that there were some parts of their stories which particularly aroused my curiosity, and I wondered if it would be OK if I asked some questions about these. They agreed, so I said that there seemed to be some things that didn't quite fit the overall pattern of how unwanted tensions had invaded the relationship. I turned to Melanie and said, 'Melanie, I understand that except on those rare occasions when Neville forgets to tell you he has to go to work early, he always shares the early morning tasks. Is that right?' She said it was, so I asked very specific and detailed questions about exactly how this worked. They each had set routines which complemented what the other did, which had been discussed and agreed. Usually, things went like clockwork; for example, Melanie was largely responsible for seeing to the children, and Neville laid the table, cooked the breakfasts, and afterwards loaded the dishwasher. I asked many more questions – what did Neville cook, who was responsible for deciding the breakfast menu, what other domestic tasks did Neville share, did he take equal responsibility for dealing with the girls or leave it to her, how long had these arrangements been in place, and so forth. I asked Melanie if she thought all married couples shared these sorts of tasks, or was it rather unusual for a man to take an equal share in domestic routines and responsibilities? She said that with most couples they knew, the woman did all or nearly all of these things. So what did she think this might tell me about Neville? She didn't know, she said. What does it say about him as a man and as a husband, I asked? What does it reveal about his values? With some prompting, Melanie replied that it showed commitment, good organizing ability, a caring attitude, the ability to 'do different' from many men and not feel ashamed, and consistency. His father was a nice man but very traditional in these matters and she thought Neville had decided not to emulate him. I wondered if Neville's consistently sharing domestic responsibilities was a good thing or a bad thing? Did this have a positive or a negative effect on his relationship with her? Positive, she replied; it was a good thing. Thinking about it now, how did it make her feel? Pleased, she said – even cared for. My next question was, 'What else does he do, or has he done, to make you feel the same way?' and Melanie gave several examples, including details of how supportive he had been while she was ill.

I then turned to Neville and asked him how it felt to hear Melanie paying him such tributes. He said he was quite surprised, and also moved. His impression had been that she just saw him as a rather remote and indifferent husband and father.

I continued to talk to Neville, selecting a second exception to explore. I said that I had been struck by Melanie's asking him to help with her letter of complaint to the hospital. Why did he think she had done this rather than just write the letter herself? Neville said that Melanie had always found writing formal letters difficult.

I realized that my wording had been clumsy – I had unwittingly invited Neville to make a criticism of Melanie! So I immediately clarified my question by rephrasing it. What was it about their relationship which had enabled Melanie to ask for his help in such an important matter? He thought for a moment then said he supposed she trusted him. What was the nature of this trust, I asked? What was she sure he would do, and what was she sure he would not do? He said he thought she knew he would take the letter seriously and that he would not make her feel silly for needing his help with it. I expanded this theme by eliciting and exploring various other times when there had been support and trust between them. Neville talked of a period when he had work worries and Melanie discussed them with him and was a great support. Although it was still Neville's 'turn', Melanie could not resist telling me of a time when they had helped one of their girls to overcome a bed-wetting habit. I asked whether Neville thought that these examples shone a negative light or a positive light on the relationship, and he said it was positive.

9. Remind the couple of the purpose of the session, suggest a simple noticing task, and arrange the next session (5 minutes)

I briefly remind the couple that the purpose of this first session has been for all of us to get a clear picture of the problem and how it is affecting their lives, and also to look at evidence that the problem may not always be present.

As 70 minutes have now passed, readers may be wondering when the problem is going to be addressed. The answer is – not yet, and maybe not even in a counselling session but by the couple in their own time. Counselling is not likely to end after one session (though I *have* occasionally found one to be enough), but *this first session has laid a foundation on which the couple's own knowledge and skills can be built anew.* A fresh perspective on the relationship has been brought about, a situation where both parties' perceptions are less paralysingly problem-saturated and nearer to the complex reality of the relationship, a reality that has previously been fogged by the problem's power to distort the couple's memories.

I have come to trust the ability of people's minds to develop ways of resolving their problems, and I believe that this works on both conscious and unconscious levels. At an unconscious level, the mind is working towards solutions even if the person is not thinking of the problem; indeed, it works at this more efficiently if the person is not fiercely concentrating. This is common experience, ranging from remembering someone's name, or where the car keys have been put, to important scientific discoveries such as Alexander Fleming's realization of the significance of the mould in the Petri dish. This process can be blocked by excessive worry and fretting, and also by an entrenched, negative cast of mind. By (a) revisiting the positive aspects of the couple's history, but without excessive and precipitate optimism, and (b) sending them on their way at this point rather than bringing them back to

problem–talk, the maximum potential for releasing their minds' unconscious creative processes is attained. Once this starts to happen (and it can be almost at once),
a conscious recognition and embedding of movements towards resolution will play
an equally important part, with the conscious and unconscious elements feeding
into and reinforcing each other. To promote this creative mental interaction, I
often suggest a noticing task – a technique from solution-focused therapy, which I
believe fits well with a narrative approach at this point. I suggest that before we
meet again, the couple might find it interesting to notice anything, no matter how
small or apparently trivial, that suggests there may be elements of their relationship
that have not been defeated by the power of the problem. Not to *try* to make such
things happen at this stage, which could feel artificial, but just to notice them if
they do occur, and to tell each other what they have noticed.

The exceptions that come out of this observation task will be significant at this
early stage of counselling, as they will demonstrate positive strands in the relationship which have remained in place even though unrecognized, whereas determined
attempts to make lots of better things happen at once can produce disillusion if such
changes are misjudged or turn out to be temporary. Variants of 'He started to be
more considerate in the way he spoke to me, but it didn't last, so what's the point?'
are a frequent outcome if a couple attempt to make major changes without an
underpinning reassurance, demonstrated through the detailed exploration of exceptions, that the relationship is basically sound.

Arrangements are then made for the next session. It can be another joint session, or the first of two individual sessions, one for each person. Often, I prefer to
continue with both persons being seen together. This promotes a sense of common endeavour and cooperation which is therapeutic in itself. This is something
that cannot easily be achieved in individual counselling around relationship problems, because one partner is not in attendance and may not even know his or her
partner is having counselling. However, there are instances when holding two or
more individual sessions is appropriate, and it is not easy, at this point, to decide
whether or not to suggest this. I sometimes hold at least one more joint session to
gain a clearer idea of the extent to which the couple can continue to agree on a
definition of the problem that does not locate it primarily in each other, and to see
how far the couple's response to joint counselling starts to become productive.
After this, I have a clearer idea as to whether either or both might benefit from an
opportunity to talk to me alone, and I also find that having taken part in a couple
of joint sessions, the partners know me well enough to be comfortable with the
idea of each seeing me individually and in confidence.

I ended the session by thanking Melanie and Neville for giving each other, and
me, such a full and detailed picture of how unwanted tensions were affecting
their lives. I said that I was also interested that they had recognized some situations when unwanted tensions had been absent, and I suggested that they might
like to notice and remember any such occasions between now and the next session, or even times when the tensions receded very slightly. It might be best
not to try to *make* such occasions come about, I said, as this might seem rather

artificial – just look back at the end of each day, make a mental note and check out their observations with each other. Maybe they might also make literal, written notes, so they didn't forget. I'd be interested to hear about any such occasions at the next session.

Sometimes it may be *essential* to give one person, most often a woman in a heterosexual relationship, an opportunity to talk to me by herself, in case there is violence or abuse which she has not dared to mention in front of her partner. If an indication of this possibility arises in a joint session, no matter how tenuous it may be, I remind the couple that their counselling can benefit from individual sessions as well as joint sessions, and invite the woman to have the first turn. Chapter 13 describes how I then proceed.

As I had no intimations of abuse or violence with this couple, I suggested another joint session, and we arranged to meet again in two weeks' time.

Refer to the Appendices for the Memory-Jogger for First Joint Session.

LEARNING EXERCISE: REHEARSAL OF A FIRST JOINT SESSION

- The exercise is adaptable to different circumstances; for example, it can be undertaken by colleagues informally, or included as part of a workshop.
- The exercise is best undertaken by three colleagues, with one role-playing the counsellor and two role-playing the couple.
- An additional observer/commentator will be a useful addition if four colleagues are available. She/he will have this book to hand and will search for the answer to any queries on the procedures or aims of the framework.
- If only two colleagues are available, one will role-play the counsellor and the other will role-play each partner in turn.
- The counsellor and couple should use their normal voice and manner. The exercise will be slow-paced and exploratory rather than a realistic enactment.
- At any point in the exercise, anyone taking part may call for time out. Role-play will then be suspended and the person who has asked for time out will raise their questions or discussion points before role-play continues.
- Timing will depend on the progress of the exercise, and will not follow the suggested timings in the text and memory-jogger. The aim is for each stage to be rehearsed and absorbed, so the exercise will take considerably longer than 1¼ hours, possibly half a day or longer.
1. The participant/s who are to role-play a couple will invent a situation where there is a worrying but not extreme problem; alternatively, they may draw on knowledge of an actual couple, in which case fictitious names will be used. Names and background details will be decided as well as the nature and history of the problem. They should jot down notes on these details and refer to them during the exercise. At this preparatory stage, the counsellor will not be involved, and will begin the exercise with no prior knowledge of the couple or their problem.

2. After a mock telephone conversation where one of the couple makes arrangements for the session, each stage of the first session framework will be rehearsed in role-play. The counsellor will have a copy of the first session memory-jogger to refer to, and the couple will improvize based on their preparation.

3. Participants will decide at each stage whether to repeat sections of the framework or to proceed to the next section.

4. At the end of the exercise, the participants will consider some or all of the following questions:

    (a) Did the partners feel that outlining their perception of the problem while the other listened enabled them to do justice to how they were experiencing the problem?

    (b) Did listening to their partner being interviewed by the counsellor make each person more aware of how their partner was experiencing the problem?

    (c) Did deciding on and using an externalized definition of the problem make it seem more manageable?

    (d) Did the partners find that exploring exceptions made any difference to their sense of hopelessness?

    (e) Did the counsellor find that the first session framework gave coherence to the session, or was the framework too restricting?

    (f) What existing skills did the counsellor call on in this exercise?

    (g) If there was an observer, what aspects of the exercise did she/he find interesting or striking?

6
SUBSEQUENT JOINT SESSIONS

This chapter presents a framework for subsequent joint sessions. The example of my counselling with Melanie and Neville, begun in the previous chapter, is continued here to illustrate the sequence and to provide subject matter for discussion.

Compared with first sessions, subsequent sessions present the counsellor with more choice and consequently a greater variety of possible pathways to follow. These pathways become evident as sessions progress, and need to be chosen in response to the developing situation rather than planned or anticipated. The session frameworks are therefore a little more complicated than for the first session, and like that framework, they are basic structures into which various additional techniques can be introduced. However, even after many years' practice, it still surprises me how often following the basic frameworks is enough in itself to create a more cooperative atmosphere between partners, to unlock impasses of thinking and action, and to kick-start the reversal of negative feelings and behaviour.

THE SUBSEQUENT JOINT SESSION FRAMEWORK (60–75 MINUTES)

All timings given below are approximate.

Opening moments

I begin the session by asking the couple if there have been any events or developments they would like to tell me about. The deliberately neutral phrasing implies no expectation of either a negative or a positive answer. There are in fact three possible responses to this apparently simple question, approximating to: 'Bad things have happened', 'Nothing to report', or 'Good things have happened'. I pursue the conversation differently according to which response is given.

Sequence when 'Bad things have happened'

1. Invite description of the newly stated or continuing problem (20 minutes)

If the couple report worrying or negative factors, I take them seriously and ask for details. Problem-narratives may have been set aside by the end of the previous session, but now they have returned they deserve attention.

Judgement is needed as to how far to stay with the problem, and at what point to move away from the newly stated concerns once they have been described, and obviously this depends primarily upon the seriousness of the issue to the couple. Minor issues may take up a relatively small part of the session, sometimes even just a few minutes, but more central issues may need the whole session to be devoted to them. Couple therapy, like individual therapy, is hardly ever a smooth sequence where persons move in an upward curve from 'problem present' to 'problem absent'. Progress can be interrupted at any time by reversals, and, luckily, apparent stalemates and lack of progress can sometimes blossom into hope. Counsellors should expect such backwards-and-forwards movements, and also the introduction of previously unmentioned problem issues, possibly when the couple have gained enough trust in the counsellor to reveal them. In these instances, the exploration of exceptions should be postponed until the newly stated issues have been fully heard.

Sometimes the problem may be serious enough for a return to a pattern similar to the first session framework and for the whole session to be taken up by it. This may be made easier by the couple having experienced this structure already. Examples of issues serious enough to warrant returning to alternate individual interviews and comments include revelations of one partner's financial irresponsibility, so far unstated sexual problems, or sexual infidelity (later chapters offer specific suggestions for when these issues arise).

For problems mentioned almost in passing, and which on further questioning do not turn out to represent very serious concerns, it is often enough to acknowledge the difficulty, normalize it as part of the 'three steps forward, one step back' nature of overall progress, then to ask whether the problem has been balanced by more hopeful events. This puts the problem in perspective and leads seamlessly to exception-talk. Staying with a problem that might not even be mentioned if the session had been held a couple of weeks later can inflate its importance and create unnecessary anxiety. On the other hand, moving too swiftly to exception-talk can leave persons feeling unheard and may even lead to failure to address problems of real importance (though persons will usually find an opportunity to raise these again later). Flexibility is essential, a readiness to modify the nature of the session as it develops.

Where the newly revealed issues are clearly upsetting to one or both of the persons but are not intrinsically extremely serious, or if they are further examples of important problems presented in the first session, I return to the 'individual interview' technique with an expectation that this will probably need less time than in the first session. Examples of less serious issues are complaints about relatively minor acts that have taken on emotional resonance – 'As usual, she forgot to post the letters, and that's just *typical*', 'He always serves the meal the moment I get in, though he knows I need some time by myself to unwind'. I invite each person to talk about the problem with me for up to 10 minutes while the other listens without interrupting, taking notes if they wish. I hold the second interview immediately after the first then ask each person to comment for up to 5 minutes on what the other has said. I make notes as the persons speak, including logging clues to exceptions. I then sum up, using the persons' own words. This is usually enough to allow a move to exception-talk but occasionally a complete session is needed after all, if my initial judgement turns out to have underestimated the problem's importance.

2. Identify exceptions (5 minutes)

As with the first session, the procedure of individual interviews and comments plus the counsellor's summing up generally brings about in each partner a calmer and more objective view of the other's feelings and thoughts. It also prevents any suspicion that they are being hurried into an unrealistically optimistic stance. It frees all participants to return to the exploration of exceptions, and so continue to build a shared, alternative narrative to the oversimplified and problem-saturated individual stories of their relationship which previously, for each of them, reinforced their problems and blocked their ability to discover ways forward.

I have to resist a temptation to jump in and offer solutions to the couple rather than to give them space for their own ideas to emerge and solidify. But it *is* useful to promote and enhance this person-centred process by asking genuinely open-ended questions that assist the couple to discover, verbalize and focus on possibilities they might not have entertained if simply invited to state their own thoughts at this point. As I outline below, in relation to an exception revealed by Melanie and Neville, I did not say 'How about having regular family outings, then?' because this would have been an imposed suggestion rather than an invitation to bring their own thinking to bear. I asked them what *meaning* the exception might have for their relationship. If as a result of this exploration of meaning they decided to have more family outings, that would have been their own conclusion; but they might have decided to promote family cohesion in different ways, or even just to be reassured by this one occasion.

> I asked Melanie and Neville if there had been any events or developments since the first session which they would like to talk about. Melanie said bitterly that Neville hadn't given any time to the girls, and had been obsessed with work, disappearing into his study soon after coming home, and again after the evening meal. He had missed watching the girls' favourite television programme with them and hadn't asked them anything about school. The family had gone to the cinema together on Saturday and had a McDonald's meal afterwards, and had enjoyed this outing, but on Sunday Neville had spoilt things by vanishing into his study again virtually all day. When she complained about this, he got angry in front of the girls and had sworn at her, which made her furious.

I thought this might be another example of the problems outlined in the first session rather than a different and/or more serious issue, but Melanie was clearly very upset, so the setback had important meaning for her and needed to be addressed. I suggested that each might talk with me for up to 10 minutes, then comment on what the other had said, and they agreed. I gave out notebooks and pencils. Melanie said how disappointed she had been that despite Neville's apparent recognition of her feelings in the previous session, he had again withdrawn from family life. There were several quite urgent repairs needed to the house, including a leak in the roof which had stained a bedroom ceiling, and Neville had promised to see to these, but despite her reminding him several times, he had put the jobs off; this was absolutely typical and it made her furious, as she usually had to end up doing these kinds of tasks herself. She also said how offensive she found it when he got angry with her and swore, especially since the children were present. She had been hoping for a real change but it seemed that he was incapable of this. Neville fidgeted a little during this exposition but did not interrupt. When it was his turn, he stated with some indignation that Melanie was exaggerating. He *had* asked the girls about school, twice, at times when she happened to be out of the room. It had been an unusually busy week for him, with very urgent work to catch up on, which he had explained to her. But he was very sorry about losing his temper in front of the girls, and he wanted to apologize for this and to assure Melanie it wouldn't happen again. At this, she nodded and relaxed a little. She said she was glad he had apologized and had promised to watch his temper in future, and that now she thought about it, she did remember something about him saying he was exceptionally busy. Neville added that he really meant his apology, and that now the urgency of his work had passed, he would make sure not to neglect the girls or Melanie. I summed up briefly, putting particular emphasis on Neville's apology and Melanie's acceptance of it.

3. Explore the significance of exceptions (20 minutes)

Exceptions need to be explored in some detail, rather than just identified and stated, if they are to lead to the modification of persons' perceptions. And when exceptions emerge, it is important to check that they are significant to the couple themselves, not just significant to the counsellor. It is all too easy to miss this step, and to go ahead with exploring a counsellor-perceived exception that does not, in actuality, have much meaning for the couple. On the other hand, sometimes a little more persistence, with a more pointed focus, can be helpful in opening up the couple's ideas when a generalized question has produced no response.

The reason for continuing to gear the counselling to the exploration of exceptions, to make the point yet again, is to assist the couple gradually to build a view of their relationship where they recognize and internalize aspects which their difficulties have sidelined and made invisible. So it is important not just to identify exceptions, but to invite the couple to consider what light the exceptions throw on their relationship.

On the rare occasions when the couple really cannot remember any exceptions since the first session, I remind them of one or more exceptions which were identified in that session, and ask questions around these. So with Melanie and Neville, if the family outing had not taken place (and would therefore not have existed as an exception for exploration), I might have said something like, 'Melanie, did Neville opt out of his usual morning tasks this week, leaving the breakfasts and school preparations for you, or did he share them as usual?' If she affirmed that Neville had not opted out of these tasks, then this would have led me to ask questions about the significance of this – of how, despite being under pressure, Neville had still found time for these commitments whereas he might easily have used work pressure as an excuse to avoid them. However, the family outing did take place, and appeared to be the most potentially useful exception to explore.

I thanked Melanie and Neville for once more taking part in a counselling sequence designed to help them to understand each other's experience of the problem. I then said I was intrigued that despite the tension and stress brought about by Neville's unusually busy week, they had managed a quite lengthy family outing which everyone had enjoyed. Did they see this as a negative or positive event? Both said it had been positive. 'Do you think it shows anything else?' I asked. They hesitated. 'Anything about you as a couple?' Neither replied, so I realized that a more specific question might be appropriate, rather than a generalization.

I asked what it might mean that, at the end of a hectic week when resentment had been building up between Neville and Melanie, the family had gone out for most of Saturday and had a good time? They looked at each other and hesitated, then Melanie said that maybe it was a sign that she and Neville could sometimes put resentments to one side, and that they both enjoyed times when the family were doing things together. Neville agreed, adding that he had been rather pleased with himself for making sure that he was able to put urgent work aside for a day, for the sake of family life, and had been correspondingly annoyed when Melanie only told me about the way he spent time working in his study. I asked what this outing had shown them about their relationship as a couple, as well as about their enjoyment of their parental roles. How had they got on together? Were they restrained, or at ease? Were there moments when they felt affectionate? Melanie said that she had forgotten her resentments and that at one point, in the cinema, they had held hands. What did this suggest about their relationship? I asked. Neville said it showed they still cared for each other, and Melanie nodded in agreement, visibly moved.

Sequence when there is 'Nothing to report'

1. Check that there really is nothing new (10 minutes)

Sometimes, when responding to my carefully neutral question about what has occurred since the last session, the returning couple say there is nothing worth mentioning. I let a moment pass in case something does occur to them after all, then I make sure – 'Nothing worrying then, except what we've already talked about? And nothing noticeably better, either?' This allows them to reconsider, and some-times to reveal an issue they had been rather hesitant to mention, perhaps because it seemed too trivial ('He did flare up at the kids once'), but it also gives them an opportunity to state something positive, again perhaps not mentioned before because they were not sure it was important ('We watched TV together on Friday and had a laugh'). At this point, I have to make swift judgements. If I ignore the occasion when one partner flared up, I will miss two possibilities – either to use it as an exception ('So he managed to avoid flaring up more than once?') or to explore it as a problem ('His flaring up seems to have troubled you; would you like to say more about that?'). If I let the mention of watching TV pass, I may also miss the opportunity to explore an exception ('Is having a laugh while watching TV together a new or rare thing to happen at the moment? What might it mean, that you could do this despite the tensions you described last time? Has humour come back into your lives again?').

But the examples may really *be* trivial! In which case, it might have been better to pass over them fairly quickly, to avoid the dangers either of paying too much attention to a rather minor worry or criticism and unhelpfully inflating it, or of exaggerating a small exception out of all proportion. Experience of couple work gradually makes it easier to decide whether to focus on a hesitantly stated issue. Also, counsellors' experience of working with individuals will have given them sensi-tivity in making this kind of decision. Overall, it can be reassuring to bear in mind that there is little harm in over-focusing on a fairly minor exception as long as the counsellor comes to recognize what is happening and changes the direction of the conversation; and if a potentially useful exception is missed, it may return later – in any case, there will be others. Probably the most straightforward way of deciding whether or not to follow up a statement is simply to ask the couple whether the example is significant for them: 'Does it worry you that he flared up, or are you pleased he only did this once?' 'Did having a laugh at the TV programme seem a step forward for you both, or was it just an everyday thing that quite often happens?' If the event does turn out to have meaning for the couple, I can then invite them to describe it in detail.

2. Invite consideration of the exceptions' significance (25 minutes)

I encourage the couple to think about what the exceptions might signify for their relationship. 'So he managed to hold his temper once, and you didn't get at him when he came in late. What do these examples say about how each of you is acting a bit differently than before? Is this hopeful or worrying? In what way is it hopeful? What does hope feel like? Has hope been very present over the past few months? What might this new hope mean for your relationship? How will you recognize it when it recurs?' Of course, these questions are put as part of an exploratory and low-key conversation, not rattled off as interrogation.

Sequence when 'Good things have happened'

1. Check that no bad things have happened (5 minutes)

Where no further problems are mentioned and the couple immediately volunteer examples of improvements or successes, a little caution is advisable in case they have picked up on the move to exception-talk at the end of the previous session and wonder whether the counsellor only wants to hear about encouraging events. In my early days of trying to be a narrative counsellor, and to my later shame, I sometimes fell into the trap of always assuming an over-positive stance, and only took myself in hand when to my dismay some persons actually *apologized* for having 'nothing positive to report'. A brief checking-out can prevent that mistake: 'That certainly sounds encouraging, but before we look at those events, can I just check with you that no worrying things have happened which you'd like to talk about?' If, after all, the couple do mention difficulties, these will, as described above, need to be fully described and addressed before returning to the exceptions.

2. Identify and explore exceptions (25 minutes)

In most instances, the couple will confirm that no problems have arisen, in which case the session will focus on the exceptions the couple have noticed, and on other exceptions triggered in their memory as the session proceeds.

A NOTE ON QUESTIONS INVITING THE DETAILED EXPLORATION OF EXCEPTIONS

In narrative therapy, carefully framed questions are used as a reflection of a concerned and genuine interest in discovering what life is like for persons consulting the counsellor, and to encourage them to think about their situation 'outside the box' with a wider and more helpful perspective than previously. With practice, and using the session framework memory-joggers as a resource to start with, these kinds of guided conversations will feel more natural and become more unforced for counsellors whose training has not included the use of questions. It should always be borne in mind that narrative therapy is not trying to lead persons to deny or dismiss the problem, but to assist them to *extend* their accounts into aspects of their life and relationships which the dominant story has obscured. Identifying exceptions should always be followed, or accompanied, by questions inviting the person or persons to think about the exceptions' possible *meaning* in relation to the problem brought to therapy. The counsellor will have her own ideas on this, or she would not have noted the exception in the first place, but questions rather than statements

(Continued)

(Continued)

or interpretations allow persons to reflect, then offer their own conclusions (which may or may not match the counsellor's).

Family therapists sometimes use the word 'curiosity' to describe the attitude they try to develop, both when eliciting the problem-description and when moving beyond it; not a prurient or intrusive attitude, but a genuinely concerned wish to know more, proceeding at a pace acceptable to the person.

Narrative therapists have developed various categorizations and descriptions of questions designed to encourage modification of the problem-story (Epston and White 1992: 128–36; Payne 2006: ch. 5; White 1989: 39). For the counsellor new to couple work, reading these quite complex descriptions is perhaps best postponed until experience has been gained in using an easily grasped and broadly applicable mnemonic. In general, significant extensions and modifications of the problem-story will be forthcoming if the therapist's questions around exceptions are based on *What did you do? What did you think? What did you feel? What did it mean?* Writing 'do/think/feel/meaning?' at the head of in-session notes or on the session memory-jogger sheets can be helpful, and re-reading the examples of therapy in this book with the mnemonic in mind will reinforce the point.

Concluding the session

1. Invite the couple to take part in an experiment where they each undertake to make a minor change (15 minutes)

This practice is borrowed from solution-focused therapy, and I think it fits well with the narrative approach at this stage of couple counselling, where after two sessions of listening to each other's narratives and identifying and exploring exceptions, each person has gained a greater appreciation of the other's recent experience of the relationship, less distorted by their own defensiveness, and both have re-engaged with more hopeful and positive aspects of the relationship than were evident to them initially. These modified perceptions can now be enhanced through an easily achievable, mutually agreed activity designed to lead to two important steps forward: a renewed sense of cooperation through undertaking agreed changes, and finding that change is possible despite problems brought to therapy which at this stage are still unresolved.

I frame the suggestion as an 'experiment', and explain that this is because whatever the outcome, something useful will be learned. If the changes the couple agree to put in place are brought about, then the success of the experiment will lie in demonstrating that changes are possible, but if the changes do not take place, the experiment will allow the couple to examine why these particular changes were too precipitate or difficult, and perhaps to decide on others. And although I do not say this, failure to put the changes into place may be an early indication that the couple's problems are more severe than one or both (or indeed I myself) have recognized.

Such recognition is particularly useful when there has been a considerable degree of refusal by one partner to take the other's complaints and distress seriously. Couple counselling does not always lead to improvement in the relationship and/or resolution of the problems which have arisen. On the contrary, in some cases, its usefulness lies in assisting the pair to cut through illusion and enable a decision to be made for parting, perhaps with greater mutual understanding and cooperation than if counselling had not taken place.

When I have explained the experimental nature of my suggestion, I remind the couple of the exceptions they have identified. I then invite each partner to offer a possible change in *their own* behaviour; one that does not present the challenge of a crucial and emotionally loaded aspect of the couple's difficulties, but might still be pleasing to their partner. This way of inviting change encourages each to think from *the partner's* perspective, whereas if I asked what they would like their partner to offer them, they would probably stay within their own resentful perspective and might ask for an unrealistically difficult or emotionally loaded change. Usually, the groundwork of identifying and discussing the significance of exceptions will provide a clue as to what they might offer – 'Perhaps I could make sure I do post the letters?', 'How about if I serve the meal half an hour after you come home?' Sometimes offers are made which could not have been anticipated, but which come out of the experience of listening to each other closely when they were interviewed: 'You said how awful you feel when I come home late without letting you know. How about if I make sure to phone you when I'm delayed?'

I ask the couple if they would be willing to put these changes in place in the interval before the next session. Usually they agree, and when each has suggested a change they might offer, sometimes after quite a lot of thought, I check with the other partner that this is something they would indeed find pleasing and acceptable. If the response is negative, or if the partner suggests a reasonable and not too challenging alternative, I turn to the person offering and check whether they would be willing to undertake the change their partner has suggested instead of the one they thought of. Agreement may take some negotiation, but most couples find the idea of this experiment quite stimulating and intriguing, and are happy to cooperate with each other in setting it up.

Once agreement has been reached, I summarize the discoveries they have made in the session, with particular emphasis on exceptions that have had resonance for them, and check that they agree with my summary. I then return to their offered changes and repeat these, checking to make sure that I have remembered them accurately and that each understands what has been offered and accepted.

2. Offer to create a confirming document, and discuss its nature and content (10 minutes)

To reinforce partners' commitment to the experiment, I offer to create, and send to them, a mock-legal statement of agreement that will act as a reminder of what each has undertaken for the experiment, and I suggest they sign this in each other's presence as a confirmation. I also suggest they place the document in a prominent place, or if the document might be seen by others, put it somewhere secure to which they both have access. No couple has ever refused my suggestion of a confirming document, and many have told me later that reading the document together and signing it was a real step forward for them. It consolidated their determination to make changes, and acted not only as an ever-present reminder of what they had undertaken to do, but also concretely represented and symbolized a significant turning point.

I acknowledged that Neville and Melanie had had a difficult week because of Neville's work pressures, and because of the resentment this had produced in Melanie, either because she had not grasped that this week was exceptional, or because Neville had not really made this clear to her. However, despite Neville's being under so much pressure, he had put work aside for a whole day and both of them had enjoyed going out with the girls. In the cinema, they had, almost without realizing it, reconnected with their affection and held hands, which on looking back suggested to them that despite all their difficulties their love was intact. I then suggested an experiment where they would each offer a change in behaviour that they thought might be pleasing to the other. I explained that trying to alter one, relatively minor behaviour rather than an emotionally loaded one was sensible at this stage, and that they could learn from the experiment no matter what the outcome. In fact, Neville offered a significant change – to make sure he did domestic jobs soon after being asked rather than putting them off, at which Melanie nodded vigorously; in turn, she offered to be calm when reminding him if he did forget, at least the *first* time she had to, she said! We all laughed at this rejoinder and I took advantage of the light-hearted atmosphere to say that I wondered if they would like to do something which might sound a bit strange but which I knew had been helpful to other couples. This was to sign a mock-legal agreement to consolidate this experimental undertaking and to act as a reminder. They said this was OK, so I undertook to create such a document and send it to them in the next couple of days, and I repeated the offers they had made to make sure I had got them right. (See Melanie and Neville's document in Figure 6.1.)

3. Arrange the next session (5 minutes)

At the end of every joint session, a decision needs to be made about whether to continue with joint sessions, or to offer one or more individual sessions to each person. As described for the first session, there are two factors to bear in mind: the preference of the couple, and the counsellor's own judgement. Usually, these will coincide, and present no difficulty or awkwardness. When things are going well, with a basically OK couple who agree on the nature of the problem, are rediscovering the resources of their relationship and are ready to make changes, joint counselling is usually preferred by all parties. However, if the counsellor suspects there may be violence or abuse, or if he picks up continuing tensions and a sense of 'something not being said', he should remind the couple that individual sessions are to be held as well as

---

**AN EXPERIMENTAL
AGREEMENT**

between

Melanie and Neville Rossiter

Neville:

I promise where ever possible and practical to complete household jobs when asked and not to leave them for too long.

I will accept gentle reminders from Melanie.

Melanie:

I will be calm when requesting for a second time that a job is done.

This Agreement signed on 24 March 2009

....
                                                                    Neville Rossiter

....
                                                                    Melanie Rossiter

---

FIGURE 6.1   EXAMPLE OF A MOCK-LEGAL AGREEMENT

joint sessions. Such indications may appear in the first joint session, or may show themselves in subsequent sessions, when initial constraints have been relaxed through familiarity with the counsellor, the setting and the counselling process. Assuming the possible victim is a woman, to avoid creating risk for her by her partner's suspecting the counsellor's motive, the counsellor should arrange for the woman to be seen first, in a way that does not arouse suspicion. My practice is momentarily to lapse into minor patriarchy, which will disarm the man to an extent and fulfil the overriding aim of seeing the woman first. I say 'OK – ladies first, I suppose?' then make the appointment.

I rather underplay the significance of the move to individual sessions so as to protect the potentially vulnerable person, by saying that a one-to-one session will give each person twice as long to talk to me as a joint session, and that issues quite frequently arise in individual sessions that are nothing directly to do with the couple's relationship but can be helpful for the person to discuss and 'get out of the way'.

It is important to emphasize to both parties that the individual sessions are confidential, and that the other partner should not ask about what has been said in them. This will not of course prevent a very controlling partner from pressurizing the woman to reveal what she has said in her individual sessions, but it provides some degree of defence, especially in instances where the partner's domineering is relatively less oppressive and threatening than that of severely abusive partners.

Individual sessions must be arranged for both partners, not just the one who is of concern; this will help to prevent a possibly abusive partner from suspecting that the counsellor is going to ask his partner about things he himself does not want revealed. Also, in a spirit of fairness, it will allow his point of view to be heard as well.

> Neville, Melanie and I agreed to meet again in two weeks' time for a further joint session, since after a little discussion none of us felt the need for individual sessions.

OUTCOME

Melanie and Neville continued with counselling for four further joint sessions at fortnightly intervals. They upheld their experimental agreement. Neville came to acknowledge that his behaviour, rather than Melanie's reactions to it, was the main reason for the couple's tensions, and he made a firm resolution to change. He himself wrote a document of commitment to these changes, and signed it at a session, with Melanie and myself as witnesses. At a follow-up session three months later, the couple reported that they were 'back on track' and happy.

Refer to the Appendices for the Memory-Jogger for Subsequent Joint Sessions.

LEARNING EXERCISE: SUBSEQUENT JOINT SESSIONS – DISAPPOINTMENTS AND EXCEPTIONS

Not all aspects of subsequent joint sessions are included in this exercise. The exercise should last about 75 minutes.

- The exercise is for groups of a minimum of three participants, who may play the same roles as they did in the first session rehearsal exercise, or else take different roles if they prefer. A fourth participant may take part as an observer.
- The counsellor (and observer) will have to hand copies of the subsequent joint sessions memory-jogger and may refer to it at any point.

- Timing will not correspond to real-session timing, so as to allow for pauses and consultation.
- Before the exercise begins, participants playing the couple will agree on events that have taken place since the first session, including one slight disappointment – an event or action related to the problem brought to counselling – and one relatively low-key exception (they should avoid any dramatically awful events or amazingly hopeful changes for the better). These details will not be revealed to the counsellor before the role-play.
- Any participant may call time-out from the role-play for discussion and clarification.

1. Role-play of a session (45 minutes)

Brief for the counsellor:

- Welcome the couple.
- Ask about events since the previous session.
- The couple will identify a disappointing event. Decide whether to normalize this issue or to hold brief interviews with each person.
- Reflect back and summarize.
- Invite the identification of exceptions.
- Invite a detailed description of the exception identified by the couple.
- Explore with the couple the possible meaning of the exception.

2. Discussion of the session (15 minutes)

Participants to discuss the role-play session, with particular emphasis on the following:

(a) Did the couple feel 'heard' when the disappointing event was elicited and described?
(b) Did the description of the exception, and the exploration of its possible meanings, modify the couple's feelings about the disappointment?
(c) Was the counsellor aware of this change? How did the change process compare with his/her usual way of working?

3. Taking therapy further (15 minutes)

Participants to discuss:

(a) What experimental changes in behaviour might the couple offer to each other at the next session?
(b) What form of therapeutic document might the counsellor write, either to reinforce the experiment, or to embed exceptions identified in the first and second sessions?

4. Post-exercise homework

Participants each to write a version of the therapeutic document, for comparison and discussion at the next meeting.

7
SUBSEQUENT INDIVIDUAL SESSIONS

In this chapter, I offer a framework for individual sessions when these take place in the context of couple counselling. I emphasize practical and ethical factors that distinguish such sessions from those that take place in exclusively one-to-one counselling, and suggest ways of balancing the confidentiality of such sessions against the need to integrate the information gained from them into sessions when both partners are present.

REASONS FOR HOLDING INDIVIDUAL SESSIONS

When I see partners individually following a joint session, it is usually because I think there may be factors that one or both partners are not happy to discuss with the other present. At one extreme, there may be abuse or violence. More often, one or both partners have been unable to use the first session fully to express their disappointment, frustration and anger, perhaps out of embarrassment, or consideration for their partner's feelings, or because they think that doing so will make matters worse. It is also possible that I may have moved too swiftly to the exploration of exceptions, and that there are grievances not yet fully voiced. Other factors to emerge in individual sessions may include undisclosed sexual affairs, health or sex issues, worries habitually dismissed by the other partner, matters involving confidentiality towards people other than the partner, or personal issues not directly related to the couple's problems but which the person wishes to raise with me.

MAINTAINING A COUPLE-COUNSELLING STANCE

Therapists new to couple counselling may be tempted to relax into their familiar ways of working one-to-one. Certainly, existing skills will be crucial resources to draw on, but these need to be shaped and modified by the new context.

Individual counsellors new to couple counselling will be used to giving one person their undivided and close attention, and to assisting them to identify and fulfil their individual wishes and needs. In individual counselling, the focus is by definition on one person, but of course the counsellor also has a responsibility to people beyond that person. If counselling produces change, this will not be restricted to the individual as a bounded entity but will ripple outwards towards his or her intimate and wider social circles. A woman who, through counselling, has decided to move towards fulfilling her wishes and needs for herself rather than to devote herself exclusively to serving her family will affect that family profoundly by this decision, and will need encouragement to discriminate between her own legitimate needs and her responsibility towards vulnerable family members who genuinely depend on her. A man who regains self-respect by facing up to and defying his bullying boss will risk financial insecurity for his family if his dismissal is engineered as a result of this defiance, and will need to recognize this possibility and be encouraged to formulate a contingency plan.

When individual sessions are held in the context of couple counselling, it is particularly important for the counsellor to maintain, at every point, a clear awareness of responsibility to the other partner. Because of the couple counselling context, this responsibility beyond the person immediately being seen may take on even greater importance than it does in work with individuals. Only one person is being heard with respectful attention, but *this is still couple counselling*.

Consistency of approach is also important, and counsellors using the narrative-based model of this book who are new to such concepts as externalizing the problem and the exploration of exceptions should not let these practices lapse. The Subsequent Individual Session framework incorporates these elements.

THE SUBSEQUENT INDIVIDUAL SESSION FRAMEWORK (50–60 MINUTES)

I have not suggested exact timings for these sessions, since stages need to be flexible according to what the person reveals or wishes to discuss. However, an approximate pattern would be about 3–5 minutes for the introduction; 25 minutes for eliciting and exploring either newly stated problems or problems revealed in the previous session; 15 minutes either for exploring exceptions or, if there is infidelity or violence, for discussing a policy for future counselling; 5 minutes for closing the session.

My experience of couple counselling has so far been limited to working with heterosexual couples. Sometimes a man will be the first to have an individual session, but I have chosen examples of individual sessions for women, because in my experience it is the woman in a heterosexual relationship who more often needs to discuss issues involving risk.

1. Introduction

As the person may have forgotten or only vaguely remembered what I said about confidentiality, and be concerned that her partner might ask her what she talked about in this one-to-one session, I always begin by re-emphasizing confidentiality. I explain that in future joint sessions I shall not refer to anything mentioned in individual sessions unless and until I have permission, and I remind her that both partners agreed not to ask about what happens in the other's individual sessions. If she does decide to tell her partner about the session, that will be up to her and quite OK by me – but the partner has no *right* to request or receive this information.

2. Inviting description of the problem

I invite the person to talk about her concerns, explaining that these may be the same as those she has already mentioned, and that if so, she now has more time to talk about them in detail. I also say that sometimes there are issues a partner does not feel able to raise in front of the other, at least for the moment, possibly to spare them embarrassment, because the issues seem trivial, or because they involve the confidences of other people. I also make it clear that one reason for individual sessions is to allow disclosure of a sexual affair not admitted to the partner; suspicions or knowledge that the partner is having an affair; or violence. These examples allow the person to orientate herself to the purpose of the session and to choose her theme with confidence.

As she speaks, I follow standard practice by checking out and summarizing, and taking brief notes, with possible exceptions noted as well as difficulties and dilemmas. As in the first session (and later ones too), I avoid psychological terms locating the problem within the person or persons, or attributing deficiencies to their personality or identity, instead suggesting and using externalized and/or interpersonal-process language. Sometimes the same terms are used as those in the first session, and sometimes modifications are possible that define the problem more accurately. Perhaps the couple's difficulties were previously defined with a generalization such as 'trouble between us' but on further description, 'mutual short-fuse reactions' can be substituted; 'Janet's attempts to get through to Dave' might now, after a more detailed narrative, become 'Janet's despairing attempts to help Dave to understand her'.

However, if factors such as abuse or violence are revealed, externalizing language such as 'violence that has entered your lives' is *not* appropriate, as it linguistically softens the behaviour and implies some degree of letting the perpetrator off the hook of responsibility for his actions. In these instances, I use direct and unequivocal language – 'Jack hitting you', 'Jack raping you'. I discuss this situation in detail in Chapter 13.

The content of the person's narrative is taken into account when deciding how to continue the session, as described below.

3. When newly stated issues appear unrelated to the couple's problems

With more time available in this session for the person to outline her concerns, she may introduce factors which, though important to her as an individual, do not appear relevant to the couple's problems, or may only impinge on them indirectly. Perhaps she has difficulties at work, maybe she is grieving for a parent who has died, or she may be concerned about her health and not convinced her doctor is taking her symptoms seriously. I try to establish whether such problems are in fact affecting the relationship, even if the person starts by saying these are just her individual concerns. Are the work problems making her tired and bad tempered at home and exacerbating the conflicts with her partner? Is the grief for her parent something that her partner understands and accepts or does he annoy her by urging her to forget and move on? Are her health worries a source of friction with her partner? Or perhaps something she dare not tell him about?

If it emerges that an apparently irrelevant issue does in fact affect the relationship, then the session will include exploration of this.

However, if it appears that the issue really *is* irrelevant to the couple's difficulties, I have a responsibility to the other partner not to get drawn into extended individual counselling. How I continue the session will depend on the degree of intensity with which the issue is being experienced. It may almost have been mentioned in passing, and not be a major source of concern to the person, in which case it can be moved away from fairly quickly; or it may be central, and dreadful for her, in which case I certainly do not want to dismiss or marginalize it. In the latter instance, I devote all or part of the session to the problem, following a sequence similar to that of the first session. I invite a full description of the problem and its effects on her life, using externalizing language so as to begin the process of the person's objectifying her concerns and not attributing them to any assumed psychological or personal deficits. I check out, summarize and take notes, including any clues to possible exceptions. I then move to the identification and exploration of exceptions. The aim is to use the session for a fairly intensive exploration of the problem, and to identify exceptions in the person's reactions to it which will give her hope and enable her to postpone further counselling on this individual problem for the moment, in the knowledge that she has, perhaps without realizing it, already begun to call on knowledge and skills to address the problem. I may also mention some ideas and actions that other people I have counselled found useful in similar situations, in case these ideas strike a chord with her.

At the end of the session, I explain that if she wishes to explore this separate problem any further with me, it will be best to postpone such counselling until couple therapy has ended. Her partner might well feel uneasy about these sessions, despite assurances that they are to be about issues unrelated to the couple. In any case, it might be difficult to keep couple issues wholly out of sessions on separate issues, despite our best intentions. If her problems are particularly urgent, I offer the alternative of referral to a colleague, whom she could see for issues unrelated to the couple's difficulties while I continue to address the couple's problems with them.

4. When there are issues related to the couple's stated problems, or to problems not already mentioned

The most frequent topics raised by persons in individual sessions comprise an elaboration of the problem-story she told in the first session, with additional details and further examples, some of which may have taken place since. When I was new to couple counselling, I found this dismaying. After all, in the first session, I had carefully moved the conversation from problem-talk to exception-talk, and yet here was the person reverting to the problem, and apparently back at square one. I was relieved when I heard Michael White, in a workshop, stress that narrative therapy is always a forwards/backwards process and that the power of the problem-story is inevitably predominant in the early stages (White 2004c). Problems do not just fade away or switch off, and exceptions are fragile in the memory. It usually takes a number of sessions before the full significance of exceptions is absorbed and a tipping point reached where the exception-story becomes more significant than the dominant problem-story and begins to be self-fulfilling.

5. Empathy-promoting questions

When the person has told the latest version of the problem-story in full (with the usual checking out, summarizing and note-taking on my part), I do not move to exceptions, as I might in one-to-one sessions unrelated to couple work. This is a couple counselling session, even though only one person is present. What I do next is ask 'empathy-promoting' questions; I want to encourage the person to step out of her own experience for a moment and put herself imaginatively into the mental world of her partner. I convey belief in her story, making it clear that I do not wish to gain evidence *against* it – the form of my questions includes acknowledgement of her point of view as well as an invitation for her to identify with her partner's experience and to some extent break out of her own, possibly blinkered perspective.

Martin:	Laura, you were terribly upset when Jamie stormed out of the house again. You said it was another example of how he refuses to face up to the difficulties and disagreements you're both having. You once again felt dismissed and abandoned, and that the relationship was doomed if Jamie couldn't even manage to discuss how things are between you. I wonder what was going through his mind? What made this so difficult for him, that he could only cope with his feelings by getting out?
Laura:	I don't know. He just shot off. Typical!
Martin:	You were terribly upset.
Laura:	Yes, I was yelling at him and crying.
Martin:	Was he upset too?
Laura:	I suppose so.
Martin:	How do you know he was upset?
Laura:	I think *he* was crying a bit.
Martin:	Crying?
Laura:	Yes, he had tears in his eyes.
Martin:	So what might he have been thinking? Feeling?

> *Laura:*   I don't know … perhaps he was feeling a bit like I was.
> *Martin:* Despairing? Fearful for the relationship?
> *Laura:*   Yes, I suppose so.
> *Martin:* Is it a good thing or a bad thing that Jamie cares so much about your relationship that he got terribly upset when it seemed under threat?
> *Laura:*   [pauses] I hadn't thought about it like that.

Laura's final statement is an in-session exception; from Jamie-blaming, she has moved to recognizing common emotional ground. Now the pathway is open to more exception–identification and exploration: 'When else has Jamie shown he cares so much for the relationship that he choked up? Would it have been better or worse if he'd stayed and had a huge row with you? When a couple have big emotional upheavals, is the relationship dead or alive? Do quarrels show they care about the relationship or that they're indifferent to it? Which gives more hope? Many men would lash out with their fists. Jamie didn't, and never has. What does that say about him? He was crying – lots of men would see that as a weakness. Do you? No? So what does it mean to you?'

The issue of Jamie's not discussing the couple's relationship has not been addressed. Doing so would not have been a misjudgement, and useful ideas might have come out of it, but it would probably have maintained Laura's resentful attitude. Instead, Laura has modified her orientation towards the incident, the conflict it caused and Jamie's action in storming off. Maybe they will talk about the issue in a later joint session, with Laura's greater understanding playing a part, or maybe Laura's new insight will allow her to raise it with Jamie at home in a calm and less critical way.

If the person raises problems that have not been stated in the first session (as distinct from further examples of issues already made clear), the nature of the problem will, again, dictate the direction the session will take. Suppose that in their first session neither Laura nor Jamie mentioned money problems, but that in her individual session Laura says that Jamie keeps on increasing their credit card debt, that she is seriously worried about this, but that he refuses to let her know the full details. This is a serious issue and needs to be addressed. I would ask her to describe the problem in detail, its history, the amount of debt she thinks might be involved, how this worry affects her, Jamie and the family, and what might happen if the problem was not resolved. I would look for exceptions, such as any times Jamie did make a full monthly repayment, or acknowledged he was worried about the debt, or stood back from increasing it, or showed responsibility in other areas of family life. I would log these exceptions and without trying to minimize the problem, bear them in mind for exploration, in this or a later individual session. However, this newly stated problem matches the couple's known problems; it extends the problem-story into a different but related area, but does not add a wholly new and revelatory dimension to it.

Laura has been assured that her session is confidential, but she has revealed a problem, and her feelings about it, which are pretty important factors in the couple's conflicted relationship. If I ignore this problem in joint sessions, and only discuss it with Laura in her individual sessions, I shall be excluding an opportunity to assist the couple to address it together and to improve their relationship by so doing. The situation of one partner revealing problems in an individual session is, in fact, easily resolved by asking her or him if they will feel OK about talking about it in front of their partner, or if they prefer, for me to raise the issue, saying that I have permission for this. Usually, the person agrees, often with relief that a contentious issue will be opened up. So, at the end of the session, I would discuss with Laura whether the financial problems might be raised in a joint session, and if she agreed that this would be a good idea, I would discuss whether this might be an appropriate topic for the next joint session or whether she would prefer to leave it until later.

When a newly stated problem extends the couple's story into a quite different dimension than the account given in the first session, the person is usually taking the opportunity to disclose matters she does not wish her partner to know about, or does not wish him to know she has revealed. She may be afraid of her partner's reaction to the disclosure, fearing that this information would finally end the relationship, or she may even think her safety may be endangered. The disclosure may be that she is having a secret affair, or suspects that her partner is having an affair, or knows that he is having an affair which she believes he would not wish her to tell me about; it may concern sexual problems which she or her partner did not mention in the first session (and which he possibly does not want her to reveal); or it could concern violence or abuse by the partner. There are many other possibilities and no general guidelines are possible for all contingencies. The counsellor will need to decide how to proceed according to the history, nature and seriousness of the issue, bearing confidentiality in mind but also considering when confidentiality might have to be breached. Discussion with a supervisor will be invaluable if the way forward is not obvious.

6. When there is disclosure of an affair that took place in the distant past

Both the person and her partner will be thinking in terms of new beginnings, and new hope for the future, even if there is still a degree of other-blaming involved. In these circumstances, the commonly held idea that committed couples should have no secrets from each other can be very powerful, and induce much guilt when one of them is withholding information that has emotional connotations in relation to the partnership or marriage. If a person had an affair in the distant past, unknown to the other, there will be a strong temptation, presenting itself as a move to openness and honesty, to 'confess' and 'wipe the board clean'. At the same time, there may be a justified fear that this act of honesty will so shock and disillusion the partner that the relationship will be put under even greater threat. When this dilemma is presented in a one-to-one session, it is tempting for the counsellor to move into the stereotypical response that no secrets should exist between partners and to assume that disclosure *must* be made to the other partner at some point; the counsellor may also be uneasy at holding further sessions while possessing this secret knowledge.

A person may disclose a recent or continuing affair that is known to the other partner, but which was not mentioned in the first session, perhaps because of embarrassment or uncertainty about how I might react. I say that there is no general rule and
all couples and their situations are unique. There is usually a case for disclosure to the
partner, but there is also usually a case for allowing the distant past to remain unknown.
Metaphorical language around this dilemma can be unhelpful by carrying an apparent logic of implication which contradicts what might actually be helpful. If the affair
is not revealed, will this be 'letting sleeping dogs lie' or 'allowing a secret to fester'?
If revealed, will revelation of the past affair be 'bringing it out into the daylight' or
'opening a can of worms'? I try to use neutral and non-metaphorical language, and
to be objective, asking questions that invite the person to consider possible outcomes
arising from either course, and to allow herself plenty of time, including between
sessions, for these potential outcomes to settle in her mind and result in a decision. I
nevertheless point out that once disclosure is made, it cannot be retracted, but that a
decision to keep the affair secret can always be reviewed.

I believe that when an affair is firmly in the distant past, with the decision to end
it fully maintained, my keeping the person's confidence does not constitute a breach
of the ethics of couple counselling any more than keeping confidence about other
types of regretted past behaviours. My responsibility lies in assisting the person to
consider how the hidden history might affect the couple's future if revealed now or
at a future time, either deliberately or accidentally, or if not revealed at all.

If she does decide to disclose, I encourage her to look, once again, at possible consequences. If her decision is unchanged after this second scrutiny of possible outcomes,
I ask whether she wishes to tell her partner privately or in a joint session, and if she
decides for the latter, when this might be. I also make it clear that the revelation
must come from her, not from me. When the disclosure has been made, I proceed as
described in Chapter 12.

If she decides not to tell her partner of the historically distant affair, she may continue
to feel under considerable psychological pressure, with guilt still urging her towards disclosure despite her decision. She may think that she is a bad person and unworthy of
her partner, and these ideas could distort her perception of both his and her own contributions to the relationship's problems. Such feelings and thoughts will be explored in
further individual sessions, as their resolution is directly relevant to her capacity to
contribute, without inhibition or excessive self-blame, to the couple's overcoming their
present problems. I presume she may still change her mind; on further consideration, she
may decide to reveal the affair after all, in which case I revert to the procedures above.

7. When a recent or continuing affair is disclosed

If the person indicates that both partners know of the infidelity but that they did not
mention it in the joint session, perhaps because of embarrassment or uncertainty
about how I might react, I say that such an important matter will need to be acknowledged and addressed when joint counselling is resumed (Chapter 12 discusses how to
proceed).

The disclosure of a recently ended affair that is unknown to the other partner needs to be addressed differently, especially since the disclosing person may be rationalizing the affair as no longer relevant because it is over, and does not wish her partner to know about it. But if I hold joint sessions without the recent affair becoming known to the other partner, I am colluding in hiding a crucial factor from him. Counselling will become false and unrealistic, and also if he does eventually discover the truth, he will no longer trust me. In this situation, and also when a continuing affair is disclosed, I explain my position to the disclosing partner. I say, as tactfully and non-judgementally as possible, that now I know about the affair, I must ask her to disclose it to the other partner if counselling is to continue, because if he were to remain ignorant, I would be in such a false position that joint counselling would be impossible. I have never known a person to argue against this, and sometimes the prospect of full disclosure produces relief as well as apprehension.

Usually, the next step is to discuss when and how the person will disclose – possibly in private at home, possibly at the next joint session, but in any case by the person herself, not by me. If she needs time to think, I arrange a further individual session with her, then after this arrange a joint session. She may disclose at that joint session, or if she has already done so at home, the session will deal with the situation as it then stands. The other partner may wish to have individual sessions to address his reactions to the disclosure, or of course he may decide to end the relationship. Chapter 12 discusses how to proceed if further counselling does take place.

If the person refused to consider disclosing the affair to her partner, I would keep her confidence but postpone further joint sessions. I would be in a delicate and difficult ethical and practical dilemma. As I have never actually had to face this situation, I would discuss my options with my supervisor. These options might include giving the person further time for reflection before holding more individual sessions with her, and/or holding an individual session with her partner in case he then reveals to me suspicions about her infidelity, or even that he knows about it without her realizing. Clearly, I would not then reveal what she has said to me, but I would discuss with him the pros and cons of his telling her what he suspects or knows. As a last resort, if it becomes clear that he is ignorant of her infidelity and that she is not going to disclose it to him, I might have to hold one more session with his partner, then consider telling the couple that I cannot continue to counsel them, perhaps apologizing that their problems appear beyond my competence, so as to avoid compromising confidentiality towards the person who has had the affair.

8. When abuse or violence is disclosed

This is the most difficult and serious situation a counsellor can face in couple work. The standard framework for subsequent individual sessions should be abandoned, and the session used to hear full details, then promote safety for the victim, her children, staff of the counselling organization, and the counsellor. The whole session will need to be devoted to what has been disclosed. Confidentiality must be maintained, unless there is a threat to children, in which case the counsellor has a legal and moral duty to ensure that Social Services are informed. No further joint sessions should be held unless and until the victim is safe to take part in them. An individual session should be held with the perpetrator, to safeguard the victim from suspicion that she has disclosed, and unless the counsellor is confident in counselling victims of violence, it may be best to refer the victim to a therapist who specializes in this work. Chapter 13 discusses the situation of domestic violence in detail.

Refer to the Appendices for the Memory-Jogger for Subsequent Individual Sessions.

LEARNING EXERCISE: SUBSEQUENT INDIVIDUAL SESSIONS

This exercise requires 110 minutes if an observer presents a summary of the role-plays, 180 minutes if recording equipment is used.

- Participants role-play the same invented couple as in the previous exercises.
- The exercise is for three participants, one role-playing the counsellor and the other two the couple. The roles taken by participants in previous exercises may be changed if they wish, but in this case the new roles should be maintained during this present exercise.
- It is useful to video-or audio-record the role-plays, or if this is not possible, for a fourth participant to act as an observer and take notes.
- The counsellor has the subsequent individual session memory-jogger to hand for reference.
- Each participant may call time-out for discussion and clarification.
- No attempt should be made to keep to realistic session timing.
- Before the role-play begins, the couple decide on an issue which is a source of conflict or disagreement but which was not raised in the first session. It should be fairly important, but not about current or recent infidelity, or violence. The counsellor will not know the nature of the issue in advance of the role-play.

1. **First role-play (30 minutes)**
   (a) The counsellor holds an abbreviated individual session with one of the partners, encouraging descriptions of (i) the newly mentioned problem, (ii) exceptions to this or any other difficulties, and their significance.
   (b) The other partner is not present during this role-play and will not learn anything about it until stage (4) of the exercise (Playback).

2. **Break (10 minutes)**
   During the break, the role-play session will not be described or discussed by any of the participants.
   (a) The counsellor may wish to review his/her notes for the first session and prepare for the next.
   (b) The partner already counselled may wish to de-role.
   (c) The partner about to be counselled may wish to finalize preparation for the coming role-play.

3. Second role-play (30 minutes)

The first partner to be counselled will not be present during this session.

(a) The counsellor holds an abbreviated individual session with the other partner, encouraging description of (i) any newly mentioned problem, (ii) exceptions to this or other difficulties, and their significance.

4. Playback

60 minutes will be required for all participants to watch/listen to recordings of the sessions.

20 minutes will be required if there is no video or sound recording and the observer summarizes each session in turn.

5. Discussion and conclusions, including consideration of the following (45 minutes)

(a) What were the limitations, and what the advantages, of these individual sessions compared with the initial joint session?

(b) What differences of opinion and perspective were presented by the persons about the newly described problem?

(c) What might have been the possible dangers to the couple's relationship, *arising out of the counselling itself*, if just one of them had come to individual counselling rather than both to couple counselling?

(d) Did the counsellor find it possible to consider both stories valid despite the partners having different perspectives?

(e) Did the transition to exceptions appear natural or artificial?

(f) Did the persons feel that the exploration of exceptions eased anxieties about their problems, even slightly? If so, how did this come about?

8
ADVANCED PRACTICES

In this chapter, I describe three narrative therapy practices that were either specifically developed for couple work or are particularly suited to it. They are more complex, and perhaps more difficult to grasp and put into practice, than those described in the previous chapters. I suggest that these practices are best not considered for use until there is full familiarity with using the first and subsequent session frameworks, and the original authors' detailed accounts should be consulted in addition to my summaries.

'INTERNALIZING OTHER' QUESTIONING

Warring couples

David Epston discusses this practice in a paper published in Gilligan and Price (1993). The 'internalizing other' format for asking questions was developed as a means of '[disrupting] those warring couples who construed couple counselling as a venue to contest their differences' (1993: 183). What follows is a modified account of Epston's paper, with some ideas given extended exposition, and with an emphasis on practicality. The original account is more detailed overall, and related more fully to narrative theory.

Epston defines warring couples as two people who have become self-focused and isolated from each other rather than having a sense of being in a relationship. Most couples I work with *do* feel they have a relationship. They have a painful sense of something precious which has gone astray; they want to overcome issues, problems or situations which have led to conflict and disappointment. I think of these couples as 'basically OK' and have found that they respond quite quickly to the practices outlined in earlier chapters of this book. However, I certainly recognize Epston's description! Occasionally, I see couples whose anger and resentment is so intense that there is an immediate danger of the session becoming a forum for the unstoppable expression of bitter aggression. My request that the partner who is not being addressed by me should maintain silence until it is his turn may be agreed to, but then swiftly negated, with squirming, sighs and grunts leading to interruptions, denials and counter-accusations, whereupon the person being interviewed responds in kind and the session deteriorates into the kind of confrontation the couple have in private, with myself as a hapless witness.

Epston suggests that when confronted with a warring couple, the therapist runs the risk of being drawn into one of three roles, none of which is desirable or useful:

- *Therapist as Legal Judge:* The couple accuse each other like lawyers in a courtroom, with attack and counter-attack, defence and counter-defence. They expect the therapist to make a judgment concerning the validity of their evidence against each other, with each believing that their 'case' will be supported, that they will be found innocent, and the other will be found guilty.
- *Therapist as Moral Judge:* Here the arguments used to present each 'case' are in terms of right and wrong, rather than factual innocence and guilt. Each partner presents as the morally innocent party and accuses the other of being wicked. Each expects the counsellor to agree with their position of moral superiority, and to 'assign penance' to the other.
- *Therapist as Consultant Psychiatrist:* One or both partners take on the role of a psychiatrist who has diagnosed a mental disorder in the other. The counsellor is put in the position of a consultant who will confirm both the diagnosis and the prescription for treatment ('He's afraid of intimacy because of rejection by his parents so he needs to learn how to trust'). I would add to Epston's argument that, encouraged by the media and pop psychology texts, persons sometimes assign psychiatric or psychological causes to their *own* behaviour, expecting the counsellor to confirm this to the partner ('She should recognize that my childhood made me insecure and she should make more allowances for this').

Sometimes I have been in danger not just of falling into one inappropriate 'expert assessor' role but of floundering between all three! I am encouraged that a therapist of Epston's status can also admit to being pushed into these dilemmas. The problem is how to escape from the role or roles and change the tenor of the sessions: 'couples often become both perplexed and vexed if I decline to participate accordingly' (1993: 185). It does no good simply to veer into a change of tactics, as this will puzzle and alienate the couple, so preparing them and gaining their agreement is essential.

Epston suggests that the couple's attempts to ask each other helpful questions should be acknowledged: 'I give you full credit for having tried your questions ...' (1993: 185). I myself am wary of such congratulation, which might appear patronizing or ironic since the couple's attempts to get through to each other will have also taken forms other than asking questions, such as yelling or snapping at each other and making angry assertions and denials. I prefer simply to acknowledge that despite all their efforts, their attempts to resolve their problems have not yet succeeded.

Epston asks the couple's permission to experiment with a rather unusual or different kind of question, which they have probably not asked each other. When they agree, he warns them that these questions will be rather difficult, stretching and possibly uncomfortable – would they still like him to go ahead? Perhaps couples become intrigued by the mystery of these suggestions, switch off from their accusatory, self-justifying and psychologizing comments, and ask him to continue so as to see what he means. He asks who would like to go first, requests the other partner to listen to their partner's answers, and makes it clear that they too will be asked similar questions when their turn comes. Both will then be able to comment. Readers of this present book will notice a similarity of procedure to the individual interviews in the first joint session framework. If 'internalizing other questioning' is taking place in a subsequent session rather than in the first session, the couple have already been to some extent prepared for this more complex development.

Promoting empathy

Epston's aim is not just to assist each person to consider the couple's problems from the other's point of view. This is unlikely to succeed with a couple who are very resentful and angry with each other, as any small degree of empathy might be resisted, partial and temporary, with each swiftly springing back to their own strongly held convictions concerning the other's guilt. The *internalizing* of the other's perspective is the point, and the reason for the technique's name. Each person will for a short while 'become' the other partner through role-play (though I imagine Epston does not openly define it as this, as for many persons the term could be worrying or imply a kind of childish play-acting, not to be taken seriously).

He starts by inviting one partner to identify how they think the other would account for the deterioration of the relationship: 'Jill, what do you think Jack would say if I asked him the following question: "Jack, how do you account for the deterioration in your relationship with Jill over the past 10 years?"' (1993: 186). Epston's brief paper does not do justice to the subtlety of this apparently simple opening question. In saying that the relationship has 'deteriorated', Epston implies that in the past the relationship was OK, thus implicitly reminding the couple that there may be something retrievable. It puts the onus for describing the reasons for the deterioration onto the couple, with the therapist stepping back from an expert position of assessing or analysing their history. It holds back a full invitation to role-play while preparing the ground for it – Jill is not initially addressed *as* Jack but is asked what Jack might think or say. The problem is externalized; by referring to the deterioration of the relationship rather than to the behaviour of the partners, it invites not accusatory language, but the language of objective consideration brought to bear on a shared problem.

Jill will nevertheless probably attribute to Jack the idea that the deterioration is caused by her, not him ('I suppose he'd say it's my fault because I …'). Accusatory language is being used but, Epston suggests, with the vindictiveness taken out of it; and Jack is hearing Jill say things she realizes he himself might say. So Jill is entering into Jack's perceptions, and Jack is hearing her do so, recognizing that she does have some grasp of what he thinks and feels. As I see it (not a point made by Epston), the subject matter of the dispute is becoming less important than the immediate, in-session, here-and-now experience of a mutual growth of, and recognition of, empathy. A new atmosphere is being encouraged, of mutual understanding rather than isolated, self-righteous defensiveness and accusation.

As the session proceeds, Epston does address the person *as* her partner, using his name. To quote Epston's own example (speaking to Jill), 'Jack, what effect has this "lovelessness" had on your relationship?' (1993: 186). (Note the continuing externalization of the problem: 'the 'lovelessness', not 'Jill not showing any love for you'). Epston continues his paper with a quite complex series of questions he might ask Jill-as-Jack, with further examples from other couples, but for the purpose of this present book, it may be enough to refer the reader back to the first joint session framework. Jill-as-Jack will be asked the same kind of questions, with the same exploratory clarifications, as if Jack himself were being interviewed. (The identification and exploration of exceptions might need to be reserved for later sessions, in this very conflicted situation.)

Similarly, when it is Jack's turn to be addressed (as Jill), 'she' will be asked to comment on what 'she' has heard and to discuss whether 'she' feels that 'Jack' has understood how 'she' experiences the deterioration of the relationship.

Epston deals briefly with how he follows the internalizing other interviews in the final part of the session. The partners' answers are 'cross-referenced', so that 'an ambience of thoughtfulness, curiosity, and a degree of generosity' (1993: 187) can be created. My own suggestion for ending the session would be to continue addressing the persons in their roles, and to summarize what each has said, using their actual words where possible and identifying any areas of agreement between them. Then I would revert to addressing the persons by their own names, and ask questions around their reactions to the session. These cross-referenced reactions might be elicited by questions such as the following, asked tentatively and conversationally and with an element of solution-focused 'scaling' to encourage precision of thought and statement:

- To Jack [*addressing Jack as himself now*]: Did Jill's representation of your thoughts and feelings about the decline of the relationship seem close to, fairly similar to, or rather different from, what you yourself might have said?
- To Jill [*addressing Jill as herself now*]: Did Jack say what you might have said about why the relationship has declined, was he reasonably close, or was he rather wide of the mark?
- To Jack: From hearing Jill speaking as if she were you, how close do you think she is to understanding your point of view about why the relationship has declined, on a scale from 0 to 10 where 0 is 'not at all' and 10 is 'completely'?
- To Jill: If I ask you the same question about how close Jack is to understanding your point of view about why the relationship has declined, where would you put him, using the same scale of 0–10?
- To both: Where would you have put her/him on that scale before today? What conclusions do you draw from that – is that hopeful, or worrying, or neither of those?
- To both: When you were answering my questions as if you were your partner, did you find your understanding of his/her thoughts and feelings becoming at all clearer?
- To Jill: You said you think Jack now has a 4/10 understanding of your point of view. What would he need to understand to move up the scale a point, to 5/10?
- Similar question to Jack.
- To both: What have you both learned from today's exercise that will remain with you?

It may be appropriate to end the session on this note, so that newly established empathy can take root in the couple's out-of-session life and lead to the identification of exceptions later in counselling. However, if things have gone either very well, or badly, one of the following may be useful:

- [*If appropriate*] Have either of you any ideas, at this point, about how you might use the understandings you have gained today to offer each other one small but important change, which might make things a bit better and start to halt or even reverse the decline of the relationship?
- [*If appropriate*] This session seems to have shown that there's quite a long way to go before the decline in your relationship is halted. You might even think that this is not likely to happen. Do you think you are working towards separation? Or are you willing to come back next time to try another experiment in increasing mutual understanding? (This next session may be a repeat of internalizing other questioning or, if the counsellor is comfortable with it, a session run according to White's 'conflict dissolution' – see below.)

CONFLICT DISSOLUTION

Michael White describes conflict dissolution in *Narrative Practice and Exotic Lives* (2004a: ch. 1). Like Epston's internalizing other questioning, it offers a way of assisting warring couples to step out of their unproductive and damaging quarrelling habits and to engage with each other from a different perspective. White suggests that the advantage of this practice, for therapists, lies in avoiding a situation where they 'find that things start off badly, then get worse, and then deteriorate still further … [and] experience an impasse in their work … I have certainly experienced such impasses' (2004a: 5). It is a long chapter which includes much closely argued theory, and also precise, detailed explanation of how to cover various eventualities and outcomes, and I shall not attempt to cover all the points White makes. My aim is to give a flavour of 'conflict dissolution' and to refer the reader to the original description if she or he is intrigued enough to take learning further.

A critique of traditional assumptions in couple therapy

White begins his account of conflict dissolution with an acknowledgement that couple therapy can be difficult and discouraging. He then suggests that there are considerable limitations to three traditional assumptions about couple interaction, and that a different basis of attempting to resolve conflict is needed when these assumptions stand in the way of effective counselling.

The traditional assumptions identified by White are:

(a) In the West, *the greatest value socially and culturally is given to the assumed norm of heterosexual marriage*, so that other sexualities and forms of committed relating are implicitly seen as falling short of this ideal. (Counsellors who hold to this position risk undervaluing and invalidating other forms of couple relationship, and/or reinforcing heterosexual married couples' sense that the form of their relationship is intrinsically superior to other forms.)

(b) *There is a powerful social assumption that partners should fulfil all of each other's needs,* and that significant relationships outside the couple should not exist – and that if they do, they are a betrayal of the partner ('relationship' is not here used in the sense of an affair). (Counsellors who hold to this position risk reinforcing a limiting and impoverishing attitude which excludes many possibilities for enrichment of the lives of each individual and of the couple relationship.)

(c) *Most conflicts and stresses experienced by a couple can be attributed to a failure of communication.* (Counsellors who hold to this position, and primarily attempt to improve the couple's 'communication skills', risk reinforcing and embedding the couple's mutual antagonism, and also they ignore important personal, political and cultural influences on the problem.)

White suggests that conflict dissolution can counter the above limitations.

Interviews and responses

Conflict dissolution resembles Epston's internalizing other questioning in that each partner is interviewed while the other listens then responds, but White takes the imaginative element further.

Rather than taking on the role of the other partner, the person interviewed remains him- or herself. The counsellor asks the *listening* partner to assume the beliefs, attitudes and values of someone whom he admires and has experienced as supportive, and who the other partner is comfortable with as an invisible 'participant' contributing to the counselling process. This 'admired other' might be a friend or relative, colleague, teacher etc. and may be alive or deceased. The listening partner does not role-play this admired other, but remains himself, reacting to his partner's account *as he thinks the admired person would.*

After the initial interview with one partner, the therapist asks the listening partner a series of carefully structured questions designed to assist him to re-tell his partner's account with identification and empathy. These questions are centred on how the listener (having taken on the values and attitudes of the admired other) has responded to the expressions and images of his partner's account, why he was drawn to these, and what in his own life echoes those elements. In taking on the values and attitudes of the admired other, the listener attempts to keep true to how he has experienced these qualities himself, perhaps at a time when he needed the admired other's support in a crisis. This enables him to step out of the reflex reaction of resentment, blaming and anger which usually overcomes him when in dialogue with his partner, or when talking about the couple's problems, and to respond with a new measure of understanding and supportiveness; and this, in turn, starts to become internalized, to modify his behaviour, and to enhance his empathy further. The interviewed partner notices this change, and realizes that the antagonistic pattern has been put aside, which in turn promotes hope for a better way of relating.

The interviewed person then takes her turn to listen, while her partner is interviewed by the therapist. Before the interview begins, she identifies her (different) admired other and agrees to respond to what is said in ways that correspond to this admired person's attitudes and values. When the second interview has taken place, with the therapist asking the same kind of questions designed to enhance the empathy which the now-listening partner has begun to develop, the session ends with the counsellor inviting both partners to reflect on it, and in particular to discuss what each has newly come to recognize about the other's experience of the relationship.

Where practicable, after further sessions, the two actual admired other people might (with the couple's permission) be invited to a session to hear how their invisible presence has assisted the couple to move forward in the repair of their relationship, and to comment on this transformation. This session follows the pattern of 'outsider witness' interviewing described in the next section of this chapter. I imagine that this session also reinforces couples' ability to take on the attitudes and values of their admired others in the remaining sessions, and boosts the internalization of those attitudes and values.

White ends the paper by claiming that he has 'consistently found this approach effective in achieving conflict dissolution with couples in high and longstanding conflict', and also useful in work with couples facing other, commonly experienced difficulties in their relationship (2004a: 40).

RECRUITING AN AUDIENCE FOR THE DEVELOPING STORY

White and Epston have always emphasized that it is helpful for persons' developing stories to be told to, and commented on by, people additional to the therapist. This idea can strike traditionally trained counsellors as odd, or even unethical. In person-centred therapy, for example, there is an assumption that the relationship with the therapist, with sessions taking place in private and in confidence, is always the central means of bringing about change. However, White's and Epston's ideas arise from the family therapy tradition, where therapists often work in teams, with the duty of confidentiality extended to the team. White and Epston believe that persons' relationships with significant others, who already play an important part in their lives and who will be part of their lives after therapy ends, are the most important and truly therapeutic relationships, and that these relationships can be honoured and drawn on, with counsellors finding ways to enhance them rather than placing themselves at the centre of the therapeutic process.

In the early years of narrative therapy, White and Epston asked persons to consider who, in their personal lives, might be interested in hearing about their struggles and their progress, then suggested that talking to these people might be helpful. From this, they developed the practice of inviting significant others to take part in one or more sessions, once the person had given permission, so that they could act as 'outsider witnesses' by hearing the person tell their developing story then reinforcing and enriching it by responding to questions put by the therapist.

Over time, White elaborated this practice into a quite lengthy, complex and specific sequence, with carefully structured and controlled stages to the session. He sometimes used teams of therapists instead of, or in addition to, persons' friends or family members (White 1995: ch. 7; 2007: ch. 4). The aim was to widen and enrich the couple's story by linking it to the lives and experiences of others, so that they do not feel so isolated in their struggle, and also to bring multiple perspectives to bear on the story which go beyond the three-way interaction of therapist and couple. Other narrative therapists have followed White's lead, and where resources are available, holding 'outsider witness' sessions (also called 'definitional ceremonies') has become standard practice. Persons and therapists who have taken part in such sessions attest to their power, effectiveness and helpfulness (Russell and Carey 2003: 13–15).

I shall not attempt fully to describe these elaborate and lengthy sessions. Most counsellors are unlikely to have the resources of time and colleagues available to White and Epston, and in any case would need further training before being able to undertake such demanding approaches with confidence. I outline below a simplified version of outsider witness practice which, although advanced compared with the basic first and second session frameworks, could be undertaken by couple counsellors who have become comfortable with working to those frameworks, and which would significantly enhance their more conventional sessions. However, before undertaking such sessions, it is important to prepare by reading more detailed accounts than I give here, for example Payne (2006: ch. 7); Russell and Carey (2003: 3–16); White (2007: ch. 4).

Outsider witnesses

Some couples regard their conflicts as wholly private to themselves. Many are very skilful at hiding their difficulties and if they split up, their friends and relatives express astonishment – 'You were the last people we would have thought were in trouble'. But other couples do discuss their problems with trusted friends or family members, and going to counselling may have been a last resort after these people's attempts to help or advise have been unsuccessful.

The good will and concern of others can be activated to reinforce and embed the progress of counselling, by inviting them to attend one or more sessions when counselling has begun to go well (this is not suitable for early, more conflicted sessions). The procedure through which they and the couple are taken reinforces the couple's progress, and also avoids repetition of the unproductive ways in which the visitors may have already attempted to assist them. Similar results can be brought about by recruiting a 'reflecting team' of one or more of the counsellor's colleagues instead of persons close to the couple, but there can be practical disadvantages to this – it is difficult to organize, the additional counsellors add to the cost of the session, and the couple are likely to feel less at ease with strangers than with people they already know and trust. Nevertheless, using a colleague or colleagues can be effective, especially if they are fully familiar with the session's rationale and procedure. Couples soon sense the colleagues' commitment, are moved by their contribution and lose any initial unease.

It is important for the therapist to remain firmly in charge so that the allotted time is adhered to, the complete procedure is followed and there is no lapse into unstructured discussion. The atmosphere of the session should be purposeful, yet friendly and informal.

THE SESSION (75 MINUTES)

1. Briefing the outsider witnesses (5 minutes)

The therapist explains that the session will follow a specific pattern which has been found helpful by other couples:

(a) The couple will be interviewed by the therapist with the visitors listening, but not yet commenting. The most helpful thing the visitors can do, in preparation for their own part of the session, is simply to be open to how the couple's story affects them.

(b) The visitors will be interviewed about what they have just heard, with the couple listening, but not yet commenting. The therapist will ask the visitors for their reactions on very specific aspects of what the couple said, and request they restrict their responses to this. It will be unhelpful if they advise, interpret, analyse motives, or congratulate – the therapist will not ask questions leading to such answers, and they should avoid volunteering them.

(c) The couple will be invited to respond to what the visitors have said.

(d) Finally, all participants will come together to discuss the session.

2. Interviewing the couple (about 20 minutes)

With the outsider witnesses listening, but preferably out of the couple's direct view, the therapist invites the couple to give an account of why they came to therapy, and in particular what changes have happened since therapy began. He also invites them to speculate on what their future will be like once they have reached a point where therapy can end and their relationship is fully re-established. This is a thoughtful, low key and exploratory interview with an emphasis on exceptions, their meaning for the couple and what they have led to in the couple's life.

3. Interviewing the outsider witnesses (about 20 minutes)

The therapist requests the couple to sit out of direct eye contact with the visitors and to listen to what they say in response to his questions. He then asks the outsider witnesses to identify and talk about:

(a) any particularly striking or significant *words, phrases or images* used by the couple when describing their thoughts, feelings and actions, both when the relationship was threatened, and now the relationship is being rescued

(b) any *aspects of their own lives and histories* which were evoked by the couple's account, how this felt and what it was in the couple's struggle to overcome their difficulties which resonated for them.

4. Re-interviewing the couple (about 20 minutes)

Again, if possible, the couple and the outsider witnesses sit out of each other's vision. The therapist asks the couple to respond to the outsider witness interview that has just taken place by identifying and talking about:

(a) any particularly helpful, powerful, interesting, moving or thought-provoking statements made by the outsider witnesses
(b) any ways in which the outsider witnesses' comments have thrown new or significant light on the couple's own experience.

5. Final discussion (about 10 minutes)

The therapist groups all the participants so they can be in eye contact, and initiates a brief discussion on how everyone experienced the session.

LEARNING EXERCISE: 'INTERNALIZING OTHER' QUESTIONING (60 MINUTES)

- Three participants take part.
- Two participants role-play a warring couple, and a third participant has the role of counsellor.
- It is helpful to video- or audio-record the role-play but if this is not possible, an additional participant takes notes and in later discussion clarifies what happened in the session.
- This is a first session role-play, but the 'internalizing other' format is used rather than the usual first session framework, because of the intensity of the couple's mutual antagonism.
- The participants playing the couple agree on their names, and some details of the conflict and its history.
- Before the session, the counsellor will know nothing but the couple's names.
- The counsellor will have to hand a brief summary she/he has prepared of the internalizing other procedure, and may refer to this during the exercise, calling time-out if necessary.
- The other two participants may also call time-out for consultation and clarification.

1. An abbreviated session (40 minutes)

Brief for the counsellor:

(a) Welcome the couple.
(b) Invite them to describe the problems which have brought them to counselling.

(c) When you can manage it, acknowledge their attempts to get through to each other and to resolve the problem by this means.

(d) Run the session as an 'internalizing other' questioning session, interviewing the partners (as the other) for 20 minutes each. Refer to your notes if necessary, and call time-out if you wish.

(e) When the couple slip out of role-playing their partner, and return to direct quarrelling, tactfully bring them back to the agreed format.

Brief for the couple:

(a) When the counsellor asks you to describe your problems, launch immediately into a bitter and escalating exchange full of recrimination and accusation, with each of you asking the counsellor to support your case and put the other partner right. Keep this up until the counsellor finally manages to get a word in.

(b) Agree to the counsellor's suggestions about how the session will be run, but occasionally revert for a moment to quarrelling until you settle down once the questioning is under way.

2. Discussion and conclusions (20 minutes)

Consider the following points:

(a) How difficult did the counsellor find it to interrupt the quarrelling and to suggest how the session might be run? Was she/he tactful? Was he/she able to avoid both bossiness and an apparent fear of losing control of the session?

(b) How swiftly were the couple able to take on each other's roles? How soon did this appear natural and intriguing to them?

(c) When listening to the other being interviewed in role, what differences did the partners feel compared with the first joint session learning exercise, when they were being interviewed as themselves?

(d) By the end of the session, had an atmosphere emerged of 'thoughtfulness, curiosity and a degree of generosity'? If so, how was this achieved? If not, what made it fall short?

(e) Doing this exercise might have been quite good fun, especially at the beginning, as the couple quarrelled violently and the counsellor tried to rescue the situation. In a real session, it would probably be far from amusing. Are humour and seriousness always at odds, or can humour sometimes teach us something seriousness cannot?

(f) What have you learned from this exercise which will stay with you?

PART 4
SPECIFIC ISSUES

Part 4 discusses some areas of couple conflict that are frequently presented in counselling, together with one (violence and abuse) that is important enough to require attention even though it may not be met so often as the others. The issues are separated by chapters but their themes are not mutually exclusive, and may overlap as part of the complexity of a troubled relationship. It would take a much longer book than a short introductory text to do justice to the range of painful situations brought to this work. What follows is a sample only. However, the reader who has absorbed the session frameworks will find that these may be applied successfully to most couple counselling situations, as I hope these examples demonstrate.

9
TENSIONS THAT ESCALATE TO CRISIS POINT

In this chapter, I discuss some of the most common problems partners bring to counselling. Mostly, these problems fall short of the more extreme situations described later in this book, but of course, couples themselves do not have this perspective. To them, these are major crises which threaten their relationship, and their distressed and chaotic thoughts and feelings reflect this. For the counsellor new to working with couples, however, following the session frameworks closely for the problems discussed in this chapter is likely to be effective and reassuring.

CHANGE FOR THE WORSE

Couples frequently bring to counselling a bewildered sense of their relationship having veered from joy to antagonism. In Western culture, when two people first start to realize that they are becoming special to each other, they usually enter into that heady process of mutual recognition and absorption, opening up of possibilities, sexual attraction and energizing and heady optimism which is the subject matter of so many songs, poems, novels, films, plays and advertisements. But as Aaron Beck, the originator of cognitive therapy, suggests, 'Love is never enough' (1988) – never enough, that is, if it is ultimately dislocated from the ordinary, the boring, the stresses and tensions of everyday life. Perhaps this is why there are so many songs on the theme of, 'Why did it all go wrong?'

Western partners usually choose each other on emotional grounds, strongly influenced by the images, assumptions and values of their culture, including taking for granted that emotions alone are the only proper guide to that choice. Beck argues that mutual idealization is a powerful component, both in a sense of excitement and discovery, and in later disillusion and recrimination (1988: 32–3). Many couples progress smoothly from the dizzy heights of falling in love to a less continuously intense but still exciting and satisfying mode of life together, and would be puzzled by Beck's reservations. But some couples become mired in reciprocating patterns of over-interpretation of the other's attitudes and motives, and a sense of loss of the person the other was believed to be, with the relationship veering into mutual resentment. Disillusion and disappointment can develop at any stage of a relationship, from newly committed couples who discover they have to an extent been living an illusion, to established couples who realize that their relationship has imperceptibly deteriorated. Some couples seek counselling only when the problem has become even more embedded through failed attempts to overcome it.

When these kinds of problems emerge in the first session, I acknowledge the distress and disillusion being experienced, and I am wary of introducing exceptions precipitately. In some instances, problem-accounts may spill over into a second session. But when the problem-story has been fully told, I follow Nichols' practice of saying 'I'd like to shift gears' (1988: 114). I ask how the couple met, what attracted them to each other, what the period of dating and courtship was like, how they reached the decision to commit to each other, and what was good about the early days of their relationship. 'Frequently the clients begin to soften and relax somewhat as they move from current unhappiness to contemplation of days when things were different' (Nichols 1988: 114). As a systemic therapist also calling on object relations theory, Nichols then moves to exploration of the systemic interactions and psycho-logical factors he sees as underpinning the couple's problems. I myself prefer not to do this, but to give prominence to their narrative, exploring it with many questions and clarifications, so that good memories return fully into the couple's awareness and form the foundation of an alternative story of their relationship. The narrative becomes, in other words, a rich accumulation of historical and recent exceptions. Unlike Nichols, I do not then ask where things went off track, but ask questions around two related themes. The informal way in which these questions are put, and their integration into a natural and conversational mode of dialogue, is not reproduced in the bare examples below.

(a)   *What evidence is there that, despite the problems you have outlined, the qualities of caring and loving so evident at the start of the relationship are still in place, even if they have become obscured?* What did you, and do you still, love and value in each other? How does this show itself? What indications of your continuing love swiftly get forgotten at the moment? Can you think of other examples? Why did you decide to go to counselling rather then split up at once? What would you each lose from your lives if the relationship ended? These are difficult questions for a couple who have lost track of loving elements, but almost always, when given time for thought, they can identify some evidence of continuing affection for each other, or some moments of mutual pleasure when conflicts subsided.

(b)   *What can you do re-create and build on the successful foundation you established in the early days, which still shows itself from time to time despite the problems?* This is a rather different question from what the couple may have been expecting; the usual response is 'I don't know'. Nevertheless, with patience and persistence by the counsellor, couples can usually always identify some action, or change, that might enhance the tenuously recognized positive aspects still underpinning the relationship. This opens the way to an experiment in making minor changes, the results of which sometimes surprise couples – and sometimes me, too:

John and Erica, married for 20 years, with two teenage children, and running a successful business together, had reached what they called a 'crisis of affection' and were seriously considering divorce. Life had become dull, routine and stressed. Erica resented what she saw as John's possessiveness, and his lack of responsiveness and emotional warmth, and felt she had lost her own identity. John resented the diminution of their sex life, and experienced recurring depression which he attributed to marital stress. They had attended Relate for sexual counselling and found this quite helpful, but had reverted to inhibition and resentment, as the suggested intimate sexual exercises made them feel embarrassed and exposed.

My invitation to talk about the early years of John and Erica's relationship and the present evidence of its subterranean existence was quite productive, with both of them gradually relaxing, recalling earlier happy times, exchanging knowing glances and occasionally smiling. They spoke of recent occasions when there had been momentary surges of affection, and a few times when they had managed to discuss their differences without getting angry. All the same, it was hard for them to identify any small changes each might offer the other, so they agreed to think about this at home and discuss their ideas at the next session.

At the second session, Erica and John said no, they hadn't thought of any small changes to offer each other. This session was going to be difficult, I thought! Then John said, 'When we got home we decided to look at *everything*, sat up all night discussing what changes were needed, wrote them down, then started to put them into practice the next day.' We examined how they had metaphorically torn up the 'one-small-step-at-a-time' rule-book, what this said about their ability to review their relationship, and what this might imply for their future. At the third session, they reported that things were still going well. Three weeks later, in what turned out to be the final session, they felt their relationship had improved by at least 60%, and that counselling could end. I have my notes in front of me as I write, and the little Smiley symbols for exceptions, which I have coloured yellow, cover the page like exploding fireworks.

GENDER ASSUMPTIONS

There is a powerful undercurrent of gender stereotyping in Western culture. More enlightened ideas have a far more limited influence than might be assumed by the minority who take them for granted (including counsellors, I suspect). Even among this minority, gender stereotyping often demonstrates its tenacity in subtle ways.

Dissatisfaction and confusion around gender roles can play a significant part in the deterioration of a heterosexual couple's relationship, not least because one or both of the partners may be ambivalent concerning their own attitudes and beliefs in this regard. The woman who resents her male partner's refusal to help with household chores might also harbour a degree of contempt for men who wear aprons; a man who encourages his female partner to change career may feel insecure and threatened when she does so, especially if her new career has higher social status than his own. Situations such as this can exacerbate resentment and misunderstanding when a relationship is already in trouble, and can lead to trouble where none existed before. In sexual matters, male and female stereotyping can produce real tension.

Gender-based behaviour can also result in unrecognized jockeying for power. It is tempting to attribute this kind of conflict to modern, culturally derived gender-role confusions, but Chaucer's *Wife of Bath's Tale* shows that struggle between heterosexual partners for the 'maistrie' (boss position) was alive and well in the fourteenth century (Robinson 1957: II. 103–4). Most commonly, in my experience, each partner defines his or her attempts to control the other as expressions of their own concern and caring.

The attempt at dominance is not always on an equal basis:

Dee, age 31, was referred by her doctor because she wanted counselling rather than antidepressant medication. Ben, her husband, came with her. She said she was happily married and that Ben very much loved and cared for her, that she liked her job as a hotel receptionist, and that there were no money worries. She was puzzled as to why she had become tearful, in low spirits and sleepless. It was Ben's idea that she should seek counselling rather than take pills, as he was convinced she would become addicted to medication. Ben frequently interrupted her, and he was persistent in explaining to me that her depression arose out of her basic insecurity, which she needed to deal with. This was not a couple counselling session in the usual sense, as there was no overt conflict between the couple. As Dee had been referred as an individual, I arranged for the second appointment to be with her alone. At that session, Dee revealed that she felt very guilty; she appreciated Ben's caring, protective feelings for her but she was finding it difficult to respond to him with warmth and affection, and their sex life was suffering. I asked for examples of Ben's caringly protective attitude. Dee said that he took all responsibility for the household finances; he shopped for her underwear; he chose the clothes she should wear for work and when they went out together; he sometimes stood in the lobby of the hotel where she worked to make sure she was not being subject to male guests' attempts at flirtation; he had worked out a weight-loss diet for her which he monitored by a twice-daily written record of her calorie intake, which she had to sign; he had bought an illustrated sex manual to help her to reach orgasm; and he had come to the first counselling session to satisfy himself that this male therapist could be trusted. There were even more extreme examples, which I will not quote here.

When suspecting male dominance rationalized and disguised as solicitude, I usually arrange joint counselling with the aim of assisting both persons to examine the nature and effects of such actions, to discuss the cultural sources of excessive male protectiveness, and ultimately to encourage the man to stop such suffocating behaviour. However, Ben's actions and attitudes were so extreme, and his skill in making Dee feel subservient and guilty was so great, that I feared for her. But it was essential to avoid another situation where a man, this time a male therapist, told her or implied what she should do or think, so I was particularly careful to avoid 'leading' questions. I encouraged her to describe in detail what Ben did, how it affected her, what name might be given to these actions, and the processes by which self-condemnation, guilt and depression had been encouraged to enter her life. She began to recognize her unacknowledged feelings about the relationship, including her fear of Ben, and finally defined his actions as 'psychological exploitation'. She also considered the choices open to her, including leaving him.

Less extreme gender-role behaviour than shown by the above example is often woven into other couple problems, permeating and affecting the way they attempt to resolve these issues. The most common form this takes in heterosexual relationships is where the man assumes a dominant position implying superior knowledge and judgement and asserts how the conflict should be resolved, thus putting the woman in the subordinate position, with her consequently feeling undervalued, unheard and resentful. The first session framework can to some extent counteract this, but outside the counselling room it will continue. If the woman tries to follow the man's advice to make a more definite contribution, she will be subordinating herself to his prescription, whereas if she does not, she still remains in the subordinate position (White 1983: 34–40).

A direct approach is called for, where the pattern of interaction between the couple is exposed, defined and tactfully questioned. Couples are fully capable of recognizing and discussing interactive patterns, and often find this fascinating. The externalized problem is addressed by calling on their thoughtfulness and intelligence. The counsellor is not working to a hidden agenda ('I am running the session according to my expert awareness of how relational dynamics are expressed through gender conflict') but inviting cooperative consideration of the issue in a wholly respectful and open manner. I adapt a technique described by White in an early paper on counselling couples where there is male violence – it fits this less obviously damaging situation of male dominance equally well (White 1989: 101–5).

I thank the man for the cooperative and active way he is responding in the session, which shows his motivation to play a full part in trying to overcome the couple's problems. This acknowledgement prevents him from feeling criticized or attacked. I then add that I have noticed his partner does not seem to be making her viewpoint fully heard. I ask if perhaps they both believe, like some other couples I have counselled, that the man should make all the decisions, with the woman always following his lead? I have never known a man admit he agrees with this idea, so I say that as a man, I myself am influenced by this common attitude, and try to avoid it, but that I sometimes slip up, and my partner could give plenty of examples! The atmosphere created by my own admission can lead to useful discussion, with an emphasis on identifying aspects of society that encourage and maintain attitudes of dominance in men, the limitations these impose on their relationships with women, ways in which men might resist them, and the potential benefits of so doing.

A woman counsellor can acknowledge the man's cooperation as suggested above, then discuss how she has experienced dominant attitudes in men she knows, saying that she thinks she may be detecting echoes of this in the way the male partner is contributing to the session. Naturally, there are some heterosexual couples where the dominant partner is the woman, and dominance can feature in same-sex partnerships. The same pattern would be followed, with the dominant person's positive contribution acknowledged then the dominant/submissive interaction tactfully being brought into the open and explored.

LOSS OF FORMER WAYS OF LIFE

Couples beginning to live together, or newly married couples who have not previously shared a home, sometimes unexpectedly find that they very much miss aspects of their previous lives and that the new couple-unit does not compensate for these losses. Classically, the man may grieve for the laddish life he has lost (perhaps regular sport and frequent drinking with mates) and the woman may feel the lack of her own social circle and family of origin. If the partners are not dominated by an assumption that they should mean everything to each other and find all their satisfactions and pleasures in each other's company, they usually manage, in time, to establish a way of life where previous ties are maintained but integrated into the life of the couple. But problems can arise if each brings different norms of thought and behaviour from their families of origin and social circles. They may be dismayed that the partner turns out to have quite different norms and expectations in aspects such as who should do the shopping or organize the finances, or whose career should take precedence, and about much else not discussed during the heady days of courtship. Each partner will see their own assumptions as right and may try to impose them, imputing negative meanings to the other's beliefs and attitudes:

> Each was oblivious to the meaning the other attached to the situation ... they both believed that the reasonableness of their own interpretations would be apparent to anybody, and that the other's attitude was, likewise, *obviously unreasonable* ... they were left flailing away in a futile attempt to force each other to accept their own frames of reference ... When partners hammer away at each other, they only bolster each other's resistance ... the partners' positions become completely polarised ... both partners foresee catastrophe ... (Beck 1989: 44)

In these instances, I normalize the partners' situation by assuring them that I have seen quite a number of couples whose relationship has included similar conflicts. I suggest that they have become caught in a well-known *process* unrelated to blame or fault in either, and I spend some time sharing with them, for their consideration, the idea of socially derived (not 'self-evidently correct') ways of thinking and acting which it now might be helpful to look at and perhaps re-think. I may engage them in internalizing other questioning sessions or, if the division is particularly bitter, in conflict dissolution sessions. I also encourage them to reconnect with what they love and value in each other, and to consider small changes that will begin a reversal of mutual blaming and lead to a calmer atmosphere for the negotiation of wider change and compromise.

FINANCIAL STRESS

Financial problems do not usually bring couples to counselling, but they may be a significant indicator, or result, of existing stresses and opposed attitudes. The corrosive effect of money worries can be particularly powerful when there is a divergence of attitude towards spending, saving and the sharing of responsibility for the household finances.

The following is a composite account of several couples:

Jerry and Marcia, partners expecting their first child, identified financial problems as the main source of their relationship's deterioration. Jerry was a self-employed plumber. His income paid the rent, he gave Marcia money for housekeeping, and he kept the rest to spend on himself, including social drinking and attending football matches. Marcia worked a few hours a week in a shop, bought her clothes and make-up out of this income, and otherwise saved for when the baby arrived. Marcia had just discovered that Jerry had a huge credit card debt from before they started to live together and was being pressured by the credit company. She felt betrayed at his keeping the debt from her, angry at his spending so much on himself, worried about whether they would be able to provide for the baby, and terrified that if Jerry's business failed, they might become homeless and destitute. Jerry was intensely irritated and annoyed by Marcia's attitude, which he described as panicky, nagging and unfair. He had kept the debt from her to save her worry, he said, and clearing it was well within his means. Although work had decreased recently, plumbers would always be in demand and he expected the business to grow rather than fail. Marcia lacked for nothing and only had to ask if she wanted money for anything; he himself worked hard, deserved his pleasures, and considered his income was his own to do what he liked with, once the rent and housekeeping were paid.

There are many issues here, including Jerry's patriarchal attitude and the consequent imbalance of power between the partners. However, the core issue in this instance is an immediate financial crisis. The reality of the situation needs to be acknowledged and faced, then practical measures decided so as to make the debt manageable. When faced with an account such as this, I ask questions to establish the exact financial situation and its possible consequences. Frequently, the problem is worse than appeared at the first telling. I ask what ideas the couple have about how to deal with the debt, but often they are uncertain, and find it hard to escape from the falsely self-protective attitudes one or both of them have brought to bear on the problem.

Sometimes, as with Marcia and Jerry, there are opposing attitudes that have become hardened as part of a wider conflict.

I have no expertise in the legal aspects of debt so I do not see my role as advisory. However, bringing the actuality of the financial crisis fully and nakedly into the couple's awareness usually paves the way for my suggestion that they consult the Citizen's Advice Bureau for financial advice and possible legal help, and most agree to this.

If a couple such as Jerry and Marcia continue with counselling, a dialogue would ensue where I would encourage Jerry to identify and explore the specific, concrete, unmistakeable results of his actions and attitudes. I would ask questions inviting him to identify the source (in his family of origin, in the male culture and in the media) of his sense of personal entitlement to most of his income, his tendency to dismiss or ignore mounting problems and his rationalization of secrecy as protectiveness. Once he began to allow that his previously fixed ideas were open to question, I would engage him in a discussion of how, in specific ways identified by him, not by me, modifying these attitudes might result in greater happiness and harmony in his relationship with his partner. This would be a tentative and respectful process, not a confrontational one. Exploration of exceptions would play an essential part, including those aspects of his relationship with Marcia which they both value, so that Jerry would see the possibility of change-with-continuity rather than feel a challenge to his identity.

COMMUNICATION FAILURE?

Ray and Sally's problems included the virtually out-of-control behaviour of their teenage daughter, who was to appear in court on a theft charge and who had an alcohol problem. Sally was afraid that Ray had ceased to love her, because he had become remote and self-absorbed and their sex life had completely ceased. Ray spent many hours on the Internet attempting to add to his already large collection of stone ginger beer bottles, which took up most of their garage space and some of the attic, and Sally was continuously exhausted by an exacting job where she worked shifts.

Despite all the problems revealed in the first session, Ray repeatedly said that his and Sally's problem was 'failure of communication'. It appeared true that he found Sally's concerns about his attitudes and behaviour hard to take seriously, and the couple told me they had frequent quarrels, but they certainly 'communicated' in the sense that they clearly demonstrated their anger with each other, said why they were angry and remembered each other's criticisms. Ray knew that Sally resented much of his behaviour, and why; he just didn't take her criticisms seriously. He appeared to be using the fashionable idea of 'communication failure' to distance himself from Sally's attempts to get him to see how hurt she was, and to avoid focused thoughtfulness concerning the effects of his actions. Where their daughter was concerned, they *were* fully able to share with each other, and with me, their frustrations and anxieties.

Michael White suggests that although many conflicted couples can benefit from some attention being given to the communication aspects of their relationship, it is possible to over-emphasize this, and not to recognize the limitations of the approach. He identifies four of these limitations (2004a: 9–11):

(a) If attempting to address problems through a focus on communication appears unsuccessful, it usually leads to an ever-greater emphasis on communication, and even more lack of success.

(b) An exclusive focus on communication leaves each partner's negative view of the other intact. The meaning of their conflict is obscured, and they are discouraged from taking responsibility for their actions.

(c) An emphasis on communication can mask situations where there is an imbalance of power, and will be dangerous if a woman in an abusive heterosexual relationship is encouraged in joint sessions to speak unguardedly of what she thinks and feels.

(d) The concept of full and open communication as 'healthy' is a cultural construct of middle-class Western society and ignores other forms of conflict resolution in tune with the norms of other cultures.

If I had responded to Ray's implied invitation to address the couple's alleged communication failures, my counselling might have had the limitations of (a) and (b) above, with Ray maintaining his distancing and self-excusing stance and Sally's distress growing. By tacitly refusing this invitation, I was able to invite Ray to consider the effects of his attitudes and actions, to assist the couple in reactivating their physical relationship, and to discuss strategies with regard to their teenage daughter. These were the actual problems, not 'communication failure'.

Mishearing, misunderstanding

Sometimes the partners' preconceptions and absorption into their own viewpoint make them unable to grasp what the other is saying. This may have become a habit, exacerbating their problems and showing itself in sessions when the listening person is asked to respond to their partner's problem-story.

In these instances, I am likely to try a simple extension to the first session framework – simple in conception, that is, but sometimes surprisingly difficult for the couple to do. I ask the listening partner to repeat the main points the other has made, and at this stage not to comment on them. In extreme instances, the listening partner finds this almost impossible – they miss important statements, misunderstand others, and in general show that their partner's viewpoint and experience has passed them by. I normalize this reaction by saying something like, 'People often find it difficult to summarize what their partner has said, because, naturally, their own emotions and thoughts get in the way, but perhaps we could have another try?' I ask the partner who has been interviewed to make their points again, and once again invite the listener to repeat them. It may take a couple more tries but usually this ends by working well enough. If it does fail, I abandon the attempt and sum up myself, point by point, and then move to the next stage of the session by inviting the listener to comment.

Mars versus Venus?

Ideas from John Gray's best-seller *Men Are From Mars, Women Are From Venus* (1992) and other books which claim to define innate and/or socially conditioned differences between the ways in which men and women use and understand language, have seeped into popular consciousness. I often see heterosexual couples who believe that all men, unlike women, have difficulty in talking about feelings; and that men, unlike women, are comfortable with logical and practical language. There is a widespread belief that many of the apparent communication problems between the sexes can be attributed to men and women simply not understanding each other's language. In counselling sessions, some men do act in a rather withdrawn and uncomfortable manner, with the woman quite loquacious and forthcoming, and it may be tempting for them and the counsellor to attribute this to the Mars/Venus dichotomy.

Deborah Cameron has, to my mind, convincingly demonstrated that Mars/Venus assumptions are a myth; she concludes that they are stereotypes, and that research demonstrates that insofar as there *are* actual distinctions, they are evenly spread in both sexes (2007: 163–5). Cameron also argues that the myth directly reflects and contributes to male power in Western society and in some heterosexual couple relationships. Men can find it quite convenient to withdraw from discussing the complexity of a couple's problems with the excuse that they find this almost impossible, and I have counselled a considerable number of women who take on the responsibility for addressing the couple's problems, with the rueful explanation that 'He finds this sort of talk difficult'. Cameron counters this idea by quoting research evidence that so-called 'feminine' verbal and listening skills are widely distributed among both males and females, with extremes of ability existing in both groups (2007: 44–5). She argues that historically widespread oversimplifications about the contrast between men's and women's use of language recently made fashionable by Gray are unhelpful to both genders, as they imply innate and unalterable differences in cognitive ability and sensitivity to feelings. The myth has seeped into popular and professional consciousness and has become a limiting factor in people's lives, affecting how they and others believe they can communicate. (An even greater danger, Cameron suggests, is that men have a ready-made excuse for rape by claiming they misunderstood the woman's verbal refusals (2007: 89–97).)

When faced with such explanations, I might mention Cameron's conclusions to the couple as something they could find intriguing. Primarily, I simply persist with my questions, as tactfully but firmly as possible. Most men *can* talk about feelings (though they may not want to) and most women can be just as skilful as men in discussing practicalities.

ENCOURAGING A FUTURE PERSPECTIVE

Our personal narratives are not limited to selected memories; they include imagined futures, ranging from the relatively trivial and transitory, such as tactile and olfactory mental images anticipating the evening meal, to the centrally important, such as what life will be like when we move house, start the new job, settle down with our partner. Troubled partners have frequently lost sight of any positive future for themselves, and their images of times to come may be blank, blurred or painful. It is a mistake to encourage future-thinking at too early a stage of couple counselling, as the response will reflect and embed this negativity, but when the relationship has started to improve it can be useful.

I do not use the standard 'miracle question' format of solution-focused therapy (de Shazer 1988: 5–6; George et al. 1999: 23–7) but I like the idea behind it – encouraging couples to imagine, then formulate, very precise images of the future they would like to move into. From these future-images, I proceed to draw forth future-narratives. I invite the couple to give me detailed imagined accounts of what life will be like, so that (by a self-fulfilling prophesy) they may ultimately move into, and live, their already-imagined 'preferred future'. I ask specific and concrete questions: 'What exactly will you be doing when you're at home together and enjoying each other's company? What will you be seeing, hearing, at those times? Which of you will suggest that activity? What will you be saying to each other? How will it feel to spend time together, compared with the past? And compared with now? How will you let each other know that? What else in your lives will be different? Can you describe that for me?'

DISCUSSION POINTS

Consider these questions, if possible in discussion with a colleague:

1. What conflicts, other than those discussed above, can result from differences in the outlook and values of partners' families of origin?
2. What conflicts, other than those discussed above, can result from differences in the outlook and values of partners' peer groups?
3. What social and cultural influences, other than those discussed above, can contribute to a growth of stress and tension between partners?
4. Although Michael White stresses the limitations of focusing on 'failure of communication', he does not deny it may contribute to some couple's difficulties. How might it do so, and how might a counsellor assist partners who experience this problem?

10
PROBLEMS WITH FRIENDS AND FAMILY MEMBERS

This chapter discusses occasions when a couple's relationship is unexpectedly and adversely affected by the feelings, wishes and influences of other people with whom they feel closely connected and to whom they owe loyalty. Counsellors accustomed only to working with individuals will find this situation particularly challenging, as the partners' differences of opinion and perceptions are likely to be powerfully emotive.

I also discuss and illustrate an approach to dealing with difficult teenage behaviour which has been found effective by parents who have consulted me, usually at a point when their own relationship is becoming endangered by stresses arising from this situation.

DIVIDED LOYALTIES

In the previous chapter, I touched on stresses arising from each partner bringing different expectations to the new relationship based on the norms, values and practices of their families of origin and previous social circles. Such tensions can be created or exacerbated by the attitudes and actions of family members and friends who may try to maintain the relationship exactly as it was before, especially the partners' parents, who may have difficulty in accepting that their grown-up children are now in a different position in relation to them. It can be puzzling and painful to friends and close relatives when a couple's relationship appears to diminish their importance to one of the partners, especially if the partners are insensitive to this possibility. Tensions can also arise when one partner hopes the other will diminish, or withdraw from, previous close relationships. Dislike of or resentment towards the friend or relative may have been held in check previously, but emerge when the couple are fully committed to each other.

In most instances, the couple will eventually get the balance right, continuing to maintain and value friends and family members, and to include them in their lives, yet negotiating changed patterns of contact and in some instances a modified way of relating – the friend who has previously been the first recipient of confidences may find her friend's partner now has this role. Negotiating such changes is often far from easy.

The partners themselves may be uncertain or ambivalent about the nature and extent of appropriate boundaries. The couple may become self-enclosed and excluding, looking unrealistically to each other for every satisfaction, and assuming that their relationship has primacy over every other – a dangerous situation, as Michael White points out:

> This exclusivity ... is profoundly isolating of couples ... the outcome of this is the deferment of much that is precious to each partner ... In these circumstances, relationships can so easily be failed ... even the sharing of a confidence with a person outside of the relationship that is not shared with the partner is perceived to be a betrayal ... (2004a: 12)

At the other extreme, the partners may try to maintain other relationships exactly as they always have been, resulting in pressures on the couple's own relationship. Or, one or both may be torn between the new partner and the demands and assumptions of previously dominant loyalties and expectations.

Richard and Rose came to counselling because Richard was feeling increasingly stressed, to the extent of yelling uncontrollably at Rose over minor disagreements and sometimes even smashing crockery in his anger. This had frightened him, and he was worried he might become physically violent towards Rose. He was having problems at work, where he felt under-valued and exploited, but the main issue was his conflict of loyalties between Rose and his mother. He said that according to Rose, his mother disliked and resented her, but he himself couldn't see this – in fact, he thought it was Rose who was being unreasonably resentful.

Rose, in her turn, claimed that Richard's lifelong habits of deference to his mother blinded him to the many subtle ways in which his mother insulted and demeaned her, and that he refused to see how his mother was trying to continue to dominate him as she had in the past, and perhaps even to destroy his marriage.

In this couple's therapy, the main factors allowing them to resolve their problem were: (a) listening to each other's detailed narration of how each was experiencing the triangular situation; (b) through this, gaining empathic insight into the other partner's feelings, perceptions and thoughts; (c) in Richard's case, gradually shifting his position and recognizing that that there was truth in what Rose said; (d) recognizing and building on exceptions – loving aspects of their relationship which had become sidelined.

In the transcript extract below, Richard shows considerable confusion and divided loyalties, but is beginning to move towards change. His tentative, convoluted and uncertain phrasing indicates that he is struggling with a new, rather disturbing intimation that his previous view of the situation may have been mistaken, while still feeling unable to let it go completely:

> *Richard:*   There was a time earlier in our relationship where I just thought Rose was being stupid or 'Why should Mum ever want to be nasty to you?' In some ways, I could see it as well – 'She is being nasty to you – she is hurting you' – because what's the point of Rose upsetting me? Whereas now I think I understand there must be something more there …

The process of mutually entering into the other's experience allowed Richard and Rose to listen more accurately to each other's viewpoints, and enabled Richard to reconsider his ideas on the central issue brought to therapy. But what consolidated the positive changes in this couple's relationship was not so much their tentative new agreement about Richard's mother's attitude and actions, as a more general growth in mutuality between them, with Richard, in particular, re-focusing on what was valuable in the relationship and what he needed to do in order to reclaim it. He withdrew from excessive attention to his job, refusing some unreasonable demands from his employer which would have severely diminished his time at home, and decided to look for alternative employment. He and Rose, after watching a television programme on marital therapy, quite independently of our counselling, decided to try out a technique discussed in the programme which was designed to promote more productive talk between couples. They found this worked well. Richard also started to spend less time with his mother. An extract from a later session shows Richard's increased self-confidence and awareness:

> *Richard:*   I feel that Rose understands me a lot more than I ever thought before. I'd always felt that there was this kind of brick wall between us, we were always trying to shout over it, and the person on the other side couldn't really understand what was going on, whereas what Rose was saying seems to have opened up a lot more, when she says things I can understand are true …

When counselling this couple, I spent considerable time encouraging them to bring the presenting problem into the open and to describe its effects. But the issue of Richard's divided loyalties was not immediately addressed in the counselling room.

Once a couple's problem has been fully described, I usually explain that, for the moment, I would like to postpone discussion of it for a short while, in order to gain a wider picture of their relationship. My assurance that the problem is going to be considered prevents the couple from feeling that their central concerns are being ignored or passed over. Drawing forth exceptions from the couple's history, and exploring the meaning of those exceptions, then allows the problem to be returned to with a more positive perspective, and can sometimes lead to spontaneous resolution of the problem.

With Richard and Rose, the *indirect* aspect of the couple's therapy made the greatest difference – the rediscovery, reactivation and renewed conscious attention paid to their commitment to each other. This became the central theme of later sessions and demonstrated that a general enhancement of a couple's relationship in therapy allows destructive dominant stories to recede, freeing the partners to rediscover and to tell positive narratives of their relationship, and within this enriched perspective to discover their own solutions. A similar process is illustrated in Michael White's counselling of a couple, described below under 'Rediscovering cooperation'.

An extended account of Rose and Richard's therapy, including longer extracts from transcripts, appears in Payne (2000: 48–9, 90–101).

EXERCISE (60 MINUTES)

Work in pairs.

1. **(10 minutes) each** Each describe an occasion when difficulties arose in a close relationship because of a conflict between the relationship and the wishes or expectations of someone outside it. The example can be from your own life; from the life of someone known to you; or from persons you have counselled.
2. **(15 minutes)** If these conflicts were resolved satisfactorily, how was this brought about? If not, what in retrospect do you think one or both persons might have done to try to resolve them?
3. **(25 minutes)** Work with another pair. Share one example per pair and discuss the following:

   (a) What conclusions do you draw from this exercise about the difficulties couples sometimes face in coping with the feelings and attitudes of people outside the couple relationship?
   (b) What have you learned from this exercise which might benefit your counselling of couples who face similar problems?

CHILDREN'S UPBRINGING

When partners have very different or opposed opinions on aspects of bringing up their children, they sometimes find their relationship affected by mutual blaming, which builds into vicious circles of frustration and resentment. Each then clings even more fiercely to their own ideas, and becomes deaf to the other's opinions. In this crisis, they may expect adjudication from their counsellor, with expert advice on what to do, or what to stop doing, with each hoping or expecting that their own point of view will be upheld.

Some counsellors, while avoiding taking an expert position on child-rearing, might see their task as attempting to encourage a respectful exploration and discussion of both points of view with the aim of the parents' reaching agreement or at least compromise. This approach could be fruitful with some couples but is not, perhaps, very likely to succeed with parents who have become entrenched in their fixed positions.

Counsellors who have read this present book might carefully avoid being drawn into becoming an expert 'referee', but might also feel they must keep the presenting problem at the forefront. They might encourage each parent to describe the problem and comment on the other's description; identify exceptions (occasions when the parents managed to agree even slightly on the contentious issues they have just described); invite detailed accounts of these occasions; link them with similar occasions in the past; then discuss how these exceptions came about, and might be built on. There is much to be said for this way of organizing the session, and it might succeed – as long as exceptions *are* forthcoming. Swift judgement is necessary as to whether the couple's differences and antagonism appear too extreme and entrenched for this approach to be fruitful. There is a risk that in this very specific situation, where firmly held beliefs have themselves become the ammunition for mutual antagonism, exceptions around issues of the child's upbringing may be few, tenuous or non-existent. There is a danger of the counsellor's being drawn into evermore desperate attempts to discover exceptions, and/or falling into the trap of attributing more significance to minor exceptions than they can carry, with the couple's opposed opinions remaining firmly in place, or even reinforced as each hears increasing confirmation that the problem is apparently insoluble.

Rediscovering cooperation

A potentially more successful approach, which eliminates the risks outlined above, is temporarily to put the issue of child-rearing aside once problem-descriptions have been given and acknowledged, and to build on exceptions from the wider context of the couple's relationship. Even with opposed views on aspects of how to bring up their children, it is likely that they will be able to give examples of compromise, agreement and cooperation which they have achieved outside this relatively limited (though important and emotionally resonant) area of concern. This can weaken the problem-saturated story of 'We have never, and never will, agree on this issue' by modifying it into something like 'We agree on lots of issues, but haven't yet managed to do so on this one'. There is a re-positioning towards each other and a re-engagement with more positive aspects of the relationship which have been lost sight of. This promotes a new situation where the couple can address their child-rearing disagreements with rancour dissolved, having discovered that they, not the therapist, are after all the experts in problem resolution.

This is impressively illustrated in a demonstration video of Michael White counselling Shannon and Kenny, a heterosexual couple who disagree on whether their young daughter should be made to attend church, or whether her attendance should be left until she is old enough to decide for herself. White picks up a throwaway comment from Shannon that implies the couple have more or less sorted out problems of sex and money, and spends most of the long session exploring and expanding these exceptions, and other examples of mutual decision-making which emerge. In the course of the session, by responding to exploratory and clarifying questions from White, the couple reach a new understanding of the basis of their relationship. Kenny takes the initiative of defining this relationship as based on 'friendship' and describes the qualities in Shannon that have allowed this friendship to flourish in the relationship, and she reciprocates. The perhaps rather clichéd idea of friendship being an essential aspect of a committed relationship does not remain just a vaguely stated and passing idea, but is given freshness and conviction by the concrete detail of these extended descriptions elicited by White. When the question of their daughter's church attendance is returned to towards the end of the session, they have gained a new perspective on the rich basis of their relationship, recognizing that it is based on spiritual values they have in common, and which are underpinned by the quality of their friendship as they have defined it. They express certainty that they will now be able to resolve the issue of their daughter's church attendance (White 1994).

TEENAGE BEHAVIOUR AND PARENTAL RIGHTS

When parents discuss their worry (and sometimes despair) at the difficult and antisocial behaviour of their teenage children, their story is often permeated with conflict between the couple themselves. Gender issues can further complicate matters.

In the individual sessions that began our counselling, Tracey complained that her and Eric's 14-year-old son, Darren, was repeatedly rude and insulting to her, refused to do anything she told him to, and that Eric never backed her up in her attempts to make Darren come home at the allotted time, put his towels in the washing machine rather than strew them around the bathroom for her to pick up, speak respectfully to her and stop swearing. Darren had started smoking cigarettes in his bedroom and she had forbidden this, but Eric smoked himself and was indulgent of Darren's habit. She was reduced to screaming at Darren when all this got too much for her, and she knew that Darren then complained to his father. The two of them often made mocking comments about her while she was present, which made her feel defeated and marginalized.

After three individual sessions, and with Tracey's agreement, I wrote to Eric to invite him to a joint session. He did not take up this invitation at once, but when there had been two further individual sessions with Tracey, he did come with her, and Tracey took first turn to speak of her concerns. Eric's response, in an indulgent tone of voice accompanied by smiles and occasional laughter, was that Tracey exaggerated the problem. Darren was a bit of a handful but basically OK, he said, and was no different from himself at that age. He was a lot better behaved than many teenagers. He would grow out of his bad habits in time and meanwhile there was nothing to be gained by yelling at him. And Tracey was too sensitive about being teased – it was all just done in fun.

Looking back at this early example of my attempts at narrative therapy, I realize that it would have been better to invite Eric to take the first turn, and that I should have paid him more attention at the start of the session. It would have been appropriate to acknowledge the unease he might be feeling when meeting a stranger, a man who had already heard his wife's worries about her home life in detail. I should have reassured him that I was there to assist them both, not to take sides or criticize. As it was, the session did nothing to open Eric's mind to Tracey's experience, and my attempts to ask him what he thought her feelings might be when he smiled, laughed and refused to take her seriously, and encouraged their son in this attitude by his example, were met with an amused shake of the head and a bland repetition that she was exaggerating and over-sensitive. Eric refused to come to more than one session, and counselling again became one-to-one with Tracey, who had much more to say about unhappiness in her marriage.

Where, unlike Eric and Tracey, both parents are equally concerned about the behaviour of their teenagers, they usually tell a dominant story of being failures as parents. This sense of failure is continually reinforced by their continuing inability to do anything to alter the teenager's attitude and actions no matter what they try, resulting in a build-up of irritability, impatience and disconnectedness between the couple themselves.

Teenage behaviour is usually more intractable and extreme than that of younger children, and the approaches outlined earlier in this chapter may not be appropriate. Exceptions are likely to relate to when the teenager was younger, and the situation has changed since then. Teenagers are likely to be more resistant to any solutions decided on by the parents, even if the parents regain confidence in their problem-solving abilities. If the parents' relationship is not yet profoundly affected by the situation, there is little point in following practices designed to reconnect them with the positive aspects of their relationship and their problem-solving skills. What can a narrative approach offer? The following example amalgamates two separate examples, to illustrate the points I wish to make.

Edward and Jo's 15-year-old son, Terry, their only child, was a great cause for concern to them, and his actions and attitudes had made them feel total failures as parents. They described him as an amiable boy, who nevertheless continually surprised and disappointed them. He had a bad school record and was likely to leave with poor examination results. All their attempts to encourage him to work at his studies had failed, including serious discussions, punishments such as grounding him and bribery (a promise of £50 for each pass grade). His bedroom was 'a tip' and he steadfastly refused to tidy or clean it, so that in the end Jo always had to set to and do it herself.

He never put out clothes for washing and Jo was tired of having to scour the house for them on washdays. He hardly ever took a shower or bath, and had started to smell. No matter what they said to him, Terry just refused to change or to take any responsibility for his actions, and this had led to a considerable division of opinion, and a conflicted atmosphere, between Jo and Edward. Edward thought Terry needed firm, imposed discipline, whereas Jo's approach was to explain the consequences of his actions to Terry and to appeal to the good nature which she knew was there beneath his apparent intransigence. She and Edward had begun accusing each other of undermining their individual attempts to control the situation and this, combined with the stress of living with a quite difficult teenager, had led to some disturbing quarrels. Although these quarrels had not yet endangered their relationship, they realized there might be a risk of this should things continue without any hope of change. A quite large amount of money had gone missing from Edward's wallet and it was clear from the circumstances that Terry must have taken it, but he refused to admit it, or to say where he had got the money for the new mobile phone they found hidden in his room. While searching Terry's room, they had also come across a stash of hardcore pornographic magazines, but when faced with this, Terry had just shrugged and said, 'So what?' Jo was terrified that this discovery meant her son was psychologically disturbed. There was a sickly-sweet odour clinging to this clothes which led them to suspect he was smoking cannabis, though he vehemently denied the accusation.

Driving home from work one day, Edward had seen Terry riding an old motorbike in the lanes near their home, at considerable speed but without wearing a helmet or other protection. When faced with this, Terry said he had bought the motorbike some months earlier, from an older boy at school, and was keeping it at this boy's house. Jo and Edward knew he was below the legal age for riding a motorcycle and so had not passed a road test, and must be unlicensed and uninsured, but were unable to convince him of the seriousness of this situation. He point-blank refused to tell them where the machine was, or to undertake not to ride it again. Edward had exploded with rage and nearly hit Terry. It was then the couple had decided to seek help from counselling. They wanted advice on what to do, and I suspected each hoped I would support them in their own approach to the problem, even though those approaches had not succeeded.

Michael White suggests that historically there has never been so much pressure for people to judge themselves against culturally validated but unrealistic standards in all aspects of life:

It would now be very rare for me to meet a person ... who hasn't experienced, at different times and to different degrees, the spectre of personal failure (here I am talking about a sense of inadequacy, incompetence, insufficiency, deficit, backwardness, and so on) looming large in their lives. (2004a: 153)

This was certainly true of Edward and Jo with regard to their parenting, and in the first session I attempted to follow White's 'failure conversation map' where the therapist invites persons to define the culturally approved areas of life where they consider they have failed, such as education, job progression, success in relationships, success in parenthood. He then invites them to identify their successes outside these culturally approved areas, and to define the personal values and beliefs that have underpinned these previously undervalued successes (2004a: 196–201). I soon realized, however, that I was imposing my own agenda on this couple, by seizing on the theme of failure and gratefully remembering White's ideas on how to address it. Jo and Edward were much more concerned about their son than themselves, and *their* agenda was not to explore and amend their sense of failure, but to address the urgent issue of what to do that might work.

I nevertheless realized that certain culturally derived assumptions ('taken-for-granted truths') were informing their narrative, producing not just a sense of failure but also blocking their attempts to address the problem in ways not validated by those assumptions. Before Jo and Edward could consider any ideas beyond those informed by these assumptions, their narrative needed to be 'deconstructed' – re-thought by examining its underpinning 'taken-for-granted truths'.

As I understood it, these assumptions were:

(a) that parental influence creates a child's character, therefore a badly behaving child derives this behaviour from parental incompetence and failure;
(b) that parents are responsible for monitoring and correcting the actions of their children, and for the results of those actions, no matter what the child's age;
(c) that parents should always put their own wishes and needs second to those of their children.

These assumptions and expectations had added to their distress at what Jo and Edward believed to be their son's 'disturbed' behaviour springing from a 'disturbed' and possibly 'damaged' personality. They were using, and being distressed by, worryingly pathologizing language derived from the popular culture of psychological explanation.

I asked Jo and Edward to describe how Terry's chosen way of behaving was affecting their own happiness and wellbeing, and had no difficulty in drawing out an extended story of anxiety, watchfulness, worry, tension and guilt. Much of their own life as a couple had been lost or put on hold because all they could think or talk about was Terry – for example, they never invited friends for a meal now, because although Terry was quite sociable, they were afraid he would spoil the occasion by inappropriate behaviour.

I needed to resist the temptation to bring into the open, and discuss, all the unhelpful assumptions I sensed behind their problem-story. It was important to avoid too much emphasis on these aspects at the expense of addressing the main issue concerning the couple. The session could easily have turned into a kind of lesson on social constructionism, with myself as 'expert'. So I limited myself to raising the aspect that seemed most relevant, and asked Edward and Jo at what age they thought young persons were able to understand the consequences of their actions, and take full responsibility for these consequences – at age 2? No, of course not. Five? Seven? Twelve? Sixteen? Eighteen? There was no easy answer, no exact point at which a child moves from being unable to see why he or she should behave, or not behave, in certain ways, to gaining an adult conceptualization of personal choice and responsibility. However, the couple agreed that Terry, at age 15, was certainly old enough for this, and indeed much of their unsuccessful campaign to alter his attitudes and behaviour had been based on trying to impress him with the need to act responsibly.

I asked if they might be interested in ideas that some other parents with badly behaving teenagers had found helpful. I said that these ideas might seem rather strange and dismaying at first, as they went against many commonly held beliefs about responsible parenting, including some which they themselves appeared to hold. Also, I said, the strategy deriving from these ideas is quite difficult to put into practice. In fact, sometimes these practices made the problem worse before it got better. Edward and Jo were interested at once, and willing to consider any-thing that might help. I then outlined the approach advocated by Bayard and Bayard (1982) where a distinction is made between 'kid's life' and 'parents' life', with each being given equal importance. The parents are encouraged by the ther-apist to consider making a firm decision to step back from their previous habits of taking responsibility for the teenager's actions, and to give the teenager a pre-cise date from when responsibility for the consequences of his actions will become his alone. He is also told that his parents will henceforth insist, and enforce, that their own lives must be respected and not impinged upon by his antisocial habits. This would mean, for example, that should Edward and Jo decide to follow this strategy, they would no longer exert pressure for Terry's bedroom to be cleaned or for him to put out his clothes for washing – if he chose to have a chaotic bedroom and wear dirty, smelly clothes, that would be up to him, but his bedroom door must be kept closed at all times, and as long as he smelled he must keep some distance between himself and his parents. Unless he put out his clothes for the wash and took baths or showers, he would be made to eat in his room, not at the dining table with his parents, and he would also be denied access to the television when they were watching it. Also, they would no longer pressur-ize him to do his homework, and if he got into trouble with his teachers, failed his examinations and faced a limited future, this would be his choice. As con-cerned parents, they would point out the dangers of this to him, but no longer take on themselves the responsibility of trying to make him work. Wherever his irresponsible actions affected their lives directly, the parents would unite in stand-ing firm against them; and, in particular, if he was ever caught stealing from them, or seen riding the motorcycle again, they would report him to the police, just as they would any other person they knew was breaking the law.

I lent the couple my copy of Bayard and Bayard's book to read and discuss, as my brief summary of its main ideas had perforce omitted the strategy's more subtle argu-ments and suggestions (as does the outline above). We arranged an appointment for a month's time. At that appointment, they returned the book, saying that they had been excited and convinced by it and had ordered their own copy. They had also discussed, and agreed on, a date when the policy would begin. They had explained the new house rules to Terry, who responded less resentfully than they anticipated. We clarified some of the policy's implications and agreed to meet monthly to monitor how things were going, and to discuss any problems that might emerge.

I reminded Jo and Edward that it was unlikely they would achieve 100% success or avoid some slipping back into former habits, but they agreed that even a 50% improvement in the situation would be well worth achieving.

> Over the next few months, Jo and Edward reported that on the whole they had managed to implement the new policy, despite some lapses. Edward did see Terry riding the motorcycle again, and despite feeling guilty and worried about reporting him to the police, he had plucked up the courage to do this. A policeman called, noted their statements, and in their presence told Terry what would be likely to happen if the offence was repeated. Terry was frightened by this lecture, delivered by the uniformed policemen in a weighty and uncompromising manner, and Jo and Edward felt it had been a salutary experience for him. The motorcycle had been retrieved, and was being stored until Terry was old enough to take lessons and had shown enough general responsibility to deserve them. There was a rather better atmosphere at home as Terry was beginning to respond to the challenge of taking responsibility – his behaviour had improved somewhat, and he now put out his dirty clothes for washing and took regular showers, admitting ruefully that his friends had begun to criticize him for smelling.

The greatest benefit was that Edward and Jo no longer felt burdened by a sense of guilt and inadequacy. By their cooperation and mutual support, they had regained their relationship, affirmed its importance and assumed control of their lives. They also concluded that, paradoxically, by withdrawing from taking responsibility for Terry's actions, and passing the responsibility to him, they had actually shown a greater demonstration of parental concern than by their previous attempts at persuasion and control. By narrating their experiences of the new policy in our sessions, they were able to re-cast the occasional lapses or failures as 'hiccups' in an overall success story rather than be discouraged by them.

LEARNING EXERCISE (60 MINUTES)

Work in pairs.

1. **(40 minutes)** Discuss the following points:

    (a) What cultural and social sources might have contributed to the assumptions about parental influence, and taking responsibility for their teenager's behaviour, which informed Jo and Edward's problem-narrative?

    (b) Could the Bayard and Bayard strategy have been considered successful if Terry had continued to behave as badly as before but his parents had nevertheless successfully re-engaged with their own relationship and ceased to take responsibility for Terry's actions?

    (c) Terry's behaviour was less extreme than that of some teenagers. Would the Bayard and Bayard strategy have been appropriate if he was becoming addicted to alcohol, taking hard drugs, taking part in violent gang crime? What other choices might be open to parents in this kind of extreme situation? Why might these choices be better, or worse, than applying Bayard and Bayard's strategy? How might these parents maintain or regain the integrity of their own relationship despite their child's extreme behaviour and the anxiety this produces in them?

2. **(20 minutes)** Work with another pair. Share and discuss your conclusions on one or more of the above questions.

11
SEXUAL DIFFICULTIES

This chapter attempts to demystify some of the sexual problems frequently brought to counselling, and to suggest practical ways in which the non-specialist counsellor can assist couples to address these difficulties. Examples are of heterosexual couples but the general principles are relevant whatever the partners' sexuality.

DIFFIDENCE

Despite the twenty-first century Western openness about sex reflected in films, television, fiction, the written media and self-help books, some couples experiencing sexual difficulties find it hard to mention the subject in counselling. For many, a sexual problem is such an intimate, private and emotionally laden topic, with such powerful overtones of socially derived value judgements, that any sense of 'failure' is inhibiting - they may discuss their overall relationship in general terms but be uncertain whether or how to raise the sex issue. They may postpone such revelations, hoping that a general improvement in their relationship will be enough to bring about a better sex life, and this is not necessarily a foolish decision. Counsellors may also feel diffidence. Asking directly about the couple's sex life, when the couple themselves have not mentioned it, might appear insensitive and intrusive. Counsellors may assume that this area is best not asked about by therapists who have not received specialist training, and if the couple do mention sexual problems, suggest referral rather than risk getting out of their depth.

There are some sexual difficulties which are best addressed by therapists who have undergone training in sex therapy, but there are some commonly experienced sexual problems which the general counsellor can assist a couple to overcome, especially if an approach is used that normalizes the problem, is practical and builds on positive aspects of the relationship. Green and Flemons, writing about brief solution-focused therapy in terms that could equally be applied to narrative therapy, suggest that when a therapist fails to raise the issue of sex with clients, this can give the impression that he or she is 'unwilling to address issues of intimacy', and that this is particularly unfortunate since 'brief therapists have unique skills and clinical understandings that offer nonpathologizing, liberating possibilities for clients experiencing sexual difficulties' (2004: xxiv–xxv). My own experience is that a flexible narrative approach, incorporating the general ideas and practices outlined in this book together with the specific guidelines offered in this chapter, is usually enough to assist couples experiencing the most common sexual problems and obviates any need to refer on.

Terminology

Couples may be uncertain how to describe sexual issues in language acceptable to the counsellor or not embarrassing to themselves. No vocabulary is neutral since language develops in particular social contexts where assumptions and value judgements become interwoven with it. This certainly applies to sex, where despite the existence of a huge range of words and phrases for sexual parts of the body and for sexual acts, there is generally no socially acceptable terminology. The choice is between popular usage with its overtones of humour, insult, obscenity or negativity, or anatomical and physiological terms which are cold and distancing when used for physical lovemaking. But both kinds of vocabulary are potentially embarrassing, simply because they relate to an area of life that has powerful emotional resonance and is fraught with social and emotional ambiguity. Usually, persons stumblingly use the more formal phraseology and I follow their lead, repeating their words in a conversational tone, so as to convey my own lack of embarrassment and to counter the words' colder associations. If I myself initiate the use of sexual language, I use this kind of language, with an engaged and matter-of-fact manner which conveys that I regard such vocabulary as ordinary and everyday. This tends to counter embarrassment, perhaps after a slight initial shock. By this means, the couple are implicitly invited to follow my example, and usually in a very short time, the words are used freely by them as well.

Very occasionally, a person initiates discussion of sex by using informal or 'street' terminology (such as 'prick' rather than 'penis') and when this happens, I take up their vocabulary. The most important thing, as with more formal terminology, is to use it in a natural and unforced manner so that any embarrassment or verbal inhibition on the part of the couple is overcome, including any worry that I might find this language inappropriate.

Sometimes couples use euphemisms which are ambiguous, such as 'We aren't close very often, and Derek has intimacy problems'. I could offend the couple if I assume these statements refer to physical sex, and continue on that basis, if what they really mean is that they seldom cuddle, or even that they seldom talk about other than trivial matters, and that Derek is reticent about talking affectionately. In such instances, I check out by using direct language – 'Can I just make sure I've understood you? You don't often make love – is that what you're saying? And am I right in thinking that Derek has problems with the physical side of lovemaking?' If the couple confirm they are talking about physical sex, my own language can move into a tentative combination of using their euphemisms when the meaning has been clarified, and more direct vocabulary so as to clarify the situation further, after asking permission to pursue this delicate area. 'Is it OK if I ask some questions about what you've said so I can get a better understanding of the problem? Right, thank you. I wonder what you mean about not being close very often. Couples vary so much in what they think of as the "usual" or "normal" frequency. Do you mean you make love once a year? Once a month? Once a week? And you say Derek has some problems here. I quite often see men who have premature ejaculations or who have difficulty in getting or maintaining an erection. Derek, do these kinds of difficulties affect you, or have I misunderstood?'

Initiating the topic

If sexual information is not volunteered, this may, of course, mean that there is no problem. But since in many instances the couple's diffidence or uncertainty will be the reason for sex not being mentioned, it is the responsibility of the counsellor to ensure that such a potentially important area does not go unstated and therefore unexplored. A matter-of-fact and unembarrassed direct question at a point where a degree of rapport has begun to exist between the counsellor and the couple, and perhaps when understanding has started to increase between the couple themselves, is usually either welcomed with relief if there is a problem, or simply met with a reply that there is no such problem, which provides an immediate exception, as in Michael White's video 'The Best of Friends' described in the previous chapter (White 1994). I usually ask the question in the first joint session, at the point when each partner has explained how they are experiencing the relationship and has heard the other's response to their story. A simple query such as 'How about your intimate life – are there any problems around sex?' is best addressed to both partners together, rather than asked of one partner at the point in joint sessions when they are responding to my questions as the other listens. This prevents the possibility of one partner saying there is no problem, with the other then feeling either that they cannot admit to the difficulty, or on the other hand building up frustration and annoyance until it is their turn to speak (*'He* may think there's no problem, but I do! And he didn't realize! *Absolutely typical!*') Of course, resentment can build around a statement about anything where the other partner has a different viewpoint, but the strongly emotional nature of sex problems can make such reactions particularly emphatic. I ask the question 'down the centre' of the partners when each has heard the other's viewpoint on the relationship without interruption, and if a sexual problem is then identified by one partner, I can immediately ask the other for their perspective.

  If a problem with sex emerges, I do not immediately pursue it, but ask the couple if they see the issue as related to those they have already outlined. It is important to get an appropriate balance between assuming that sex difficulties are the principal reason for the couple's deteriorated relationship and, on the other hand, considering whether the sex problems spring from the relationship's wider stresses. Of course, a vicious circle may have developed where these causes and effects are intermingled, and if so, it can be helpful for the couple to recognize this pattern and to see it as something that has the potential to be reversed.

MEDICAL FACTORS

When the problem involves a diminution of sexual response, it is not always appropriate to begin by exploring possible psychological or relationship issues.

> Harry and Anne, a heterosexual married couple in their mid-fifties, explained that their relationship had become fraught with tension and, on Anne's part, mistrust. Anne said that she had become unattractive to Harry, and as a result he had increasingly withdrawn from sexual activity. Despite all her efforts to look nice and to be affectionate, Harry now hardly ever initiated lovemaking, and when he did he seemed tense and uninvolved. She was rather shy, and found it difficult to initiate sex herself, especially since the pattern of their lovemaking had always been for Harry to take the lead. His erections had become either non-existent or weak, and she herself became inhibited when the problem occurred. Harry had assured her he loved her and still found her attractive but Anne felt that this was not true; she was very aware of the effects of ageing on her appearance and she thought his body was revealing the true state of his feelings. She felt ugly, unfeminine, unloved and rejected, and had recently begun to wonder whether there might be another woman in Harry's life. When it was his turn to speak, Harry vehemently denied that there was another woman involved. He was puzzled and distressed at his lack of sexual potency and the effect this was having on their relationship, and could only conclude that his age was responsible. He had heard that men became less capable of sex as they grew older, though he did think he was rather young for this to happen to him.

I assumed that this couple had become trapped in a self-fulfilling prophesy where awareness of the possibility of Harry having a poor erection led to anxiety, lack of spontaneity and inhibition. In the second session, I began to address the problem on this basis (see 'Vicious circles' below). Towards the end of the session, Harry returned to his idea that his age might be the problem, and wondered whether seeing his doctor to ask for Viagra might be the answer. He had an appointment soon anyway, he said, to discuss his diabetes medication.

Harry's diabetes was news to me. Although not medically trained, I knew that one of the effects of diabetes can be a diminution of sexual function, so I asked him what his doctor had said about this. Harry looked surprised and said it had never been mentioned. His doctor had not warned him of the possibility, and he had never told his doctor about the change in his erections. This was a turning point in the session. Anne visibly brightened with relief and said that she also had no idea that diabetes could be responsible – it probably meant that Harry's medical condition was the culprit, not that he had stopped caring for her. She said she didn't mind not having what she called 'full' sex – this was unimportant – there were other ways they could make love. Only one further counselling session was held. Harry told me his doctor had confirmed that diabetes was undoubtedly the cause of his weak erections, and the couple were feeling happier and closer than for a very long time.

Many couples turn to psychological hypotheses before considering whether there might be a medical reason for physical sexual problems, perhaps being influenced by Western media obsessed with 'pop' psychological explanations for so many aspects of life and relationships. This is also a temptation for counsellors. When there are problems around physical sex, I now always ask if there are any medical issues, and whether the person's doctor knows about the sexual limitations he or she has described.

INFLUENCE OF TRAUMA

A couple's story of sexual difficulties will, like all accounts of experience, leave much out, including elements that might provide clues to seeing the problem in a less despairing light, or with a wider and more helpful perspective. As with all narrative therapy, it is important to gain as full a description of the problem as possible, including its history and its effects on the couple's thoughts, feelings and attitudes, not only in their relationship itself but in their wider life (such as whether sexual frustration and sleeplessness is making them short-tempered with friends and colleagues). Through the detailed telling of the problem-story, it may become obvious that the sexual problems are a reflection of a general deterioration in the relationship, or it may become clear that the sexual problems came about unexpectedly, when the relationship was fine, but that they have now led to tension and distress. Many couples with sexual problems are *not* conflicted; they are loving and committed, very much wanting their sex problems to be overcome but unable to see how.

It is important to consult the couple themselves for their views about the problem's origin. Their opinions might be totally opposed ('She's never interested in having sex', 'Well, he's just not interested in anything else!'), or, unlike in most other couple counselling situations, they may be in complete agreement ('It all started last year when we both got exhausted running the business, and we've never had a good sex life since'). Significant information can emerge that might never have been brought out had the couple not been consulted on why the problem has arisen.

Dean and Holly were a young couple whose sex life had virtually ceased. There were some differences of opinion between them, especially an open conflict between Dean's traditionally patriarchal ideas and Holly's feminism, and we spent some time exploring these to little avail. I was becoming puzzled about the reasons for the failure of their sex lives – there was some lively debate about feminism in our sessions, but it was reasonably good-humoured, and the couple's differences of opinion did not seem enough to account for the sexual problem. It was not until the third session that I thought to ask the couple what they thought lay behind the problem, whereupon Dean hesitantly revealed that as a boy he had been subject to prolonged sexual abuse by two men. He had told Holly about this early in their relationship but had underplayed it in order to spare her, and because she had never heard the full story, she had not suspected the abuse as a factor in the couple's sexual difficulties. Images of these events had increasingly invaded Dean's mind when he began to be sexually aroused, and had led to feelings of shame, uncertainty and worry about his sexual orientation, and eventually to his avoiding sexual activity altogether. Counselling became geared to his recovery from sexual abuse rather than to couple conflict, with Holly attending sessions and fulfilling an invaluable supportive role. The eventual outcome was positive, with Dean reassured, the images from the past fading and the couple's sex life renewed.

Counselling for sexual trauma is beyond the scope of this book, but there is ample coverage in the narrative therapy literature (Durrant and White 1990; Fraser 2006; Mann 2001, 2004; Mann and Russell 2002; McPhie and Chaffey 1999; White 1995: ch. 4; White 2004b).

PHYSICAL PROBLEMS

Sometimes couples with a good relationship, to their dismay, develop problems in their physical capacity to have sex. Men may have unexpected difficulty in having or maintaining erections, or they may have premature ejaculations, and women in heterosexual relationships sometimes experience a tightening which makes it difficult or impossible to accept the man's penis into her vagina. Sometimes a doctor has given reassurance that there is no medical complication, but doctors vary widely in their ability to make useful suggestions about how to overcome such difficulties. I have no doubt that many doctors do this well, and of course I am unlikely to see couples where this is the case. However, I have been consulted by persons whose doctor has told them that in time the problem will just go away (it hasn't), or that they should have a glass or two of wine before going to bed (no result), or that they should just try to relax and not worry (they haven't been able to), or that they should use a lubricant and/or have longer fore-play (problem still there). They may have begun to tell themselves a story of failure and possibly despair, suspecting that there is something wrong with them as individuals and/or with their relationship. Some couples hope that I will give them some practical suggestions as to what to do, but others seek counselling thinking that there must be hidden conflicts or unrecognized 'complexes' that I can uncover and resolve.

Reassurance and normalization

Facile reassurance is, of course, unhelpful in counselling, as it assumes a future that the counsellor cannot be sure of, and puts him or her in the role of knowing expert. It is also mismatched with persons' present experience and therefore likely to be seen as unhelpful and insensitive. However, there is a place for tentative and provisional reassurance that does not promise resolution of the problem but quotes the experience of other couples to give a degree of hope. Where there are physical problems such as the above, I say that although each couple is unique, and it can be unwise to make direct comparisons, they might like to know that their problem is similar to that of other couples I have counselled who have overcome their physical difficulties and regained a happy and fulfilling sex life. Usually, the couple respond to this information with relief. The atmosphere of the session lightens, and the couple become more open to considering practical solutions and less inclined to stay with the dominant story of sexual anxiety and failure.

Humour

Michael White suggests that using externalizing language 'frees persons to take a lighter, more effective, and less stressed approach to "deadly serious" problems' (White and Epston 1990: 40). Sex is, of course, the subject of many jokes, comedy sketches and other forms of humour, but is it appropriate to introduce humour into such a 'deadly serious' and painful aspect of a couple's life as their sexual dilemmas, confusions, disagreements and tensions, let alone their sense of failure and inadequacy? Michael White was clearly justified in encouraging a soiling child's problem to be called 'Sneaky Poo' (White and Epston 1990: 46–8) but how many men would take kindly to their erectile problem being called 'Droopy Dong?'

I wonder if this book's readers responded to that last sentence with a slightly embarrassed smile or laugh? Well, sex *is* comical in many ways. I hope I would never be so crass as to introduce such a jokey term myself, especially in a first session; my externalizing language takes the more sober form of phrases like 'erection problems affecting your lovemaking' or 'early ejaculation causing problems for you'. However, a lightening of atmosphere through a sensitively timed use of humour can be invaluable. I agree with Green and Flemons that 'you and your clients needn't check your humor at the door when touching on sexual issues. Indeed, it might be the very thing that helps turn around a serious, relationship-threatening situation' (2004: xxiii). Humour around the topic can be an early casualty of sexual difficulty – and, correspondingly, regaining humour can be both a sign, and a means, of recovery. I am not suggesting that counsellors should tell bawdy jokes as a therapeutic technique! But as things begin to improve, the relief and hope experienced by the couple often lead quite naturally to a more humorous tone in sessions, especially since the English language is rich in ambiguity and double meaning. This should be welcomed. Once, when a couple reported that they were beginning to improve their sex life, I asked them in all innocence how they might keep it up. After a moment's uncertain silence, we all three burst into laughter and when we regained our equilibrium, I was able to use the moment as an exception, asking what their laughter told them about where they were now compared with when they first came to counselling.

Vicious circles

The most useful ideas I have come across with regard to counselling couples experiencing difficulties with the physical aspect of sex comprise three linked propositions:

- Physical sexual responses are not amenable to conscious control.
- The more problems of physical response are consciously thought about at the point of lovemaking, the less likely sex is to improve, because anxiety inhibits bodily responses, and the resultant sexual failure leads to increased anxiety, which inhibits bodily responses even more.
- Therefore, the most useful approach to improving or recovering physical sex is to recognize this vicious circle and find ways to step out of it.

Kathy and George had been married for 24 years, had two grown-up children and led busy working lives. For several years, George had begun to lose erections soon after lovemaking began, and Kathy had become inhibited in her responses. Intercourse had become sporadic, and in the last few months had ceased. Both had become nervous about any kind of sensual contact, even kissing or cuddling, because each immediately thought this might be a prelude to intercourse, and anxiety set in at once. They had discussed these problems together and made various unsuccessful attempts to solve them. Thinking they might have become too routine and unadventurous, they bought a book on sexual positions and tried some of them, but found these experiments embarrassing and unproductive. Kathy bought some sexy nightwear but had never felt like wearing it. They had gone out for a 'romantic' meal, only to find that their conversation in the restaurant was rather unnatural and forced, and that when they got home and went to bed, the sexual inhibitions were fully in place.

The atmosphere between the couple in this first session was comfortable and cooperative – they agreed on the nature of their sexual difficulties and expressed rueful amusement at some of the unsuccessful ways they had tried to solve them. After briefly checking out the nature of the problem, I said, 'I'd now like to ask you both to do something important. Is that OK? Well, please *don't think about onions.* Onions have nothing to do with why you've come to counselling, so please put them right out of your mind. Don't visualize them, don't recall the papery texture of the skins when you peel them, don't imagine the tangy smell when you slice them, and don't have any sense of how your eyes water. In fact, *don't think of onions at all'*. Kathy and George looked at me in amazed dismay for a moment, then Kathy got the point and laughed. George still looked puzzled and anxious, so I said, 'George, what are you thinking about?' 'Onions!' he replied.

Having established that the more one tries to put something out of mind, the more firmly it tends to establish itself, I discussed the vicious circles which had invaded the couple's intimate life, so that the harder they tried to overcome their sexual inhibitions, the more powerful the thoughts and worries became, with anxiety feeding the process and leading to the story of failure and frustration which they had told me. I externalized the problem as 'vicious circles of anxiety' so that the physical limitations were characterized as the *result* of the problem, not as the problem itself. I said I had seen other couples who had experienced the same vicious circle, and I asked Kathy and George what ideas occurred to them about how to reverse the process. How could they, paradoxically, improve their sex life by forgetting about its problems? Trying to forget obviously wouldn't work – the 'onion effect' – so what else might they do? They had no answer, so I wondered whether other couples' solutions might be worth considering.

The ideas I offer for consideration when sexual inhibition has developed between loving couples have two aims: firstly, to alleviate 'performance anxiety' and, secondly, to promote re-engagement with sensuality in acceptable and non-threatening stages. Taken together, these practices can usually overcome the vicious circle described above.

George and Kathy were only too pleased to attempt methods that other couples found had worked. I explained that this would be an experiment and – whatever the outcome – we could learn from it. It would consist of two temporary changes. There would be an agreement not to attempt intercourse for the next two months. This was designed to interrupt the anxiety/inhibition/anxiety vicious circle. Secondly, they would spend 15 minutes a day holding hands, at an agreed time – not in bed, but when watching television, going for a walk, listening to music, or during any other leisure activity. No other sensual contact would take place. The idea was to re-learn sensual contact in slow stages *without proceeding to the next stage until they were completely comfortable with the stage they were at.* It would be like re-learning tennis strokes or playing a musical instrument or driving a car again after a long period without these activities. Each stage would feel awkward at first but should gradually become natural and unforced with acclimatization.

Kathy and George chose the evening as their experiment time, when they usually sat watching their favourite television 'soap'. At the next session, they described with amusement how at first they sat apart on the sofa, stiffly holding hands. But in a few days, they relaxed, sat closer and held hands almost without realizing it. It had also felt good going to bed knowing that there would be no unease about whether they should try to have sex. The next stage, discussed in the session and chosen by the couple after considering various possibilities, would be to sit holding hands with their bodies just touching.

> Over the next few weeks, George and Kathy moved through small, graduated stages of contact, not deciding on the next until wholly at ease with the present stage. They reached a point of feeling at ease when lying together in bed, embracing, with their bodies in contact. The agreed prohibition on having intercourse was still in place when they unexpectedly found themselves overwhelmed with tenderness, and rediscovered full lovemaking. They decided they needed no further counselling. A few weeks later, they sent me a postcard from Venice saying they were enjoying a second honeymoon.

INTERNALIZED SOCIO-CULTURAL NORMS AND VALUES

Disagreement or conflict around sexual issues can frequently be traced to discrepancies in attitude or belief that have not been fully recognized as such, with each partner indignant at the other's apparently irrational or mistaken ideas. It is also possible for partners to *share* socially constructed assumptions about sex which are unhelpful to their relationship. Freedman and Combs suggest that, especially with heterosexual couples, it can be vitally important to bring socially constructed sexist and patriarchal assumptions about sex and gender to the forefront for recognition and reconsideration (2002: 67–84).

Socially constructed assumptions I have met in my counselling include:

- Full penetration is essential, and anything short of this is failure.
- Women are not sexually attractive unless they are slim.
- Mutual orgasm is always the goal, and anything short of this is failure.
- It is normal to have sex four or more times a night/very occasionally/only when trying for a baby.
- The proper way to have sex is with one partner underneath the other, in the dark. Anything else is dirty and perverted, including oral sex, anal sex, cross-dressing, fantasy enactment, use of sex toys, etc.
- Unless the partner agrees to oral sex, anal sex, cross-dressing, fantasy enactment, use of sex toys, etc., she/he is clinically inhibited and needs therapy.
- The man should always take the lead in lovemaking.
- When a woman says no to sex, she is just teasing and needs to be persuaded.
- When a woman says no to sex, she will always respond to a passionate and insistent approach.
- Sex is a sacred and solemn activity profoundly linked to the spiritual side of human nature.
- Sex is nothing but recreational fun.
- Masturbation is sinful/harmful/a sign of sexual inadequacy.
- Men and women have different/incompatible sexual needs.

Counsellors are not, of course, immune to taking on socially constructed attitudes and beliefs about sex, and my own socialization may be partly responsible for my critical attitude to all the ideas listed above! However, when I come across assumptions like these in my work, I try to hold fast to two parallel obligations: (a) I have a duty to invite persons to take a fresh look at ideas that my thinking, reading and experience have indicated to be suspect, mistaken or dangerous, but (b) I also have a duty not to impose my views on persons with a different lifestyle or belief system to my own.

It is essential to *discriminate* between these two different kinds of divergence. To take two examples: I wholly disagree that when a woman says no to sex, she is just teasing and needs to be persuaded, and I always invite an examination of this idea in the hope that it will be modified. On the other hand, if I counsel a couple who both genuinely see sex as nothing but recreational fun, I respect this opinion and work within its parameters even though this is not my own view.

Where one or both of the partners reveal socially constructed views that appear to be a factor in the couple's problems, I follow a four-point procedure:

1. *I invite them to be explicit:* And I repeat, summarize or paraphrase, using clear and direct language. I also prepare the ground for a re-examination of the idea, sometimes by extending it to a broader conclusion which demonstrates its fragility:

'Pete, I think what you're saying is that when women say no to sex, they are really just teasing and will always agree to sex after some persuasion. This applies to all women in all circumstances at all times. Is that what you mean?'

2. *I invite them to consider where their opinions originated:* 'OK, Pete, I've got it clear now. Can I ask you to think about where that idea came from? We develop our thinking partly from our experience and partly from other people's opinions. So who or what influenced you to believe that most women are just teasing when they refuse sex?'

3. *I tentatively offer an alternative viewpoint for consideration:* 'So you found that some women eventually agreed to sex if you persisted, and your mates often boast about overcoming women's resistance. And there are films which show women just falling at a man's feet when he suggests sex – maybe James Bond has a lot to answer for! Pete, I'd like to talk about a rather different way of seeing things which I've come across, which you might find interesting, but I'm not sure whether this would be acceptable. Shall I risk it? Thanks, I will. I have counselled a lot of women who told me that when they say no to sex, they really mean it, even if the man is some-one they love and like having sex with. They tell me that sometimes all they need is a kiss or a cuddle, or just time to themselves. When the man persists, this feels as if he's not respecting them, not showing a really loving and understanding attitude.'

4. *I invite them to examine how their ideas affect the relationship:* 'You and Jenny live together, love each other and are committed, and OK – there are times when Jenny just doesn't feel like sex. You've heard her describe how she feels pressured and upset when you persist, and how frightened she is when you get angry at her for not wanting sex at that particular time. You probably know her better than anyone else in the world. When she says no to sex, is she just teasing, or does she mean it? Does not wanting sex on some occasions mean she never wants it, or never will again, or that she doesn't love you?'

The neat sequence given above for the sake of clarity is rarely followed exactly. I may ask the questions in a different order, or revert to one I have already asked. The aim is gently to dislodge certainty, opening up the possibility for persons to modify or change their received opinions. Exceptions may emerge – perhaps Pete denies that he was referring to all women at all times, or Jenny may remember occasions when he accepted her refusal of sex with more grace than usual. The significance of these occasions, which indicate his potential for a more sensitive interaction with Jenny, would be fully explored. Ideally, as therapy progresses, Pete's gradually modifying his damaging, socially constructed ideas about women would reinforce the process.

LEARNING EXERCISE: TAKEN-FOR-GRANTED 'TRUTHS' ABOUT COUPLE RELATIONSHIPS (45 MINUTES)

- Work in pairs.
- Choose examples from the socially constructed ideas given below.
- Consider the possible socio-cultural sources of these ideas, such as family of origin, social class, peer groups, ethnicity, political ideology, 'pop' psychology, religious community, teachers, gurus, role models, authors, mass media, professional culture.

- Consider these points:
    (a) If couples hold these ideas, how this might affect their sex life?
    (b) If the therapist holds these ideas, how might they affect her/his work with couples who are experiencing sexual problems?

Socially constructed ideas:

1. Couples who do not want children are selfish.
2. Unmarried couples living together have less commitment than married couples.
3. Everybody needs a partner or spouse in order to live a fulfilled life.
4. A man needs a large penis to give his partner sexual satisfaction.
5. Small penises are a legitimate source of derision.
6. The larger a woman's breasts, the more attractive she is.
7. Unless a couple have mutual orgasms, their sex life is a failure.
8. Unless a man has regular orgasms, he will become ill.
9. Women have an instinctive need to be faithful to their partners, but men are psychologically programmed to seek relationships outside the partnership.
10. A person who wants intercourse much more frequently than his or her partner is addicted to sex and needs therapy.

12
INFIDELITY

In this chapter, I define infidelity, one of the most frequent issues brought to couple coun-selling and one of the most distressing. I discuss how the counsellor might acknowledge the pain and confusion felt by the 'betrayed' partner, yet maintain a non-judgemental stance towards the partner who has strayed outside the couple relationship. The issue of forgiveness is addressed in some detail, illustrated by a description of practice.

DEFINITIONS

'Infidelity' is usually taken to mean sexual intercourse with someone outside a committed relationship. I have counselled many individuals who have discovered their partner to be unfaithful in this sense, and who are in emotional turmoil as a result; also individuals who, rather to their surprise, are feeling relieved at the revela-tion, having recognized for some time that things have not been right. After the initial shock, they are rebuilding their lives with a sense of release. I have counselled couples who despite the initially devastating effects of the affair wish to make a new start and rescue their relationship; and couples still reeling from the effects of infidelity and its disclosure, and not at all sure what they want for the future.

Counselling has also been sought by persons whose partner has secretly turned to someone else for comfort, support and affection but not for a sexual relationship. The revelation of this last kind of emotional intimacy often produces reactions just as powerful as if the relationship had included physical sex, since trust has been broken. 'Infidelity' is often an entirely appropriate name for this situation, and I have frequently found the definition welcomed by the betrayed partner with relief as a validation of their chaotic and disoriented feelings, powerfully present despite the other partner's puzzled or indignant protests that since no sex happened, the outside relationship was not infidelity at all.

Revelation of the secret life of an unfaithful partner comes as a tremendous shock because it suggests that the couple's relationship, and the person's long-held image of her/his partner, are built on illusion.

This trust violation frequently is the most significant aspect of what occurs: it is not necessarily what the partner does with someone else, but the fact that he or she is deceiving ... that produces the greatest amounts of anger and damage to the ... relationship. (Nichols 1988: 186)

The novelist Henri Troyat evokes the shock of discovery with telling detail:

It was enough for Sophie to recall the last conversation she held with her husband, Nicholas's kindness just as he was leaving, his suggestions, his smile, his kiss, for a wave of disgust to choke her. All memories of her marriage were poisoned by this. She wanted to forget them at once, to wash herself clean from head to foot. Her confusion had nothing to do with the base tumults of jealousy. It was not Nicholas's infidelity which tormented her the most, but the apparatus of falsity with which he had surrounded his affair. Wounded in her self-respect more than in her love, she could not bear the idea that, for such a long time, she had trusted a man who had now made her a laughing-stock. (2000: 471, my translation)

Not all affairs arise from one partner's straying thoughtlessly and irresponsibly outside a valuable relationship. Sometimes an affair starts when the existing relationship is unsatisfactory, dead or damaging. In these instances, the new relationship can begin a wholly beneficial and positive new phase of life for the 'unfaithful' partner, and sometimes the 'deceived' partner may receive a much-needed wake-up call:

Daniel and Kate married followed an exciting whirlwind courtship at a time when both had been lonely. There were two young sons from Kate's previous marriage. Once married, Daniel found he could not cope with his stepchildren, and immersed himself in his work. He stayed late at the office every night, brought paperwork home most weekends, and became habitually irritable. Kate felt excluded and demeaned. She had an affair, which Daniel discovered. He at once sued for divorce, and Kate and her children went to live with her lover. When Daniel's immediate reactions subsided, he felt immense loss and became affected by depression. Through individual counselling, he began to acknowledge his own contribution to the break-up and to re-examine his lifestyle and values. He retreated from excessive work, saw more of friends he had neglected, and took up lapsed interests, including singing in the local church choir. He described himself as 'becoming the man I once was'.

Care is always needed in choosing vocabulary when counselling people who are emotionally and perhaps physically involved with someone outside the couple. Words like 'infidelity', 'unfaithfulness', 'affair' and 'extramarital sex' carry negative resonances. They are inappropriate when referring to a situation where a partner in an unsatisfactory, dead or abusive relationship has found love and fulfilment with someone else.

The meaning and nature of relationships other than with the established partner cannot be generalized and should not be oversimplified. Such relationships may be a fulfilling rediscovery of the possibility of being loved; or a continuous, cynical and calculated betrayal; or a genuinely regretted one-off occasion when drunk. As in my earlier example of John and Lynn (Chapter 3), such relationships can include unconventional forms which some counsellors might find surprising or distasteful but which are acceptable to both partners. Respecting persons' opinions and lifestyles rather than basing counselling on the therapist's own socially constructed values is particularly important here.

The key is to address not so much the acts of infidelity themselves but the *meaning* of the infidelity to one or both of the partners, especially when each sees the situation differently, and to make sure of these meanings from the beginning.

EMOTIONAL IMPACT

Most couples who have already decided to part do not seek counselling. They turn to solicitors and perhaps to mediation for the practical aspects, and to friends and relatives for emotional support. If they do have counselling, individual therapy with two therapists is usually appropriate rather than couple counselling, with the aim of assisting each partner to adapt to a new phase of life. It is worth noting that unless separation comes as a welcome relief, and sometimes even then, it can be emotionally devastating, with problems of finance and accommodation adding frustration and anxiety. Disbelief, anger, disorientation, damaged self-view and depression are common reactions. Images of the partner with the other party may haunt the imagination, both preventing sleep, and contributing to a waking nightmare. Recovery from separation or divorce can sometimes take longer than recovery from the death of a loved person.

Emotional meaning for the counsellor

If the counsellor has direct personal experience of infidelity, it may be important to raise this with the supervisor, since the lingering emotional effects of this most powerful of distressing experiences may make it difficult to avoid over-identification either with the 'betrayed' partner if the counsellor has been in this position, or with the other partner if the counsellor found happiness and fulfilment outside an established but unsatisfactory relationship. However, I have already made the point (in Chapter 1) that a counsellor's personal experience may provide insights and sensitivities which, far from negatively affecting his or her counselling, may play a significant part in its effectiveness.

Contrasting situations

Broadly speaking, two contrasting situations are brought to counselling by couples where one has been unfaithful. The first is where one partner has been told that the relationship is over but has persuaded his/her partner to come to counselling in the hope that the relationship can be rescued after all. The second is where both partners wish to put the infidelity behind them and rescue their relationship, but are finding it impossible to do this.

WHEN PARTNERS HAVE DIFFERENT AIMS

When only one of the partners wishes the relationship to continue, counselling does not usually last long, since the counsellor should not aim to rescue the relationship (which would mean respecting one partner's wishes but going against the other partner's) but to clarify the situation and explore realistic possibilities. One joint session when each person has time to tell their story, listen to the other and comment, is sometimes enough.

Steve and Samantha, married and in their late thirties, came for counselling following Samantha's brief affair with Dave, previously Steve's best friend. Samantha spoke first and expressed bitter regret, saying that 'it had just happened' one evening when Steve was out. Tearfully, she described how she and Dave had drunk a bottle of wine together, 'one thing led to another' and they ended up in bed. In the next few weeks, she and Dave had sex once or twice at his flat, but she realized this was not what she wanted and had ended the affair. In his anger at being rejected, Dave told Steve what had occurred, whereupon Steve immediately told Samantha the marriage was over. She loved Steve, she said, not Dave, and wanted things between them to get back to where they were before the affair. She was dreadfully sorry, had learned her lesson, and would never do anything like this again.

Steve listened to Samantha calmly, without taking notes. When it was his turn to speak, he said clearly and firmly that he had only come to counselling at her request and that nothing she said had made any difference. He could never trust her again, and he had lost a friend as well as a wife. There was no possibility of the marriage continuing and she must accept this. He was seeing a solicitor the following week to start divorce proceedings and had delayed this appointment only because of promising to try counselling first.

Samantha was too upset to comment and the session ended early. I said I would leave it to them to contact me if they wished to continue, but they did not return.

Not all couples where one partner wishes to rescue the relationship end counselling after just one session, but where there appears to be little chance of reconciliation, it can be futile and misleading to continue with joint sessions in case things change. Individual sessions with each partner are invaluable here. The deceived partner may be less certain of his decision than Steve was in the above example, and be experiencing soul-searching, guilt and ambivalence. Self-blame at this stage can be less painful than taking fully on board the implications of the deceiving partner's actions, since it lessens the sense of bewilderment and disorientation and maintains some fragile sense of the other's integrity. Fretting about questions such as 'What did I do to make him/her look elsewhere?' can postpone recognizing the full implications of the infidelity, yet be torture to the deceived partner. A clear-sighted exploration of such chaotic feelings in individual sessions can be beneficial.

Dawn's partner Patrick had been having sex with other women for about three years before she suspected what was happening, faced Patrick with her suspicions, and he admitted the affairs. In the first joint session, Patrick said he had been unhappy in the relationship for a long time, largely because Dawn had become sexually unresponsive. He had tried to improve their sex life by adding an aphrodisiac to Dawn's bedtime drink without her knowing, but this had not worked. He also felt frustrated and trapped by the limitations of what had become a rather conventional relationship and way of life. He did not want them to split up but he wanted to be a 'free spirit', and wondered if she too might benefit from the excitement of occasional sex with other men – he would not object to this.

Patrick's individual sessions largely consisted of him repeating and enlarging on what he had said in the joint session, and my questions were unsuccessful in encouraging him to examine his ideas and actions. In her individual sessions, Dawn expressed great confusion. Her previously taken-for-granted view of what constituted a valuable relationship had been blown apart – Patrick spoke very convincingly, and she sometimes wondered if he might be justified in what he thought and had done. She knew she had become sexually unresponsive, and she could see that their life together had become rather staid. But she also had unexpected moments of rage, especially when she thought of Patrick's secretly adding a drug to her drink. When I invited her to give a name to this action, she was unable to think of one, so I suggested a range of possibilities, including 'thoughtfulness for Dawn's sex life', 'a concerned initiative', 'a well-intentioned misjudgement', 'an inconsiderate action' and 'a selfish abuse of trust'. At once, Dawn seized on 'a selfish abuse of trust', and from then onwards gradually came to decide that Patrick's actions had been based on selfishness and disrespect for her, and totally contradicted what she believed made a relationship valuable. In what turned out to be the final joint session, she firmly told Patrick that the relationship was over.

Helping a couple to part amicably

Sometimes when couples who are being counselled decide to part, a continuation of couple work is possible, with the aim of assisting the partners to terminate their relationship with the minimum of conflict and as little as possible emotional damage to themselves and their children. In my experience, however, most couples who decide to part also decide to end counselling at this point, and in these instances I always recommend mediation. Mediation is beyond the scope of this book but I recommend Winslade and Monk's *Narrative Mediation: a New Approach to Conflict Resolution* (2001) to interested readers.

In contrast to the above examples, I have known instances when, despite coming to counselling determined to end the relationship, the deceived partner has changed her mind after listening to the offending partner's story and taking on board for the first time how genuine unhappiness was a factor leading to the infidelity. When this happens, the couple may move to the second category – partners who both want the relationship to survive despite one of them having been unfaithful.

WHEN BOTH PARTNERS WISH TO RESCUE THEIR RELATIONSHIP

Going slowly

Although narrative therapy tends to be completed in many fewer sessions than some traditional therapies, the unfolding of possibilities for rebuilding a relationship where infidelity has occurred cannot be hurried. Attempting recovery is often difficult, uneven and at times disheartening, and there is no guarantee of success. The counsellor should be alert to any temptation to over-optimism or to over-valuing exceptions, as well as recognizing and *tentatively* acknowledging signs of positive change when they occur. I try to bear in mind family therapist John Weakland's approach, as described by Ray and Anger-Diaz (2004: 233):

> … many therapeutic approaches suggest that the appropriate response is to praise, compliment and encourage … Weakland typically heads in the other direction, voicing concern that things are moving too fast and continuing to promote change by restraining it. The logic for Weakland's stance is simple – the client is often surrounded by others who respond with reassurance and praise at the slightest sign of progress. Such advice, unfortunately, helps perpetuate rather than attenuate the problem.

Such caution is particularly necessary when there is an understandable, but premature, wish on the part of one or both partners to put the infidelity firmly into the past and, in the cliché, to 'move on'. Typically, it is the straying partner who urges this, resulting in the deceived partner finding it hard to admit that she is still overwhelmed by pain, loss and images of the infidelity. Her continuing reactions may feel to her like ungraciousness or vindictiveness, but failure to articulate them will produce a false situation for all concerned. If these persistent feelings *are* expressed, the straying partner may attempt to turn the tables by accusing the deceived partner of holding up progress, thus neatly transferring blame in an 'offender becomes victim' move. Such pressures add to any guilt or self-blame the deceived partner is already feeling, and need to be tactfully exposed and questioned by the counsellor, who should also make sure the persisting feelings are acknowledged, normalized and validated.

Pseudo-forgiveness

Another pressure frequently imposed by the offending partner and/or by others, or by the deceived partner on herself, is to forgive. Forgiveness is traditionally seen as a virtue in Western society, and an inability to forgive can be experienced as a failing. I spend time discussing the possible meanings of 'forgiveness', and in exploring the pressure of expectation it embodies, as well as identifying the prevalent overvaluation of expressions of regret and apology as somehow being enough magically to put things right. I sometimes quote the Monty Python sketch where two knights slaughter a castle's guards in order to rescue a captured maiden, discover it's the wrong castle, then leave the scene of carnage profusely and politely apologizing.

Walrond-Skinner (1998: 11–12) warns against premature, 'pseudo' forgiveness:

> Premature forgiveness is offered and/or accepted in the belief that the necessary work has been done to restore the system to its pre-conflictual relational capacity. Many games of 'let's pretend' serve to enable a relationship to continue but only on the basis of denying conflict and its consequences.

Sells and Hargreave, quoting Bass and Davis (1994), define a crucial danger of pseudo-forgiveness:

> There is an artificial forgiveness in which perpetrators maintain dominance and subtly promote a continuation of the injury. (1998: 25)

Where forgiveness is premature and unearned, the unfaithful partner is unlikely ever to know the full extent of the pain he caused, will rationalize the infidelity and will forgive *himself* too readily. He may return to the affair, or have other affairs. The deceived partner may find it hard or impossible to follow up the new beginning implied by her having forgiven, and the relationship is likely to founder sooner or later, with both partners feeling aggrieved and misunderstood.

Productive forgiveness

Some degree of *provisional* forgiveness is nevertheless necessary if the couple are to rescue the relationship. I define provisional forgiveness as a freely chosen decision to work towards rescuing the relationship despite the continuing pain of the infidelity. Full forgiveness has to be earned by the deceiving partner, not just expected or demanded, and it involves a *process* that can be facilitated by the counsellor if it has not already begun (Diblasio 1998: 77–94; Segal 2004: 100–6). It is important for both partners to recognize that when this process has been completed, there is still no guarantee that the relationship will survive, but that without it the relationship will have little chance.

Although I have counselled couples where forgiveness has turned out to be impossible, I have also counselled partners whose problems around infidelity might appear totally intractable to an outside observer, but who have managed to rescue their relationship. Below, I describe my work with such a couple, and give the sequence of the forgiveness and recovery conditions.

Helen was referred for individual counselling by her doctor, who indicated that Paul, her husband, might have mental health problems. Helen had just discovered that Paul, whose work as a sports trainer frequently took him away for quite long periods, had been having a long-term affair with a woman named Marie when training in the city where Marie lived.

Helen had emptied Paul's jacket pockets to take it for cleaning, and found a passionate love letter from Marie referring explicitly to her and Paul's sexual activities. As Marie's address and phone number headed her printed note paper, Helen immediately rang her in fury, but this conversation became a long talk that ended with both feeling baffled, incredulous and even some sense of womanly solidarity. Marie did not know of Helen's existence, and thought that she herself and Paul were about to live together with a view to getting married. Paul had told her a whole string of fantasy lies which she had believed, including that he was expecting a large legacy from his deceased grandfather, and that before going into sports training he had been a government secret agent penetrating terrorist groups, still occasionally called on in an advisory role, which explained his lengthy absences. He told Marie he had been forced to retire some years before because of a serious injury, and had been given a new identity. When Paul returned from the local office where he had been working that day, Helen had faced him with Marie's letter and told him of the phone conversation. He broke down in tears, admitted to the liaison and all that Marie had said, and shamefacedly volunteered that in addition to his relationship with Marie, he was having an affair with a woman colleague. He said he would immediately put an end to both affairs, begged Helen to forgive him and assured her it was she whom he really loved and wanted to be with. She found herself calm, beyond anger, and able to say that she needed time to absorb the situation and to think.

They had continued to live their everyday lives in an uneasy truce, although she had been in an agony of doubt when Paul went away to work. She consulted her doctor because she could not think of anyone else to turn to, but the doctor's suspecting Paul might have mental health problems had only added to her confusion and mixed feelings.

Helen took two sessions to tell the story of her discovery and its effects. She spoke of the conflict between her continuing love for Paul, which made her feel weak and foolish, and her awareness that his betrayals had been long term, extreme and deliberate. Above all, she said, she was in conflict about possible reasons for his actions. Was he mentally ill and therefore not responsible, or was he a cynical liar and betrayer who deserved divorce? She fretted about the exact details of his affairs. How had they started? How had he maintained them? What specific sexual acts had been involved? She felt she could not ask him these urgent questions, especially in the present fragile atmosphere of pretended normality. In any case, she was unsure whether her intense curiosity was appropriate. She was also worried by the lengthy periods when she felt calm, fearing that the relief of emotional numbing might not last, and that her suppressed fury might erupt destructively.

In later sessions, Helen told a wider narrative of her experience. Exceptions we focused upon were those clear-sighted moments when she called on her knowledge of Paul to rebut the idea that he had such severe mental health problems that he was not responsible for his choices. His skill in organizing his double or even triple life demonstrated that he was fully in control of his faculties. He obviously did not believe in the fantasies he had told Marie, so these were not the products of delusional illness, but elaborate lies designed to aggrandize him in Marie's eyes and account for his absences from her. But Helen could not reconcile what she now knew of his secret life with the man who for many years had always been so loving and considerate to her, and who had been seen by all their friends and relatives as a good and caring husband. She could not believe that his intense distress at being found out was feigned. Finally, she decided that Paul was not wicked, but very weak, and she recognized a temptation to feel protective towards him, which she knew was at odds with what her intelligence told her about the need to face the situation realistically.

Helen was adamant that she wanted to save her marriage. This surprised me, and went against my unexpressed opinion that this was likely to be a mistake given the degree of Paul's deliberate betrayal. However, my obligation was to take her wishes seriously and to assist her in attempting to fulfil them. I suggested couple counselling and Helen agreed, although we would have to take Paul's complicated work schedule into account when arranging sessions. We discussed the form and content of the initial joint session, and I outlined the conditions which my reading and experience suggested would need to be fulfilled for the marriage to have any chance of renewal.

Condition 1: All contact with the 'other' person must cease, and this will be monitored

At the first joint session, I welcomed Paul and explained the session's structure. When invited to give his version of events, Paul avoided my gaze and spoke very softly, with long pauses. He said that he very much wanted to rescue his marriage, and on looking back could not imagine how he had become embroiled in these other relationships. He hesitatingly described his affairs with Marie and with his colleague, and on the whole his account matched Helen's. I asked him what he valued in his marriage. He spoke of Helen's many good qualities and of the happiness he and she had experienced in the past. I asked what importance he attributed to trust, loyalty, fidelity and commitment, and he affirmed that he put a high value on these. I then asked whether, in his opinion, he had lived up to these values over the past couple of years. Paul at once admitted that he had not, but said that he was more than ready to change.

Questions inviting an unfaithful partner to state and reconnect with his/her values are an important prelude to the therapeutic process, as they create a positive launching pad for further work. By affirming his values, Paul was better able to accept my later challenges than if he had felt I was implicitly criticizing him from a superior moral position. Establishing common ground (the values) also freed me to be direct and uncompromising.

> Clients should be invited to explore whether or not they are living up to their own standards for the kind of man/woman or husband/wife they had always hoped to be. The implications of this personal appraisal are used to help clients become more aware that they are not only letting their partners down, but also ... letting themselves down. (Segal 2004: 103)

I told Paul that there were some important questions Helen wished to ask, and that since these would be very painful for her, we had agreed that I would put them to him on her behalf – would he accept this? He nodded, and repeated that he desperately wanted to save his marriage, and would do anything to make this possible. My questions, and Paul's answers, substituted for the usual second phase of a first session, and Helen continued to listen and take notes.

Had Paul made any contact with the other women since Helen's discovery of his infidelity? He looked surprised and shook his head. I reminded him that although he had assured Helen he would end the affairs, previously to this there had been a long period when Helen had been subject to consistent lies and deception. There were also two other women whose feelings had a right to be respected, and who deserved truthfulness. Was it enough simply to stop all contact abruptly? Or could he end the affairs decisively in a way that would reassure Helen, and also not leave the other women uncertain? He was at a loss for a reply, so following a procedure I had already cleared with Helen, I suggested a monitoring system that had been helpful to other couples in this situation. Would he be willing to write to both women to break off the relationships firmly, unmistakeably and decisively, stating that he had chosen to work on his marriage? Would he show the letters to Helen and re-draft them if she felt they fell short? And would he give them to Helen to post? Following this, would he take all possible steps to reassure Helen that he had not renewed these affairs or started others? Would he always let her get the post from the doormat and open any letters addressed to him that were not clearly bills or official letters? Would he make sure she saw all landline telephone bills, and explain any numbers she did not recognize? Would he change his pay-as-you-go mobile for one with a monthly billed account and show her the statements? Would he hand her his mobile at any time she asked so she could check any saved text messages? When he was away on training trips, would he tell her his hotel, agree for her to ring him at any time and show her the hotel receipt on his return? Would he make his credit card statements and bank statements available to her and explain any unclear entries? Would he undertake to accept any other checks she might request which reflected her absolute right not to trust his word, and to ensure she felt as safe as possible? And would he agree to these steps becoming routine for the rest of his life, without ever saying or implying that Helen ought to have got over her mistrust by then? Paul looked rather shocked at this list of radical conditions but Helen confirmed that she would find these steps reassuring, and he agreed to them. I undertook to type them out and send them to the couple as a document of agreement for Paul to sign, and Helen to witness.

Condition 2: If the betrayed partner wishes to know the whole truth, she/he has a right to this information

In Helen's individual sessions, I had undertaken to ask Paul, on her behalf, to reveal the unknown details she was fretting about. I had told her that, in my experience, the deceived partner's need to know exactly what happened is often felt as urgent, and is legitimate – total openness and full awareness in these circumstances is a necessary condition for the relationship's potential recovery. Offending partners need to accept that the wishes of their partner are paramount, and that after so much deceit, total honesty begins now.

Unlike Helen, some persons shy away from detailed knowledge, as it would be too painful for them. The counsellor should respect this rather than hypothesize 'denial' or any similar mechanism, and should not assume that at some future time the details must be revealed.

I asked Paul if I might question him about unanswered questions haunting Helen, which she felt needed to be clarified before any progress might be possible. Did he agree that she had a right to know these details? He agreed that she did. The rest of the session consisted of my drawing out information that Helen had told me she needed to know. This included how Paul had met Marie, how their relationship had developed, verification of the lies and fantasies he had told Marie, and the exact nature of their sexual acts. The other affair, with the colleague, was also elicited in full detail. It became a very painful session. Paul was deeply embarrassed, but answered all my questions, again speaking quietly and not meeting my gaze. Helen sat tensely, occasionally reacting with an intake of breath. At the end of the session, I asked her if there was anything more she needed to know and she said there was not. The session had over-run by 10 minutes, and after arranging the next appointment, the couple left, not speaking to each other.

Condition 3: The unfaithful partner should apologize with genuineness and a full recognition of the results of his/her infidelity

The second joint session, held several weeks later because of Paul's work commitments, began with Helen saying that she and Paul had been rather more relaxed together and there were even brief times when she forgot his infidelity. At other times, especially lying awake at night, she still continuously asked herself *why* he acted as he had. She managed to put this question to him one evening, but all he could say was that the relationships started almost unawares, and things then happened so fast he lost control. Paul nodded. I suspected that by using impersonal, distancing, 'it just happened' terminology, he was defensively attempting to deflect his actions away from personal choices and consequent responsibility for their results. In order to re-focus him on the nature and effects of his infidelity, and of his responsibility for those effects, I invited Helen to fully describe her reactions when she learned of the affairs and since. Drawing on my memory of what she had told me in our individual sessions, I asked her questions on how the revelation had affected her sense of who she was, her emotional stability, her peace of mind, her sleep, her work, her ability to understand people and life, and her faith in humanity. She also revealed how haunted and distressed she was by mental images of Paul and Marie having sex, even though she was glad she now knew the full details. Her responses revealed emotional numbing, hopelessness, a sense of betrayal, disbelief and even a perceived risk to her sanity. Her account built to a powerful and moving story of mental paralysis, confusion, disorientation and waking nightmare. While listening, Paul blushed deeply, shifting in his chair. He could not speak for some time, but finally looked at Helen and whispered, 'I'm so sorry.' I had the impression that for the first time, the full implications of his conduct and its effects on his wife had really come home to him.

Helen did not accept his apology – or at least not then, in the counselling room – but to my mind that was as well. The offending partner should not expect automatic acceptance and forgiveness. The apology is not a device to pacify the betrayed partner, but is given for its own sake to witness a genuinely changed attitude.

Condition 4: The partners agree on steps towards a renewed but different relationship

There should be no implication, explicit or implied, that the effects of infidelity have been 'healed' or that the relationship can ever wholly return to what was previously thought of as normal. There are two parallel stories being formulated by the partners at this stage of counselling: the infidelity story and the hope-for-the-future story. The counsellor's task is to assist the couple to begin building and living the new story *alongside* the history of infidelity and pain. At the same time, the counsellor should be alert to, and respect, when the infidelity story reasserts itself, and the couple need to know that this does not signify failure or a retrograde step. The infidelity story remains valid; the hope and aim is that it will gradually fade and become less dominant.

Positive aspects of the couple's past may be called on as exceptions and a source of hope and continuity, but the past may to an extent be tainted as it ultimately led to the infidelity. 'Future' exceptions are important and need to be worked towards, and I find solution-focused practices useful here, particularly the identification of small, achievable steps to promote renewal which can be discussed, tried out and then built on. As with couples who are renegotiating their relationship after problems other than infidelity, these steps may include small but significant changes such as deciding on pleasurable everyday activities together which have long been neglected, or deciding to try new ones. Renewal of the couple's sex life may present considerable problems, and patience and time are usually needed before the associations and images of sex outside the relationship can be overcome. Even holding hands again can be fraught with disturbing feelings. In contrast, some couples may experience a passionate return to full sexual activity, unexpectedly and distressingly followed by inhibition and a falling away. An unhurried step-by-step progression, with each step feeling comfortable before the next is tried, can work well.

Often, the small, achievable steps become less important in themselves than the cooperative effort of regularly agreeing them then reviewing their success. Once this is under way, the counsellor is less and less needed, and counselling can usually end well before complete reconciliation has occurred. However, some couples find it helpful to return to counselling for 'top-up' sessions, as recovery and rebuilding can be a very uneven process, with setbacks likely.

I had tentatively planned to introduce the identification of future exceptions into the third joint session with Paul and Helen, but the day before their appointment, Helen left a message saying they had decided not to continue with counselling. I was rather dismayed, and wondered whether the extreme nature of Paul's infidelity might after all have led Helen to change her mind about maintaining the marriage. But about two years later, when shopping in a local supermarket, I noticed Paul and Helen together at a checkout, absorbed in unloading their trolley and paying for their shopping.

DISCUSSION POINTS

Consider these questions, if possible in discussion with a colleague:

1. What are the main sources of people's beliefs and attitudes about:

    (a) norms of sexual fidelity?
    (b) the nature of forgiveness?

2. By what specific means do these sources influence people's beliefs and attitudes?
3. How do these sources interact?
4. In what ways do they differ in contrasting societies and cultures?
5. How possible is it for individuals to stand back from these influences and form independent opinions and conclusions?
6. Can sexual infidelity ever be fully forgiven?
7. Can trust ever be fully restored when infidelity has occurred?
8. What do your conclusions on the above imply for your work with couples?

13
VIOLENCE AND ABUSE

When planning the workshops on which this book is based, my first thought was to exclude the topic of violence and abuse altogether. Participants were to be individual-trained counsellors with no experience of counselling couples, who were going to find it pretty challenging to learn how to organize couple sessions, and to assist two persons rather than one to address their problems. Why should they be invited to consider this most dangerous of situations, more properly the province of therapists with specialist training? I was inclined to leave well alone, and to advise workshop members to do the same.

However, when I received the forms I had sent out in advance to ask what topics members would like me to include, violence was mentioned by a substantial minority. I had to reconsider. I still wanted to warn of the dangers and to discourage participants from taking on couples where there was violence, but perhaps they needed a resource plan should the issue arise unexpectedly. I also recognized from my own experience that in certain limited, very clearly defined circumstances, where violence had been spontaneous, minimal, genuinely regretted and unrepeated, a non-specialist counsellor might be able to assist the couple, aided by frequent supervision. This chapter embodies these ideas and principles.

I do not distinguish between abuse and violence, since both words indicate physical or psychological attack, and 'abuse' does not necessarily imply sexual assault. Some couples enjoy mutually agreed sado-masochistic sexual play, but this chapter refers to violence imposed by one partner on the other.

STATISTICS

A report by the UK Department of Health in 2000, based on Home Office crime surveys and circulated to a wide range of professionals such as doctors, social workers and teachers, indicated that domestic violence occurs in all ethnic groups and all income groups, ranging from psychological abuse such as threats, control of movement, denial of privacy and destruction of property, to varying degrees of physical abuse including murder and manslaughter – there is an average of two deaths per week from domestic violence. The report gave 771,000 as the total number of people attacked in domestic violence incidents that year, with women making up 74% of victims and men, 26%. These figures almost certainly under-represented the actual incidence, since domestic violence and abuse are under-reported, especially attacks on young men in domestic settings. Also, on average, a woman is assaulted 35 times by a partner or ex-partner before reporting this to the police.

More recent Home Office surveys indicate an approximate one-third overall decline in the amount of domestic violence over the past 10 years but a greater proportion of domestic violence with male victims, especially young men (Dewar Research 2009).

It is difficult to draw clear conclusions from these figures as the method of estimating them varied. Pre-2000 surveys are based on reported crime alone, whereas later surveys have supplements based on interviews of about 22,500 people selected as representative of the population as a whole, and it is these supplements which clearly indicate previous under-reporting of male victims. This suggests that men have consistently failed to report domestic abuse when they are the victims.

These more recent figures imply that the conventional assumption that domestic violence is *overwhelmingly* committed by men needs to be treated with a degree of caution, at least as far as the UK is concerned. Despite this caveat, it is important to note that in the UK, men are the majority perpetrators by a significant margin; in 2006/7, about 20% more women were attacked by men than men attacked by women (Dewar Research 2009). Statistics from other countries certainly indicate a risk factor according to gender; the American Institute on Domestic Violence (2001) estimates that in the USA at least 85% of domestic violence victims are women and the World Health Organization (2005) estimates that internationally the figure is 71%.

According to the UK Department of Health, the most common forms of physical violence are pushing, grabbing, kicking, slapping and punching. The frequency and intensity of attacks vary, but if unchecked, violence tends to escalate. When violence becomes frequent and repeated, well over half of victims are badly injured. Injuries to men are generally less serious, less frequent and made in less intimidating circumstances than injuries to women, and the injuries inflicted by female partners on male partners more often arise from self-defence than do injuries inflicted by men on women.

It is clear that at some point most counsellors are likely to meet the issue of partner-on-partner violence, and that the victims are most likely to be women attacked by men. For convenience of reference, I shall refer to women as the recipients of violence from now on, but this must not be taken to mean that violence to men is less important or should be taken less seriously by counsellors. I use the word 'victim' for convenience of reference despite its unfortunate overtones of passivity.

AN OVER-RIDING POLICY OF SAFETY

Unless the counsellor has specialist training in this area, he should beware of continuing with the couple, and his general aim should be to withdraw, while maximizing the safety of all concerned, including the victim, her children, the counselling organization and himself. The only possible exception is where violence has been untypical, minimal and perhaps one-off, sincerely regretted, and not repeated for a significant length of time.

Violence is different from any other situation met in counselling. It has the potential to put the victim, the counsellor and other people in the counselling organization (such as receptionists) at risk, and this is why it involves different priorities than other problems. Counsellors who, like me, have led relatively secure and sheltered lives may not be fully aware of the extreme nature and devastating consequences of domestic violence, and it is salutary to have one's eyes opened. When presenting workshops on couple counselling, I recommend that participants see Gary Oldman's (1997) uncompromising film *Nil by Mouth*, which is obtainable on DVD. The film is based on incidents Oldman remembers from his childhood in south-east London, where there was a subculture of macho criminality, and the film portrays extreme domestic violence with unflinching realism, including a husband beating up his wife so savagely that she has a miscarriage. Colleagues who have seen this film tell me it has left them horrified and shaken – these were my reactions as well.

Since research has shown that women are usually subject to a great many violent acts before they dare to report them to the police, the same presumably applies to their seeking counselling. Since a violent man will resent his partner's having any kind of help, her coming to counselling will put the woman in even greater danger, and this needs to be clearly understood by anyone and everyone who might inadvertently add to this danger. Reception and administrative staff will already have been briefed to keep confidence, for example by never letting anyone outside the immediate organization know details of who is attending for counselling. However, when violence is known or suspected, this standing policy should be reinforced by a specific reminder, since violent men can be devious and convincing when attempting to discover if, when and where their partners are receiving any kind of support.

Violence is a crime, and it may be necessary to involve the police and/or Social Services at some point. Keeping confidentiality is secondary to ensuring safety for all concerned, including the victim's children, and any well-meant temptation to become 'the hero who liberates' (Anderson 1997: 32) should be recognized and resisted.

Once violence is suspected or revealed, experienced counsellors as well as those new to couple work and/or untrained in counselling persons who are violent, should immediately seek their supervisor's advice on how to proceed. This is not to advocate a panic reaction with immediate refusal to continue; the counsellor has a responsibility not to let the couple vanish from sight, since this would endanger the victim further and also pre-empt an opportunity for promoting change. The following guidelines should assist counsellors to deal with immediate dilemmas arising from the situation.

When severe and/or repeated violence is revealed at first contact

It is highly unlikely that a couple where one partner uses extreme and/or repeated violence will agree between themselves to seek counselling. If this unlikely scenario does occur, the counsellor should make it clear that this particular problem is beyond her competence, and direct the couple to where they can receive appropriate help. The counsellor's supervisor should be consulted about such local resources if they are not known, and the couple referred on.

If a victim of violence makes initial contact either with or without her partner's knowledge, she should be referred to a specialist in domestic violence, even if this means asking her to make contact again to allow the counsellor time to seek information on the availability and contact details of such a service.

WHEN VIOLENCE IS REVEALED

When violence is suspected or revealed in a joint session

Sometimes acts of violence may not come to light until counselling is under way, but extreme violence is unlikely to be disclosed in a joint session, and if violence is acknowledged at all, it is likely to be understated. For their own protection, victims are likely to have developed skills in concealing or denying the degree and extent of the violence, and of course the perpetrator will almost certainly conceal it. It is very difficult to distinguish between the minimizing or concealment of extreme violence and situations where violence has indeed been minimal as yet. Once alerted to the possibility, the counsellor, even if she believes the violence is minimal, should *not* pursue the matter in the session but, possibly to the temporary disappointment of the victim and relief of the perpetrator, take the stated degree of the violence at face value, say this is a subject to return to, and focus on other aspects of the relationship. At the end of the session, the counsellor should remind the couple that both joint and individual sessions are usually held, and an early appointment should then be made for the person the counsellor thinks may be experiencing violence. In order to protect a woman victim as far as possible, the counsellor might quite casually say 'Ladies first, perhaps?' and make the appointment. An individual appointment must also be made for her partner, to be held at a later date than hers. The supervisor should be consulted immediately and any further sessions closely supervised and monitored, with safety the priority.

When violence is revealed in an individual session

When the partner who might be at risk comes to her individual session, assurances that what she says will not be revealed to her partner are particularly important, and although confidentiality will already have been stressed at the previous session, this assurance should be repeated firmly and unequivocally at the beginning of the individual session. The issue of violence should then be brought into the open and the woman asked to comment and elaborate on the clues picked up by the counsellor in the joint session. These apparent clues may have been mistaken, but if violence is indeed an issue, the woman should be encouraged to expand her story by means of tactfully phrased questions in response to her answers, encouraging her to describe in her own words the events leading to violence, the violence itself and what usually follows. Where details are expressed vaguely or with softening/excusing language, it is important to ask for clarification, and to name the violence, rather than leaving description fuzzy: 'You said in the session with Darren that he sometimes shoves you, and that once he slapped you. I'd like to ask you a bit more about that, if that's OK? ... So, what kind of situation leads to Darren shoving you? Can you give me a couple of examples? ... How often does he shove you, and how long has that been going on? ... Are they just little pushes or are they really hard? Do you ever lose balance, fall over? ... What about when he slapped you? I'm not sure what that means ... So by 'slap' you mean not a light blow, but a hard punch? Has he only done this once, or have there been other times?'

Such questioning needs to be extremely sensitive and low-key, not as interrogatory as the above truncated and out-of-context examples might suggest. Male counsellors should be particularly careful in this respect so as not to echo anything like the male-dominated situation the woman faces at home. The woman may become upset and tearful, and pauses for her to recover will be necessary. None of this should deflect the counsellor from pursuing the topic until a full picture has emerged. Sometimes this process of detailed story-telling will assist the victim to see the situation clearly for the first time, as her description builds and the reality becomes unclouded by defensive justifications or self-blaming. Variations of 'He hit me, but I deserved it' are frequent responses by women whose male partners have succeeded in making them internalize responsibility for the violence.

Telling the full story of the violence and its history does not always free the victim from rationalizations which have allowed her to maintain that the man loves her and is acting under justified provocation. Many such rationalizations are powerfully supported by socially and culturally derived attitudes and beliefs that at some point in counselling will need to be exposed and examined. Even in this first individual session, when eliciting the full story is the priority, one or more of these rationalizations may emerge. A gentle questioning of these ideas and/or a suggestion that the woman might find it helpful to discuss how she came to believe them can sow the seeds of growth for revised attitudes. Such respectfully framed questions can produce cognitive change, though this may need several further individual sessions. Exceptions emerge when the victim begins to recognize that some of her rationalizations do not hold up, and perhaps that before counselling began, she had already resisted the violence, even if in small and uncertain ways. And, of course, many women do not rationalize – they resent and fear their partner's violence, know it is unjustified, feel trapped and long for a way out of the situation. In all instances, exceptions based on the woman's self-preservation and awareness of the violence's unacceptability should be elicited, drawn out in detail, and their meaning explored in terms of resistance, fortitude, self-valuing and initiatives for safety. 'Exceptions' focused on the perpetrator, such as occasions when he was less violent than usual, are *not* helpful in this context. They diminish the seriousness of the reality. However, they may be appropriate when counselling perpetrators of minimal and regretted violence, should this be undertaken (see below).

'Received truths'

Examples of socially constructed 'received truths' excusing or minimizing violence, some of which may be believed by men as well as women, include:

- It's a woman's role to please her man.
- It's a woman's duty to forgive.
- Femininity is bound up with being tolerant.
- Women with a history of violent relationships invite/send signals to violent men.
- People who stay with a violent partner are weak and feeble.
- He can't help it, because his father was violent to his mother.
- He said he was sorry so he will change from now on.
- Love is all that matters and I know he loves me despite the violence.
- He's insecure.
- He's highly sensitive.
- It's my fault because I wind him up/fail him/had an affair.
- The real problem is his stress at work/drinking/drug-taking.

The victim's view of the perpetrator's attitude

The victim should be asked how the perpetrator views his acts of violence. The following points are crucially important, and can help to determine whether or not further joint sessions will be held:

1 Has the perpetrator already committed to ceasing violence?
2 If so, was this commitment made a significant length of time ago, and has he kept to the promise since?
3 If 'yes' to both the above, do you feel totally and unreservedly safe about future joint sessions where no details of the violence will be held back?

'No' to any of the questions indicates that holding further joint sessions would be unwise, and the counsellor's aim must change from couple work to assisting the victim on an individual basis, preferably by referral to a colleague experienced in counselling for violence. It may then be best for the counsellor to withdraw, after holding the arranged individual session with the perpetrator. The victim can be protected by the counsellor's explaining regretfully at the end of that session that the problems are beyond her experience and competence, and that because of this she will no longer be able to counsel the couple.

Towards the end of the session, it can be helpful to ask the victim a 'future exception' question such as, 'What would life be like for you if he was able to stop himself being violent?' (The conditional form of the sentence – 'would' rather than 'will' and 'if' rather than 'when' – is important, as change is by no means assured.) Her answer can be drawn out in detail so that images of life without violence become firmly established in her imagination. The next question might be, 'Taking into account all that you have told me about how he treats you, how realistic is any hope that this might come about?' Victims of extreme violence are more likely to be pessimistic about the future, unless they are still holding firmly to emotionally protective rationalizations. Victims of early-stage violence may express some degree of optimism, and this is not necessarily delusional – it depends on the wider circumstances and details of the relationship. A sincerely regretted, partly held-back, one-off blow is very different from a long history of deliberate and sustained abuse.

The victim's promotion of her safety

In all instances, the next question should invite the victim to consider what she might do to maximize, or at best to ensure, her safety. Asking 'What would he have to do from now on for you to be safe?' (note – not *feel* safe) can encourage a realistic perspective and consideration of possibilities for action. According to circumstances, these might include further joint and individual counselling; leaving the perpetrator; staying with him, at least for the moment, if there would otherwise be a danger of increased violence. Information should be given concerning local and national support services for victims of domestic violence, and if the woman feels she is at immediate risk, contact details for the nearest refuge. It is no part of a therapist's role to go beyond the wishes of the person being counselled, and if the victim's response or decision seems unwise, or even dangerous, no pressure should be put on her to change her mind, though the counsellor does have a responsibility to invite her to consider the consequences.

The victim should be consulted on whether she would like referral to another counsellor, whom she could see without her partner's knowledge, preferably a colleague trained and experienced in working with victims of violence. She should be advised to tell her doctor of her situation. At the end of the session, assurances should again be given that the partner will not be told what the victim has said. Another individual appointment should be made for her. It is also essential to hold the individual appointment already made for her partner, since not doing so might arouse suspicion that the victim has disclosed the violence, with consequent heightened risk to her.

Children's safety

If there is a present or potential danger of violence to the couple's children, the counsellor has a clear and unequivocal duty of protection which transcends confidentiality. The victim should be reminded or made aware of this and tactfully but firmly informed that unless she herself undertakes to contact Social Services or the police about the situation, the counsellor has a legal duty to do so (at least in the UK). It should be made clear that protection and safety of the children are the immediate and main considerations. No action should be precipitate, however, and all precautions must be taken to prevent the disclosure to officialdom increasing risk to any of the parties concerned. The procedure and timing for the disclosure needs to be discussed and agreed with the victim.

The individual session with the perpetrator

The counsellor should discuss with her supervisor how to manage the individual session with the perpetrator – it is likely to be difficult. My own practice is to run this session very much as a 'listening and checking-out' occasion, giving the man an opportunity to describe his view of the relationship and its history, and I do not mention violence if he does not raise it himself. If he does, I do not challenge his account of its extent and nature, although as I describe below, I do invite him to say more about what he *has* disclosed. The man may ask what his partner has said about what goes on in the relationship. If so, I remind him that individual sessions in couple counselling are confidential (I have already said this in the joint session) then ask for his own views on the relationship. I cannot, of course, prevent him from subsequently pressurizing his partner to reveal what she has said, possibly with threats if she refuses, but she will know that no information about her session has been revealed and will be able to dissimulate if necessary.

An individual session with the perpetrator will leave many questions unanswered, and the counsellor should keep an open mind as to how far the person has been open and sincere. Perhaps he has, but on the other hand, he may be skilled in concealment and the presentation of apparent innocence, naivety or regret. If he does admit to violence, he may exaggerate the circumstances leading to it – 'She just kept nagging on and on at me like she always does, and it was doing my head in, and I just flipped' – and minimize the violence itself – 'I just gave her a little push to get past her and she threw herself on the floor yelling blue murder'. In some instances, the perpetrator may be anticipating legal proceedings where solicitors might (with the full support of the law) insist on the counsellor's notes being made available to the court, and he may tailor his account accordingly. The account already given by the victim in her individual session will be a balancing factor for the counsellor against this kind of biased narrative, but obviously the counsellor should not contradict the perpetrator by quoting what his partner said! Instead, patient questions aimed at eliciting a more detailed and accurate story may be fruitful, especially in instances when the perpetrator's distorted account is not deliberately dishonest, but defensively self-deceiving. A more detailed and rounded account will contain details that contradict the 'innocent' or minimized story and reveal its limitations and inadequacy. These aspects will assist the counsellor to gain a more accurate picture, more nearly matching the actual events, but more importantly, they will provide self-generated material for the perpetrator to recognize, reflect on and absorb. If by the end of the session his account has expanded to include that his 'little push' was rather more than that because he is a large, powerful man and his partner is quite small; and if the expanded account includes that in falling, she hit her head on the coffee table; and if his characterizing of her reaction moves from 'yelling blue murder' to 'crying and protesting', it may just be that some basis for future therapy is being established.

Ideally, the protection of the victim is best achieved by encouraging the perpetrator to acknowledge his actions and their results, to take full responsibility for them, to apologize with sincerity, to commit to stopping all violence at once and forever, and to agree to long-term monitoring to ensure he does not backslide. In these respects, therapy for violence is similar to that for one-sided infidelity. If the couple's counselling began at a point when the perpetrator had already committed to ending violence, and he has kept to this for a significant length of time, an approach similar to that outlined in Chapter 12 concerning infidelity may be adapted for this situation, consisting of: a process of commitment to end the violence permanently and for this to be monitored; all details of the violence to be fully told; a sincere apology to be made with no expectation of a right to forgiveness; an exploration of the perpetrator's potential to develop and internalize a respectful attitude to his former victim. No optimistic assumptions should be made about this process and the counsellor should have frequent supervision.

Michael White's paper 'The conjoint therapy of men who are violent and the women they live with' (1989: 101–6) and Alan Jenkins' book *Invitations to Responsibility* (1990) give excellent guidance, for experienced counsellors, on narrative practice with persons who have been violent. The novice couple counsellor working with a couple where the perpetrator is sincerely regretful will find these texts useful, but reading should not be taken as adequate preparation for this work or be a substitute for attending workshops or other forms of training around the issue.

Preparation and monitoring

Where violence has been brief, regretted and not repeated, the perpetrator's further acknowledgement, apology and commitment to non-violence can be prepared for in his individual sessions, then be the subject of a joint session where he signs a document confirming his commitment never to repeat violence. Individual sessions with both partners should still be interspersed with joint sessions, since situations change and develop, and either partner may at some later point wish to raise issues they are not happy for the other to know about. The couple's own monitoring of the cessation of violence may be assisted by the therapist in counselling sessions that are increasingly separated in time, until the victim feels that counselling is no longer needed. A clear option to return (at short notice if necessary) should be given.

When there has been long-term and/or severe violence

Where extreme and/or long-term violence is disclosed by the perpetrator, he should be referred to an agency or therapist specializing in work with people who are or have been violent. Local availability of such specialist counselling is uneven, and the counsellor's supervisor may need to be consulted on where it can be obtained.

Let me say it again – inexperienced counsellors *should not* risk the dangers of trying to counsel persons with a long and/or unrepented history of violence. If the perpetrator does not disclose the violence, the counsellor may have to accept that only the victim can be helped, at least for the present.

HELPFUL ASSUMPTIONS

From his analysis of a quoted example of couple therapy, Nichols extrapolates five assumptions that should underpin the counsellor's responses to an account of violence (1988: 202). Holding these assumptions firmly in mind has helped me when faced with the task of negotiating a path through the defensive and sometimes distorted stories told by individuals or couples where violence is a factor in their relationship, and I have often found it useful to make these assumptions clear to persons at an appropriate point, so there is no uncertainty about my position. Italics indicate where I have extended or slightly amended Nichols' text.

1   The abuser alone is responsible for the violence. The victim cannot cause or eliminate the violence, *and should not be expected to take responsibility for doing so.*
2   Violence is learned. *It has nothing to do with innate or unalterable tendencies or with genetic inheritance.* The abuser learned to be violent, *probably* primarily in his family of origin *but also through social and cultural pressures, especially peer group norms.* If the abuser learned to be violent, he can also learn to be non-violent.
3   Provocation does not equal justification. There are always alternatives to violence. There are no circumstances under which violence between *partners* is legitimate.
4   Violence is harmful to all family members, including the abuser. Damage to the victim may be obvious. Damage to the children may be less obvious but equally serious. Violence is illegal, and the abuser can be arrested, and jailed if convicted.
5   Once violence has occurred in a relationship, it will most likely continue *and escalate* unless changes are made.

These principles imply modification of some of the therapeutic practices discussed earlier in this book. 'Violence' and 'abuse' should never be used as externalizing definitions (such as, 'When did violence enter the relationship?') because this would diminish emphasis on the perpetrator's responsibility and capacity for choice. Michael White suggests that when the couple's situation involves any form of oppression, then externalizing is best used in relation to 'the attitudes and beliefs that appear to compel the violence and those strategies that maintain persons in their subjugation ...' (1989: 12). Examples might be: 'How did temptation to be violent overcome your better nature?', 'What beliefs and ideas influenced your bullying?', 'When did the idea that men own women take root in you?', 'What's the difference between over-protectiveness and domination?'

Normalization and reassurance should be used sparingly, if at all. The counsellor needs to take a firm position that abusive violence is in no way acceptable in loving relationships, although it may have become the norm, and he needs to bear in mind that ending violence is difficult and uncertain. Even-handed attitudes to couple conflict should also be put aside where violence and abuse occur. In many other situations, both partners will have contributed to the couple's problems (although perhaps not always equally) and both will need to work towards reversing the situation, whereas ending violence is wholly the perpetrator's responsibility, no matter what the ostensible provocation.

LEARNING EXERCISE (60 MINUTES)

The exercise may be undertaken either individually or in pairs.

- Refer to this chapter to create the following memory-jogger notes for possible future use, each on a single page:

1. A flow-chart summary framework for the first individual session with a person whom the counsellor thinks may be the victim of violence or abuse. Include (a) where violence is disclosed to the counsellor during the session and (b) where no violence is disclosed.

2. A flow-chart summary framework for an individual session with a perpetrator who has not previously revealed that he acted violently. Include (a) where he admits to violence during the session and (b) where he does not admit to violence.

3. A framework for subsequent joint sessions where the perpetrator has admitted to genuinely minimal violence, apologized unreservedly to the victim, committed to change, and already kept to that commitment for a significant amount of time.

APPENDICES

APPENDIX 1: MEMORY-JOGGER FOR FIRST JOINT SESSION (PHOTOCOPIABLE)

All times are approximate

1. *Opening moments* *(10 minutes)*

   - First names OK?
   - Confidentiality.
   - Frequency and possible number of sessions.
   - Couple details.
   - Urgent immediate issues? If yes, devote whole session. If no, go to 3.

2. *If necessary, address immediate urgent issues* *(60 minutes)*

3. *Set up the session* *(5 minutes)*

   - Agree structure of 4/5 below.
   - Agree who goes first.
   - Give out notebooks and pencils.

4/5. *Talk with each in turn, taking notes* *(15 minutes each)*

   - A speaks, B listens, takes notes. Elicit full effects of problem.
   - B comments on A's account.
   - B speaks, A listens, takes notes. Elicit full effects of problem.
   - A comments on B's account.

6. *Summarize, and name the problem* *(5 minutes)*

   - Summarize, using the persons' own words.
   - Negotiate an externalized, non-blaming name for the problem.

7. *Normalize the problem and establish commitment to continue* *(5 minutes)*

   - Reassure realistically (if appropriate).
   - Make sure the couple wish to continue.

8. *Explore one or two exceptions to the problem* *(15 minutes)*

   - Use implicit exceptions if possible.
   - If none, elicit exceptions by questions.
   - Ask questions to establish/explore significance of exceptions.

9. *Conclude the session* *(5 minutes)*

   - Affirm purpose of the session.
   - Negotiate an exception – noticing task.
   - Arrange next session – joint, or first of two individual sessions?

© *Couple Counselling: A Practical Guide* by Martin Payne (2010, SAGE)

APPENDIX 2:   MEMORY-JOGGER FOR SUBSEQUENT JOINT SESSIONS (PHOTOCOPIABLE)

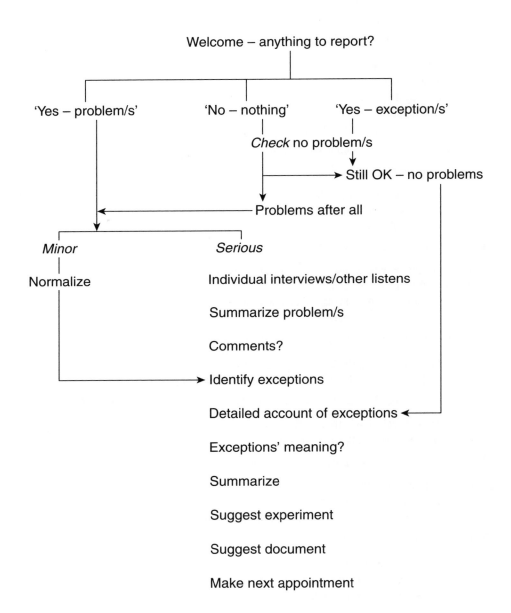

APPENDIX 3:   MEMORY-JOGGER FOR SUBSEQUENT INDIVIDUAL SESSIONS (PHOTOCOPIABLE)

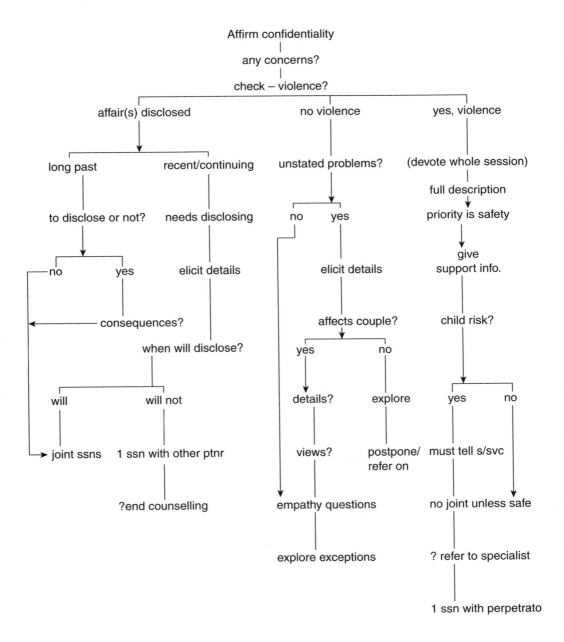

© *Couple Counselling: A Practical Guide* by Martin Payne (2010, SAGE)

FOLLOW-UP INFORMATION

SUGGESTED READING

I hope this short list of texts and other sources will be useful to readers who would like to learn more about narrative therapy. In some instances, I have stated the most easily obtainable source rather than where the text first appeared, for example where a paper in a journal has been reprinted as a chapter in a book. The recommended texts take narrative therapy further than this present book, but for the most part they are less demanding than those written for experienced narrative therapists.

INTRODUCTORY BOOKS ON NARRATIVE THERAPY

- Morgan, Alice (2000) *What is Narrative Therapy?* (Adelaide: Dulwich Centre Publications)
  Alice Morgan's book describes narrative therapy clearly and concisely, illustrating basic theory with practice examples.

- Payne, Martin (2006) *Narrative Therapy: an Introduction for Counsellors*, 2nd edition. (London: Sage)
  My book, written specifically for counsellors rather than family therapists, presents narrative theory in detail and discusses many examples of practice. One chapter is partly devoted to couple counselling, with different examples from those used in this present book.

Books by the originators of narrative therapy

- White, Michael and Epston, David (1990) *Narrative Means to Therapeutic Ends.* (New York: Norton)
  This seminal text includes a chapter on externalizing the problem, with some delightful examples of work with children, and a comprehensive chapter on therapeutic documents.

- White, Michael (1995) *Re-authoring Lives: Interviews and Essays.* (Adelaide: Dulwich Centre Publications)
  This is possibly Michael White's most accessible book. It covers a wide range of theory and practice including the narrative perspective, counselling for abuse, and a follow-up from his previous writing about therapeutic documents. His conversational tone when interviewed is particularly appealing.

- White, Michael (2007) *Maps of Narrative Practice.* (New York: Norton)
  A closely written exposition of White's most recent thinking on core narrative therapy practices.

Texts on narrative therapy with couples

- Ziegler, Philip and Heller, Tobey (2001) *Re-creating Partnership.* (New York: Norton)
  Although solution-focused therapy is the main model presented in this engaging and imaginative book, it is integrated with narrative ideas and practices.

- Freedman, Jill and Combs, Gene (2002) *Narrative Therapy with Couples – and a Whole Lot More!* (Adelaide: Dulwich Centre Publications)
  The first, long section of this book is about couple therapy, and is particularly effective in relating it to the social context.

- Doan, Robert E. (2004) 'Who really wants to sleep with the medical model?', Ch. 9 in Shelley Green and Douglas Flemons (eds), *Quickies: the Handbook of Brief Sex Therapy.* (New York: Norton)
  Doan's chapter contrasts narrative therapy with models that pathologize persons. The whole book is well worth reading, as many of the brief solution-focused practices described by the other contributors can be integrated with a narrative approach.

The following two texts are discussed in Chapter 8 of this present book:

- Epston, David (1993) 'Internalized other questioning with couples: the New Zealand version', Ch. 9 in Stephen Gilligan and Reece Price (eds), *Therapeutic Conversations.* (New York: Norton)

- White, Michael (2004) 'Narrative practice, couple therapy and conflict dissolution', Ch. 1 in *Narrative Practice and Exotic Lives.* (Adelaide: Dulwich Centre Publications)

Website and journal

The Dulwich Centre website (www.dulwichcentre.com.au) is a superb resource for all aspects of narrative therapy. It includes an online library and Michael White's workshop notes, and there is a regular, free, online newsletter.

Dulwich Centre Publications publishes the *International Journal of Narrative Therapy and Community Work,* obtainable from the Centre or from local representatives in many countries, who are listed on the Centre's website.

Training

The Dulwich Centre offers a wide range of conferences, courses and workshops in Adelaide, including a diploma in narrative therapy: for details, see www.dulwich centre.com.au

Putting 'narrative therapy training' or 'narrative therapy workshops' into Google produces a plethora of information on narrative therapy training in many countries.

In the UK, the following organizations regularly offer workshops and courses run by family therapists/clinical psychologists:

- Plymouth – Mark Hayward: www.narrativetraining.co.uk

- Manchester – Hugh Fox, Centre for Narrative Practice: www.narrativepractice.com

As this book is in preparation, these and other narrative therapy centres in the UK and the Republic of Ireland are establishing the UK Institute for Narrative Therapy: www.theinstituteofnarrativetherapy.com

Author contact

I am always pleased to hear from readers of my books: martin.payne@which.net (website: homepages.which.net/~martin.payne).

REFERENCES

American Institute on Domestic Violence (2001) 'Statistics on Domestic Violence'. www.aidv-usa.com. statistics

Anderson, Harlene (1997) *Conversation, Language and Possibilities: a Postmodern Approach to Therapy.* New York: Basic Books.

Angus, Lynn and McLeod, John (eds) (2004) *The Handbook of Narrative and Psychotherapy.* Thousand Oaks, CA: Sage.

Bass, Ellen and Davis, Laura (1994) *The Courage to Heal.* New York: Harper Perennial.

Bayard, Rohert T. and Bayard, Jean (1982) *Help! I've Got a Teenager.* Watford: Exning Publications.

Beck, Aaron (1988) *Love Is Never Enough.* London: Penguin Books.

Beck, Aaron (1989) *Cognitive Therapy and the Emotional Disorders.* London: Penguin Books.

Bruner, Jerome (1990) *Acts of Meaning.* Cambridge, MA: Harvard University Press.

Buzan, Tony and Buzan, Barry (2006) *The Mind Map Book.* London: BBC Publications.

Cameron, Deborah (2007) *The Myth of Mars and Venus.* Oxford: Oxford University Press.

Carlson, Jay (2004) 'Brief integrative therapy for individuals and couples', in Stephen Madigan (ed.), *Therapy from the Outside In.* Vancouver: Yaletown Family Therapy. pp. 73–86.

De Shazer, Steve (1988) *Clues: Investigating Solutions in Brief Therapy.* New York: Norton.

Diblasio, Frederick A. (1998) 'The use of a decision-based forgiveness intervention within inter-generational family therapy', *Journal of Family Therapy* 20 (1): 77–94.

Dewar Research (2009) 'UK Government Statistics on Domestic Violence'. www.dewar4research.org

Durrant, Michael and White, Cheryl (eds) (1990) *Ideas for Therapy with Sexual Abuse.* Adelaide: Dulwich Centre Publications.

Epston, David (1993) 'Internalizing other questioning with couples: the New Zealand version', in Stephen Gilligan and Reese Price (eds) *Therapeutic Conversations.* New York: Norton.

Epston, David and White, Michael (1992) *Experience, Contradiction, Narrative and Imagination.* Adelaide: Dulwich Centre Publications.

Falcof, Nicky (2007) *Ball and Chain.* London: Fusion Press.

Fransella, Fay, Dalton, Peggy and Weselby, Grant (2007) 'Personal construct therapy', in Windy Dryden (ed.), *Dryden's Handbook of Individual Therapy.* London: Sage.

Fraser, Michelle (2006) 'Outsider-witness practices in developing community with women who have experienced child sexual assault', *International Journal of Narrative Therapy and Community Work* 3: 52–8.

Freedman, Jill and Combs, Gene (2002) *Narrative Therapy with Couples – and a Whole Lot More!* Adelaide: Dulwich Centre Publications.

George, Ivan, Iveson, Chris and Ratner, Harvey (1999) *From Problem to Solution,* 2nd edn. London: Brief Therapy Press.

Gilligan, Stephen and Price, Reese (eds) *Therapeutic Conversations.* New York: Norton.

Gray, John (1992) *Men Are From Mars, Women Are From Venus*. New York: HarperCollins.

Green, Shelley and Flemons, Douglas (eds) (2004) *Quickies: the Handbook of Brief Sex Therapy*. New York: Norton.

Jenkins, Alan (1990) *Invitations to Responsibility*. Adelaide: Dulwich Centre Publications.

Mann, Sue and Jessie (2001) 'Jessie's story: acknowledging the work involved in addressing the effects of sexual abuse', in Cheryl White (ed.), *Working with the Stories of Women's Lives*. Adelaide: Dulwich Centre Publications.

Mann, Sue (2004) 'Deconstructing love in the context of sexual abuse', *International Journal of Narrative Therapy and Community Work* 3: 3–11.

Mann, Sue and Russell, Shona (2002) 'Narrative ways of working with women survivors of childhood sexual abuse', *International Journal of Narrative Therapy and Community Work* 3: 3–22.

McPhie, Lisa and Chaffey, Chris (1999) 'The journey of a lifetime', in David Denborough and Cheryl White (eds), *Extending Narrative Therapy*. Adelaide: Dulwich Centre Publications.

Moorey, Stirling (2007) 'Cognitive therapy', in Windy Dryden (ed.), *Dryden's Handbook of Individual Therapy*. London: Sage. pp. 297–326.

Nichols, William C. (1988) *Marital Therapy*. New York: Guilford.

Oldman, Gary (1997) *Nil by Mouth* (film/DVD). Twentieth Century Fox.

Parlett, Malcolm and Denham, Juliet (2007) 'Gestalt therapy', in Windy Dryden (ed.), *Dryden's Handbook of Individual Therapy*. London: Sage. pp. 227–55.

Payne, Martin (1993) 'Down-under innovation: a bridge between person–centred and systemic models?', *Counselling* 4 (2): 117–19; reprinted in Stephen Palmer, Sheila Dainow and Pat Milner (eds) (1996) *Counselling: the BAC Counselling Reader*. London: Sage.

Payne, Martin (2000) *Narrative Therapy: an Introduction for Counsellors*. London: Sage.

Payne, Martin (2006) *Narrative Therapy: an Introduction for Counsellors*, 2nd edn. London: Sage.

Ray, Wendel A. and Anger-Diaz, Barbara (2004) '"Don't get too bloody optimistic": John Weakland at work', in Shelley Green and Douglas Flemons (eds), *Quickies: the Handbook of Brief Sex Therapy*. New York: Norton.

Robinson, F.N. (ed.) (1957) *Complete Works of Geoffrey Chaucer*, 2nd edn. Cambridge, MA: Houghton Mifflin.

Rogers, Carl (1951) *Client Centred Therapy*. London: Constable.

Russell, Shona and Carey, Maggie (2003) 'Outsider-witness practices: some answers to commonly asked questions', *International Journal of Narrative Therapy and Community Work* 1: 3–16.

Segal, Marie (2004) 'Rebuilding trust in fractured relationships', in Stephen Madigan (ed.), *Therapy from the Outside In*. Vancouver: Yaletown Family Therapy.

Sells, James N. and Hargeave, Terry D. (1998) 'Forgiveness: a review of the theoretical and empirical literature', *Journal of Family Therapy* 20 (1): 21–36.

Spence, Donald P. (1982) *Narrative Truth and Historical Truth*. New York: Norton.

Troyat, Henri (2000) *La Lumière des Justes*. Paris: Flammarion/Omnibus.

Walrond-Skinner, Sue (1998) 'The function and role of forgiveness in working with couples and families: clearing the ground', *Journal of Family Therapy* 20 (1): 11–12.

White, Michael (1983) 'Marital therapy: practical approaches to longstanding problems', *Australian Journal of Family Therapy* 5 (1): 27–43.

White, Michael (1989) *Selected Papers*. Adelaide: Dulwich Centre Publications.

White, Michael (1994) Video: *The Best of Friends*. Los Angeles: MastersWork Video Productions.

White, Michael (1995) *Re-Authoring Lives*. Adelaide: Dulwich Centre Publications.

White, Michael (2000) *Reflections on Narrative Practice*. Adelaide: Dulwich Centre Publications.

White, Michael (2004a) *Narrative Practice and Exotic Lives*. Adelaide: Dulwich Centre Publications.

White, Michael (2004b) 'Working with people who are suffering the consequences of multiple trauma', *International Journal of Narrative Therapy and Community Work* 1: 45–6.

White, Michael (2004c) Mapping Narrative Conversations. Workshop in Maynooth, Republic of Ireland.

White, Michael (2007) *Maps of Narrative Practice*. New York: Norton.

White, Michael and Epston, David (1990) *Narrative Means to Therapeutic Ends*. New York: Norton.

Wilkinson, Mary (1992) 'How do we understand empathy systemically?', *Journal of Family Therapy* 14 (2): 193–202.

Winslade, John and Monk, Gerald (2001) *Narrative Mediation: a New Approach to Conflict Resolution*. San Francisco: Jossey–Bass.

World Health Organization (2005) 'Violence Against Women'. www.who.int/mediacentre/factsheets

INDEX

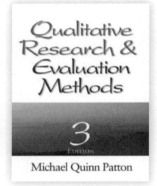
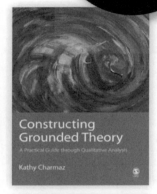
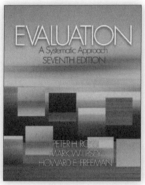
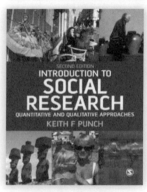
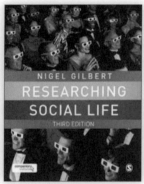

The Qualitative Research Kit

Edited by Uwe Flick

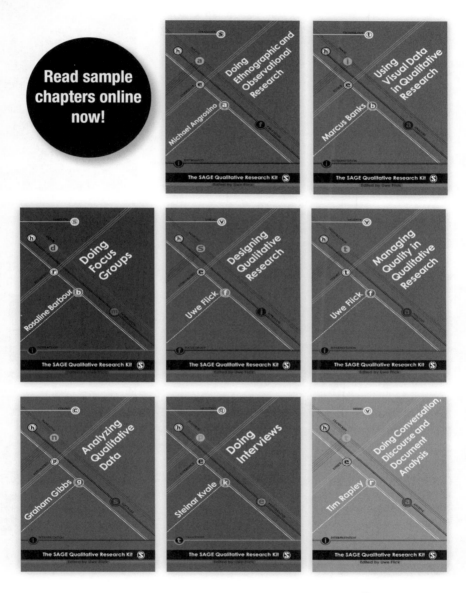

Read sample chapters online now!

Doing Ethnographic and Observational Research — Michael Angrosino

Using Visual Data in Qualitative Research — Marcus Banks

Doing Focus Groups — Rosaline Barbour

Designing Qualitative Research — Uwe Flick

Managing Quality in Qualitative Research — Uwe Flick

Analyzing Qualitative Data — Graham Gibbs

Doing Interviews — Steinar Kvale

Doing Conversation, Discourse and Document Analysis — Tim Rapley

The SAGE Qualitative Research Kit

www.sagepub.co.uk

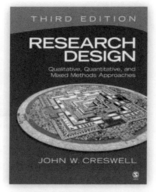
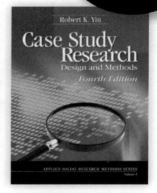

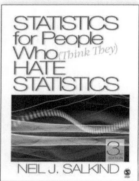

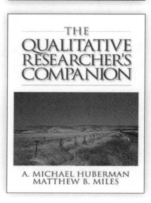